PENGUIN CLASSICS

THE JOURNEY THROUGH WALES

AND

THE DESCRIPTION OF WALES

ADVISORY EDITOR: BETTY RADICE

GERALD OF WALES, one of the formidable Geraldines, a grandson of Gerald of Windsor and the Princess Nest, was born c. 1145 in Manorbier, Pembrokeshire. He died in obscurity in 1223, possibly in Lincoln. Three parts Norman and one part Welsh, he was one of the most dynamic and colourful churchmen of the twelfth century. His dream was that he might become Bishop of St David's, be consecrated without having to acknowledge the supremacy of Canterbury and then persuade the Pope to appoint him Archbishop of Wales. For this he fought with great courage and tenacity over the years, refusing four other bishoprics in Ireland and Wales, and preferring to remain Archdeacon of Brecon if he could not realize his grand design. He knew almost everyone worth knowing in his day, kings, popes, Welsh princes, prelates; he argued his case with most of them and he criticized them with some venom in his writings. He wrote seventeen books and planned a number of others, all in Latin. *The Journey through Wales* and *The Description of Wales*, obvious counterparts to each other, are among his more amiable works. The first is a travel-diary of a preaching-tour which Archbishop Baldwin and Gerald undertook in 1188 to gain support in Wales for the Third Crusade. The second is a description of the geography of Wales, and of social and economic conditions in that country, in the last years of Henry II. They are invaluable source-books for the history of the twelfth century.

LEWIS THORPE, B.A., L.-ès-L., Ph.D., D. de l'U., LL.D., F.I.A.L., F.R.S.A., F.R.Hist.S., was Professor of French at Nottingham University from 1958 to 1977. He joined the staff of that university in 1946 after distinguished war service. He was President of the British Branch of the International Arthurian Society, and editor of the Society's *Bulletin Bibliographique*. He was also editor of *Nottingham Mediaeval Studies* and *Nottingham French Studies*. He published many articles, and his books include *La France guerrière* (1945), *Le Roman de Laurin, fils de Marques le Sénéchal* (1950), *Le Roman de Laurin, text of MS B.N.f.fr. 22548* (1960), *Guido Farina, Painter of Verona, 1896–1957* (1967), with Barbara Reynolds, *Einhard the Frank: The Life of Charlemagne* (1970), *Le Roman de Silence*, by Heldris de Cornuälle (1972) and *The Bayeux Tapestry and the Norman Invasion* (1973). He translated *Geoffrey of Monmouth: The History of the Kings of Britain*, *Two Lives of Charlemagne* and *Gregory of Tours: The History of the Franks* for the Penguin Classics. Lewis Thorpe was a member of the M.C.C. He died on 10 October 1977.

My husband's first book, *La France guerrière*, was published by Penguins in 1945. As he was then in Italy on active service, I had the privilege of correcting the proofs in his absence.

The proofs of this, his last book, arrived a few days after his death. Once again I have performed the same service, with the skilled editorial assistance of Professor Robin Storey, to whom I am most grateful.

The index was made by Brenda Hall, M.A., a registered indexer of the Society of Indexers.

Barbara Reynolds,
University of Nottingham

GERALD OF WALES

The Journey through Wales
and
The Description of Wales

TRANSLATED
WITH AN INTRODUCTION BY
LEWIS THORPE

PENGUIN BOOKS

PENGUIN BOOKS

Published by the Penguin Group
Penguin Books Ltd, 27 Wrights Lane, London W8 5TZ, England
Penguin Putnam Inc., 375 Hudson Street, New York, New York 10014, USA
Penguin Books Australia Ltd, Ringwood, Victoria, Australia
Penguin Books Canada Ltd, 10 Alcorn Avenue, Toronto, Ontario, Canada M4V 3B2
Penguin Books (NZ) Ltd, Private Bag 102902, NSMC, Auckland, New Zealand

Penguin Books Ltd, Registered Offices: Harmondsworth, Middlesex, England

This translation first published 1978
14

Set in Ehrhardt Monotype
Printed in England by Clays Ltd, St Ives plc

Gens etenim haec in omni vehemens est intentione. Unde et sicut malis nusquam pejores, sic bonis meliores non reperies.

Descriptio Kambriae, I.18

CONTENTS

7

CONTENTS

8

INTRODUCTION

I. THE LIFE OF GERALD OF WALES

Giraldus Cambrensis,[1] or Gerald of Wales as we may call him in English, wrote his own life-story, but a considerable part of it has been lost.[2] Fortunately several of his other works are largely autobiographical,[3] he had a habit of referring to himself in his writings, and he made a collection of his occasional papers, letters, polemics and poems, so that we do not lack information about him. Everything that he wrote was in Latin.

He was born and apparently spent his childhood in the castle of Manorbier, on the coast of Pembrokeshire in South Wales, and of this delightful spot he paints a nostalgic word-picture in *The Journey through Wales*.[4] The date of his birth can be inferred as 1145 or 1146.[5] His father was the Norman knight

1. In *The Journey through Wales* he is always 'archidiaconus Menevensis', the Archdeacon of St David's. Elsewhere he is 'Giraldus archidiaconus' or 'Giraldus archidiaconus de Brechene' (*De iure*, III). He rejects the name Silvester: 'non igitur tam sylvester sum sicut adversarii mentiuntur' (ibid.). Did he ever call himself Giraldus Cambrensis or Giràldus de Barri?

2. *De rebus a se gestis*, 'The events of his own life', which ends in midsentence halfway through Bk III, ch. 19. Professor H. E. Butler made a most attractive translation of the *De rebus*, inserting biographical passages from the other works at the points to which they refer: *The Autobiography of Giraldus Cambrensis*, Jonathan Cape, London, 1937.

3. E.g. *De iure et statu Menevensis ecclesiae*, 'The Rights and Privileges of the Church of St David's'.

4. *Itin.*, I.12.

5. His uncle David, Bishop of St David's, died on 23 May 1176. The canons of St David's, who met soon afterwards, 'parumper autem postea', to draw up suggestions for a replacement, decided to put forward the names of all four of their archdeacons, one of whom was Gerald, for consideration by King Henry II. According to Gerald, the people assembled outside the chapter-house imagined that the canons had gone so far as to nominate him alone, 'cum necdum tricesimum aetatis ageret annum', although he had not

William de Barri, whose family took its name from Barry Island off the Glamorgan coast, also described, but in less detail, in *The Journey through Wales*.[6] His mother was Angharad, daughter of Nest and granddaughter of Rhys ap Tewdwr, Prince of South Wales. Nest's husband was the Norman knight Gerald of Windsor, castellan of Pembroke. It follows that Angharad was only half Welsh and that the blood in Gerald's own veins was three quarters Norman. He had two older brothers, Robert and Philip, at least one sister and a half-brother Walter.

One of his mother's older brothers, David FitzGerald, had become Bishop of St David's in 1148, and from his early youth onwards Gerald was encouraged by his father and his uncle to study and to see himself as a future churchman. As soon as he was old enough to leave his home at Manorbier, he was sent to the Benedictine Abbey of St Peter in Gloucester, where a Frenchman Amelin was Abbot and where his teacher was a monk called Haimo. He approved of the instruction which he received at St Peter's and he later described his teacher there as 'that most learned scholar Master Haimo';[7] but, looking back down the years, he was critical of the wealth and worldliness of the monks of Gloucester, more perhaps of Llanthony Secunda than of St Peter's, especially when he compared them with the saintly and frugal inmates of the former's mother house at Llanthony.[8] It was at St Peter's that he began to acquire his mastery of medieval Latin and his extensive knowledge of

yet completed his thirtieth year (*De rebus*, I.9). This seems to mean that he was below the minimum canonical age for a bishop and thus cannot have been born before June 1146.

Prince Philippe Auguste of France, son of Louis VII, was born on 22 or 25 August 1165. Gerald was then in Paris, 'adolescens in urbe existens et quasi vicesimum aetatis suae tunc annum adimplens', living there in the city and about to complete his twentieth year, i.e. near his twentieth birthday (*De princ.*, III.25). This would mean that he was born in the late summer or early autumn of 1145. The two statements do not agree.

6. *Itin.*, I.6.

7. *Spec.*, I.33. The abbreviations used for citing Gerald's works are listed on p. 62. His book and chapter numbers are quoted except in the case of *De iure*, when reference is made to pages in the Rolls Series edition (Vol. III).

8. *Itin.*, I.3.

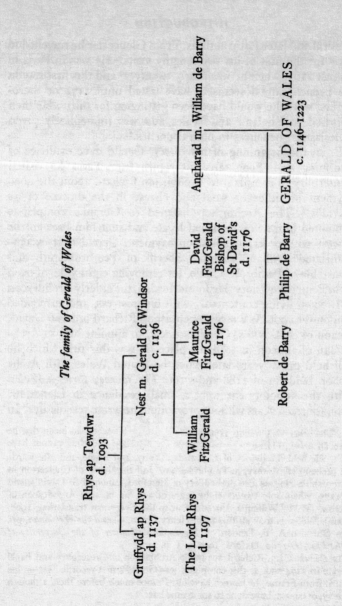

The family of Gerald of Wales

Rhys ap Tewdwr
d. 1093

Nest m. Gerald of Windsor
d. c. 1136

Angharad m. William de Barry

Gruffydd ap Rhys
d. 1137

William
FitzGerald

Maurice
FitzGerald
d. 1176

David
FitzGerald
Bishop of
St David's
d. 1176

Robert de Barry

Philip de Barry

GERALD OF WALES
c. 1146–1223

The Lord Rhys
d. 1197

classical and later Latin authors. From Gloucester he travelled to Paris for the first of his two lengthy visits.[9] He was in Paris in August 1165, when he was nearly twenty;[10] and this first stay in the French capital seems to have lasted until 1174 or thereabouts, when he would have been getting on for thirty. He then returned to England and Wales and was immediately given ecclesiastical benefices in both countries.[11]

From the beginning of his career, Gerald gave evidence of reforming zeal. Soon after his return from Paris, he visited Canterbury to complain to Archbishop Richard about the non-payment of tithes of wool and cheese in the diocese of St David's.[12] The Archbishop listened to Gerald's complaint, appointed him as his personal legate and sent him back to the diocese with orders to insist on payment. Gerald next excommunicated William Carquit, Sheriff of Pembrokeshire and Constable of Pembroke Castle, for removing eight yoke of oxen from Pembroke Priory. He found Jordan, the elderly Archdeacon of Brecon, living contentedly with his mistress, and suspended him on the spot. As a result Archbishop Richard ordered David, Bishop of St David's, Gerald's uncle, to appoint him as Archdeacon of Brecon in Jordan's place. It was this title which he still held many years later when he toured Wales with Archbishop Baldwin in 1188 and wrote *The Journey through Wales*. With the appointment went a small residence in Llanddew. After fourteen years without promotion, he wrote resignedly: 'In

9. The other visit was in 1176-9.

10. *De princ.*, III.25.

11. 'He held the livings of Llanwnda, Tenby, and Angle, and afterwards the prebend of Mathry, in Pembrokeshire, and the living of Chesterton in Oxfordshire. He was also prebendary of Hereford, canon of St David's, and in 1175, when only twenty-eight years of age, he became Archdeacon of Brecon' (W. L. Williams, Introduction to the Everyman translation, 1908, p. xiii). Williams took all this from Henry Owen, *Gerald the Welshman*, pp. 5-7. See also A. B. Emden, *A Biographical Register of the University of Oxford to AD 1500*, Oxford, 1957-9, I, p. 117.

12. *De rebus*, I.3. Richard was made Archbishop of Canterbury and Papal Legate in 1174 and, as this complaint was Gerald's first recorded act on his return from France, he cannot have left France much before then, although he may, of course, have done so some time later.

this most temperate area I myself have been appointed to a post of some importance, to use the jargon with which we are all so familiar, but it affords me no great promise of wealth and certainly no expectation of ever playing my part in the tragic pomps and ceremonies of this world. I occupy a tiny dwelling-house not far from the principal castle of Brecknockshire and, indeed, adjacent to it. This is convenient enough for my studies and my work and there I pass my time in a sort of happy-go-lucky mediocrity. The house gives me pleasure and it is conducive to thoughts of the next world.'[13] Meanwhile, with his new appointment to give him added authority and with the modest archdeaconry in Llanddew as his base, Gerald pressed on with his reforming activities. The Flemings established by Henry I in Rhos had been granted immunity from the tithes of wool and cheese, but Gerald made sure that their fellow-nationals outside Rhos should pay. He stopped the parish priest of Hay-on-Wye from sharing his benefices with his brother, who was a layman. He made a visitation of the church of Llanbadarn Fawr, despite the fact that his household had been driven off with spears and a shower of arrows. He prevented Adam, Bishop of St Asaph, from appropriating the church of Kerry, which really belonged to the diocese of St David's.

Meanwhile, on 23 May 1176, Gerald's uncle, David Fitz-Gerald, Bishop of St David's, died and the see became vacant. Gerald had set his heart on replacing his uncle in what, as he never ceases to remind us, had, in his opinion, once been the metropolitan see of Wales. The canons of St David's met in their chapter-house and decided to put forward the names of all four of their archdeacons, so that King Henry II might make his choice. As we have seen,[14] the rumour spread among the people assembled outside the cathedral that the canons had nominated Gerald alone, which was not in their power. According to Gerald, they would have done so had they dared. He realized immediately that if this rumour reached Henry's ears, it would be fatal to his cause, and he tried to counter it by attending the

13. *Itin.*, I.3.
14. See p. 9, n. 5. The reference is to *De rebus*, I.9.

chapter-house in person the next morning and refusing any specific nomination, although he allowed his name to go forward with the other three. The case came before the King. All the bishops present and Richard, Archbishop of Canterbury, himself spoke in favour of Gerald, lauding his reforming zeal and his physical courage, stressing his scholarship, and speaking at length of his noble birth and his kinship with Rhys ap Gruffydd, Prince of South Wales, and with so many other high-born Welshmen.[15] Henry was only too well aware of Gerald's dream of restoring to St David's the archiepiscopal status which he supposed it to have held until Samson fled to Dol c. 550, and of freeing it from all subservience to Canterbury. A spectre must have flickered before his eyes. Less than six years had passed since the murder of Thomas Becket. He summoned the canons of St David's to Winchester and gave them as their new bishop Peter de Leia, the Cluniac Prior of Much Wenlock, apparently an Anglo-Norman by birth.[16] Gerald had lost the bishopric and, although he did not know it, he had lost it for ever. He was still not yet thirty. He collected his books together and returned to Paris.

During his first visit to Paris, which lasted from 1165 or before until c. 1174, Gerald had been a student of the trivium: grammar, logic and rhetoric. It was as a student of canon law and theology that he returned in 1176. Soon he began to lecture on the *Decretals* of Gratian, and from his own account he was a great success.[17] He remained in Paris until the summer of 1179 and then proposed to move on to Bologna, but he was having difficulty in supporting himself and he returned to England instead.[18]

Gerald's zeal for reform remained undiminished. Immediately

15. *De rebus*, I.10.

16. ibid., I.11. Peter de Leia was consecrated on 7 November 1176. His surname means simply 'of the lea', 'of Lee'.

17. The *Concordia discordantium canonum* of c. 1140, known as the *Decretals*, a collection of some 3,800 texts, was already the basis for the teaching of canon law in Bologna and Paris. Gerald includes the beginning of one of his lectures in *De rebus*, II.2.

18. *De rebus*, II.4.

after his return from Paris he had a meal with the monks of
Christ Church, Canterbury, and complained of their behaviour
at table and their gluttony.[19] He stopped his sister from divorcing
her husband.[20] When he at last reached Wales, he found Peter
de Leia at loggerheads with his chapter and in virtual exile in
England, with the result that Richard, Archbishop of Canterbury, decided to give administrative power over the diocese of
St David's to Gerald himself.[21] Things went from bad to worse,
and they reached a point where Gerald contemplated sending an
appeal to Rome to ask that Peter should be deposed. In the end a
synod of the chapter was summoned in St David's and peace
was patched up.[22]

In 1184 Gerald was called to his presence by Henry II, then
in the Welsh marches, and appointed Court Chaplain, and for a
year or more he followed the court in its wanderings[23] and acted
as liaison-officer between the King, Rhys ap Gruffydd and the
other princes of Wales, most of whom were his blood-relations.[24]
At Easter 1185 Prince John sailed with a fleet from Pembroke
and Milford Haven and landed at Waterford. Gerald, a close
relative of the earlier conquerors of Ireland, was sent with him
as chaplain and adviser.[25] John returned home in the winter of
the same year, but Gerald remained in Ireland until some time
between Easter and Whitsun 1186.[26] While there he began to
write his first two books, the *Topographia Hibernica* or 'The
Topography of Ireland', and the *Expugnatio Hibernica* or 'The
Conquest of Ireland'. Before he came back to England, John
offered Gerald first the bishopric of Wexford and then that of
Leighlin, and, when he refused, the two bishoprics combined.[27]

In 1185, just before Gerald sailed for Ireland, Heraclius, the
Patriarch of Jerusalem, came to England and begged Henry II to
take the Cross and to defend Jerusalem against Saladin, or at
least to send one of his three sons.[28] Henry refused, but he

19. ibid., II.5.   20. ibid.
21. ibid., II.6.   22. ibid., II.7.
23. ibid., II.8.   24. ibid., II.9.
25. ibid., II.10.   26. ibid., II.13.
27. ibid.   28. ibid., II.10.

changed his mind and in 1187 he himself, Prince Richard and Philippe Auguste of France all took the Cross.[29] Richard, Archbishop of Canterbury, had died on 16 February 1184. His successor, Baldwin, was sent to Wales to travel the country and preach the Cross. With him went Gerald, and their long journey together, which took them to all four cathedrals, Llandaff, St David's, Bangor and St Asaph, and which lasted from soon after 2 March until Easter 1188, is described at length in Gerald's third book, the *Itinerarium Kambriae* or 'The Journey through Wales'. At the same time or soon after he composed the *Descriptio Kambriae* or 'The Description of Wales', as a counterpart to *The Topography of Ireland*. Among the first to take the Cross were Gerald himself and Peter de Leia, Bishop of St David's.[30]

Gerald actually set out for the Holy Land. In the company of Archbishop Baldwin and the Justiciar Ranulph de Glanville, he crossed over to France in the spring of 1189. He was probably in Le Mans in March 1189[31] and he was certainly with the English court in France in April and May of that year.[32] On 10 May 1189 he was in Chinon.[33] Henry II died there less than a month later, and, on Archbishop Baldwin's advice, King Richard I sent Gerald back to England, where he might well be of more political use than he would have been in the Near East.[34] In Dover he was given absolution from his vow to go on the Crusade by the Cardinal Legate, John of Anagni, who at the same time absolved the ageing Peter de Leia.[35] Archbishop Baldwin, on the contrary, kept his vow: he sailed from Marseilles to Tyre and then made his way to Acre, where he died in the siege on 19 November 1190.[36]

The bishopric of Bangor became vacant and William de Longchamp, the new Justiciar, offered it to Gerald, but he refused it.[37] Prince John offered him the vacant bishopric of

29. ibid., II.17.
30. ibid.
31. *De princ.*, III.13.
32. ibid.
33. *De princ.*, III.16.
34. *De rebus*, II.21.
35. ibid., II.21–22.
36. *Itin.*, II.14.
37. *De rebus*, II.22.

Llandaff, and again he refused.[38] Peter de Leia was now in failing health: and St David's was the prize on which Gerald had set his heart. Tired of waiting, he gathered his books together some time in 1196 and prepared to set off once more for Paris, but the war between Richard I and Philippe Auguste blocked him and he took refuge instead in Lincoln, where his old acquaintance William de Monte was teaching theology.[39] Peter died at long last on 16 July 1198 and the way was once more open.[40]

This new battle for the vacant bishopric of St David's lasted for more than five long years, from the death of Peter de Leia on 16 July 1198 until 10 November 1203, when Geoffrey de Henelawe, Prior of Llanthony, was eventually chosen to replace him. It was at once the highest point and the nadir of Gerald's fortunes. As his chances of success seemed to him to ebb and flow, he fought every inch of the way, with extraordinary pertinacity and superhuman courage. The story is told in the fullest detail, first in what remains of *The Events of His Own Life*, and then, when that fails, in *De iure et statu Menevensis Ecclesiae* or 'The Rights and Privileges of the Church of St David's', and there is further documentary evidence in his other works. It is a remarkable example of sustained effort, for the most part against overwhelming odds. Naturally enough, we observe the conflict from a single viewpoint, that of Gerald himself. One may say that it is a tale of personal ambition, ambition made of the sternest stuff; but it was far more than that. Four times Gerald had refused a bishopric, twice in Ireland and twice in Wales. For him it was clearly St David's or nothing. Evidence is not lacking throughout his writings that he was a fervent

38. ibid., II.24.
39. ibid., III.3. This must have been in 1196. Writing to Archbishop Hubert Walter in 1198 (*Symb.*, Letter 28), Gerald says that he had then been two years in Lincoln. He had previously spent two years in Oxford, 1194–5 (ibid.). At some time in 1191 or 1192 he had visited Glastonbury and was shown the supposed tomb of Arthur and Guinevere, which had just been discovered. He wrote two descriptions of what he saw, *De princ.*, I.22, and *Spec.*, II.8–10. For their great interest I print the two Latin texts with a new translation in Appendix III. 40. *De rebus*, III.3.

admirer of Thomas Becket.[41] His dream was not merely to become a bishop, even if the bishopric were St David's. It was to restore St David's to the metropolitan status which, according to him, it had lost when Samson fled to Dol. It was to free the Church in Wales from its subservience to Canterbury, and if necessary to forfeit his own life in the transept of his own cathedral in doing so. Henry II had seen things differently, and so now did those who came after him. Rhys ap Gruffydd, Prince of South Wales, had died in 1197, but Gerald still had far too many powerful relations in high place and he was far too dangerous a man ever to be considered as a suitable replacement for Peter de Leia.

Things began in 1198 as they had begun at the previous election in 1176. The chapter of St David's sent four nominations to Hubert Walter, Archbishop of Canterbury, until recently Justiciar of England. Gerald's name headed the list,[42] and him Hubert could not and would not accept. Hubert offered in exchange Alexander, Abbot of Ford, his own former chaplain, or Geoffrey, Prior of Llanthony, his own former medical attendant,[43] both of them Englishmen, and these were refused.

41. E.g., writing of Baldwin, *Itin.*, II.14, Gerald says: '. . . it is clear that, in our own lifetime, Saint Thomas, his predecessor [but one] as Archbishop of Canterbury, won a glorious victory for the freedom of the Church by fighting on until he was martyred.' The main reference, however, is *Exp. Hib.*, I.20. There is something ironic in the fact that, as a good Protestant, David Powel omitted the first passage about Gerald's idol and exemplar from his 1585 edition of *The Journey through Wales*, in which extraordinary action most editors and translators have followed him ever since; and that John Hooker, another good Protestant, omitted the second passage from his 1587 translation of *The Conquest of Ireland*. Did they not accept that Gerald was a Catholic living in a Catholic world?

42. The others were Walter, Abbot of St Dogmael's, Peter, Abbot of Whitland, and Reginald Foliot (*De rebus*, III.4). Walter and Peter were Welshmen. Reginald Foliot, canon of St David's, nephew of Peter de Leia, counted as an Englishman: '. . . quoniam ex Anglicis erat, et tamen Menevensis ecclesiae canonicus, utpote quem avunculus ejus, sc. proximo defunctus episcopus, canonicaverat . . .' (. . . for he was of Anglo-Norman stock, despite his holding a canonry of St David's cathedral, it having been his uncle, the late Bishop, who had raised him to that position) (*De rebus*, III.7).

43. *De rebus*, III.7.

18

Hubert then visited King Richard I at Château Gaillard and, at his request, the King summoned four canons of the chapter to confer with him there.[44] The King's letter was delayed. Geoffrey FitzPeter, the new Justiciar, sent a reminder.[45] The four canons travelled to London to meet Geoffrey FitzPeter, and while there they talked with Gerald, who had come from Lincoln. They refused Alexander of Ford and Geoffrey of Llanthony, and they sent one of their number, Elidyr, with a clerk, to the King to tell him so. In the meantime Richard I died at Chaluz on 6 April 1199. The two messengers travelled on to Chinon, where they found John, with his mother, Queen Eleanor, and his sister-in-law, Queen Berengaria.[46] John professed himself favourable to Gerald's cause, and wrote both to Gerald himself in Lincoln, and to the chapter in St David's, to make this clear, but at the same time he sent a letter to the Justiciar, Geoffrey FitzPeter, to instruct him to do nothing until he, John, had seen Gerald.[47] John was crowned King at Westminster on 27 May 1199. He summoned Gerald to London, informed him apparently, with two of the canons of St David's present, that he proposed to accept him as Bishop, but added that he could not yet make an announcement, as the Archbishop of Canterbury was still hostile.[48] Gerald travelled to St David's, and on 29 June 1199 he was unanimously elected as Bishop by the full chapter. They directed him to go to Rome to be consecrated by the Pope, instead of to Canterbury to be consecrated by the Archbishop, for otherwise he would have lost the battle for the establishing of St David's as the independent metropolitan see of Wales before it had even begun.[49]

Eleven months and more had passed since the death of Peter de Leia. It seemed that Gerald now had won at last. In effect, the struggle was to continue for another four and a half years, and he never became Bishop. He went to Ireland to consult his rela-

44. Letter of 9 November 1198, quoted in full in *De rebus*, III.8.
45. Letter of 18 December 1198, quoted in *De rebus*, III.9.
46. All this is narrated at length in *De rebus*, III.10.
47. *De rebus*, III.10.
48. ibid., III.12.   49. ibid.

tions. Letters arrived from the Archbishop and from the Justiciar ordering the chapter of St David's to accept Geoffrey, Prior of Llanthony.[50] The chapter appealed to Pope Innocent III.[51] Gerald travelled a first time to Rome, arriving on 30 November 1199 or thereabouts,[52] meeting the Pope immediately and soon gaining evidence of his consummate skill in the art of delay.[53] For the next four years he was to spend most of his time in Rome, twice returning to Wales and twice making the long and tedious journey back across the Alps. What all this cost, in the burning up of nervous energy, in physical exertion and day-to-day expenditure, it is impossible for us to imagine. The debate went on unendingly, but the possibility of a conclusion seemed to recede like a mirage. Month after month, year after year, Gerald continued to fight his case, although the world was fast coming to lose all interest in it. By now the chapter of St David's had only two desires left to them: to have a bishop and to live in peace. Harassed by debts and beset by accidents of every kind, Gerald finally said goodbye to Pope Innocent III in Ferentino in the summer of 1203.[54] He passed once more through Rome and through Bologna, traversed again the fertile plains of Lombardy, crossed the high Alps and on a lean and puny horse[55] straggled despondently into the town of Châtillon-sur-Seine, the last of a long line of returning pilgrims. The Archbishop's clerk, John of Tynemouth, had warned them of his coming, but it was only by his tall stature and his shaggy eyebrows[56] that the castellan's young brother could recognize him as the Elect of St David's. He was thrown into prison. In

50. De rebus, III.13.
51. Letters quoted in full in De rebus, III.14 and 15.
52. De rebus, III.18.
53. Gerald gave Innocent III copies of his six books, saying: 'Praesentant vobis alii libras, sed nos libros' (Others give you money, but I bring books) (De rebus, III.18).
54. De iure, V, p. 289.
55. De iure, V, p. 293: '... equum suum modicum ac maculentum ...'
56. ibid.: '... per descriptionem sibi factam, tam staturae grandis quam superciliorum quoque grandium et hirsutorum, ipsum recognovit, maxime vero per supercilia.'

INTRODUCTION

his possession he had only eight deniers of Dijon.[57] 'As a result
the Archdeacon spent all that day without food and all the next
night without sleep, being in the depths of despair when he
considered the peril of his present plight, to which there seemed
to be no remedy, and thought of his miserable captivity, which
appeared beyond all human solace or support.'[58]

Gerald was now nearly sixty years old, he was six hundred
miles or more from home, if St David's could be called his home,
he was imprisoned in a small provincial town in a country which
was at war with England, all alone in a sea of troubles and
virtually penniless. A lesser man would have turned his face to
the rough-hewn wall and died of despair; but that was not the
way of the Geraldines. The next night the Seneschal of Burgundy arrived in Châtillon-sur-Seine, freed Gerald from prison
and, being a neat-minded man, put his denouncer, John of
Tynemouth, there in his place.[59] Gerald travelled on to Troyes,
where he found money, to Paris, where he was helped by John,
the exiled Archbishop of Dublin, to Rouen, where he met
Eustace, Bishop of Ely.[60] He appeared before King John in
Elbeuf, and protested once more against the possible election
of the Abbots of St Dogmael's and Whitland, and Reginald
Foliot, on the grounds that the first was practically illiterate, the
second a bastard and the third a notorious fornicator.[61] By
August 1203 he was back in England.[62] On 17 August, on the
occasion of the consecration in Canterbury of William of Blois
as Bishop of Lincoln, he made the same protest.[63] He then wrote
to Hubert Walter, Archbishop of Canterbury, who had been ill
that day, to protest a last time.[64]

The final act in this long drama was every whit as remarkable
as all that had gone before. The canons of the chapter of St
David's were summoned to Lambeth. Gerald, who was in St

57. ibid.: '. . . nec denarios invenerunt praeter octo divionenses, qui
sterlingos duos non valebant.'
58. ibid.
59. ibid., pp. 294–5.
60. De iure, V, p. 297.
61. ibid., pp. 301–3.
62. ibid., VI, p. 304.
63. ibid., pp. 304–5.
64. Letter quoted in full, De iure, VI, pp. 305–7.

21

David's, rode there by forced marches, having a preliminary
interview with the Archbishop in Waltham.[65] On 10 November
1203 the Archbishop and the Justiciar, Geoffrey FitzPeter,
presided over a meeting of the chapter in Saint Catherine's
Chapel in Westminster Abbey and announced the election of
Geoffrey de Henelawe, Prior of Llanthony, as the new Bishop of
St David's.[66] To everyone's astonishment, Gerald accepted their
decision without demur and at the same time resigned his
archdeaconry of Brecon and the prebend of Mathry.[67] He gives
a long explanation of his actions. He could have said it all in one
short sentence. If the consecration was to be made by the
Archbishop of Canterbury, then Gerald of Wales was not
interested.

Gerald lived on for another twenty years, devoting himself to
literary composition, but certainly not dropping out of public
affairs. Just where he spent his time or what he did with it is not
clear. In addition to those already mentioned he was producing
book after book, until in the end he had seventeen to his name,
not counting those which he promised but never wrote, or
maybe started and never finished.[68] One day he mounted his
horse and rode off once more to Rome, this time as a simple
pilgrim. He says that this was two years after his resignation, but
he may mean four.[69] He was received again by Pope Innocent
III, and he was still in Rome when Stephen Langton was
consecrated Archbishop of Canterbury on 17 June 1207.[70] On
his return to England he discussed this appointment with King
John.[71] Geoffrey, Bishop of St David's, was seized with the
palsy and paralysed: he lingered on for a long time and died
eventually at the end of 1214.[72] There was some talk of Gerald
as his replacement, but it was too late, and Iorwerth, the Welsh

65. *De iure*, VI, p. 318.
66. ibid., pp. 321–2.
67. ibid., pp. 322–5.
68. A complete list is given on p. 62.
69. *Invect.*, V.12.
70. ibid., V. 12–13.
71. ibid., V. 22.
72. *De iure*, VII, pp. 354–5.

Abbot of the Premonstratensian house of Tally, near Llandeilo, was consecrated on 21 June 1215.[73] Gerald had dedicated *The Journey through Wales* and *The Description of Wales* to Stephen Langton in 1215.[74] In the same year he presented to him *The Rights and Privileges of the Church of St David's*.[75] He was with Langton in Guildford just before the latter's departure for Rome in the autumn of that year, and then set off himself for Canterbury.[76] He still had eight years to live. He passed his days in humble circumstances among his books, confessing his sins in the dim recesses of churches.[77] When he died in 1223 he was nearly eighty.[78]

Gerald of Wales was a very tall man.[79] In his thirties he had been strikingly handsome.[80] He was bustling and energetic, absolutely fearless, a magnificent horseman. He was strongly convinced of his own ability and importance, and prepared to argue his case, in public and in private, in person or by letter, with any tiresome adversary, from the Pope and the King of England down. His tongue could be very sharp and the ink in which he dipped his quill-pen was often mixed with gall. Until old age weakened him, he was resolute and undeterred by the buffets of fortune, of which he received more than his share. He was self-regarding and self-admiring; and the faults and weaknesses of other men were only too apparent to him. With his

73. See H. E. Butler, 'Some New Pages of Giraldus Cambrensis', *Medium Aevum*, IV.3 (1935), pp. 143–52.

74. See pp. 38 and 50. 75. *De iure*, Prologue.

76. *Epistola ad Stephanum Langton*, Rolls Series, *Giraldus Cambrensis*, I, p. 401.

77. *Invect.*, V. 23.

78. In that year his death was reported to the Bishop of Lincoln and his living at Chesterton in Oxfordshire was filled (*Register of Bishop Hugh of Lincoln*, II, pp. 9–10).

79. Cp. n. 56.

80. Writing of his visit to Baldwin, then Bishop of Worcester, in Blockley, at some time between 1180 and 1183, he says of himself: 'Eram autem tunc adolescens, statura procerus, facie quoque fragilique ac momentaneo naturae bono, formae nitore praeclarus . . .' (I was a young man at the time, with Nature's bounty of delicate features – they were not to last – and greatly distinguished by my handsome physique) (*Spec.*, II.33).

great height, thick straggling eyebrows and features once so delicate but now sharpened and made gaunt by age and disappointment, he must have been a dusty scarecrow of a man towards the end.

II. THE JOURNEY THROUGH WALES

The Journey through Wales was Gerald's third book. It describes, almost in diary form, the mission to South and North Wales undertaken in 1188 by Baldwin, Archbishop of Canterbury, with Gerald, Archdeacon of Brecon, as his companion. Together they crossed the Herefordshire border soon after Ash Wednesday, 2 March 1188, and rode towards Radnor. They remained in South Wales for just five weeks. On 7 April they crossed the River Dovey and so entered North Wales, where they travelled for one week only, arriving in Chester on 14 April, the Thursday before Easter.

1. *The purpose of the journey and its achievements:*

Archbishop Baldwin went to Wales to preach the Cross. Henry II, Prince Richard and Philippe Auguste of France had all taken the Cross in 1187. Baldwin, an Exeter man, one-time Abbot of the Cistercian house of Ford in Devon, later Bishop of Worcester and since 16 December 1184 Archbishop of Canterbury, had himself taken the Cross at the Council of Geddington on 11 February 1188. He had already visited Wales in 1187 as Papal Legate: and he was now sent there to further the cause of the Third Crusade. He was to meet the Princes of Elfael, Gwent, Deheubarth, Meirionnydd, Gwynedd and Powys, to make contact with the Abbots of Margam, Whitland, St Dogmael's, Strata Florida and Whitchurch, to address such gatherings of the Welsh people and of Anglo-Norman soldiery as he could assemble, and to say Mass in the four cathedrals of Llandaff, St David's, Bangor and St Asaph. Baldwin was a modest man, of humble birth. No one knows when he was born, but by 1188 he was certainly no longer young. Gerald describes him in some detail: he was swarthy, only moderately tall, of great abstinence and self-control, thin rather than corpulent.[81] He was a good Latinist and an eloquent preacher, but, in Gerald's opinion, not the leader which the church needed at that time: a better monk than an abbot, a better abbot than a bishop, and a better bishop than an archbishop.[82] He had a modest sense of humour. On the journey from Nefyn to Caernarfon, as they rode along a valley, where the going was hard, he had the whole party dismount from their horses and walk, as he thought that this would be good training for the Near East. 'We walked the whole length of the valley,' wrote Gerald, 'and we were very tired by the time we reached the farther end. The Archbishop sat himself down on an oak-tree, which had been completely uprooted and overturned by the force of the winds, for he needed to rest and recover his breath. As he reclined there, he joked with his attendants, which was a wonderful thing for so venerable a person to do. "Which of you, now, in all my company, can soothe my tired ears by whistling a tune?" he asked, although he knew very well how difficult this would be, seeing how exhausted they all were. He maintained that he himself could do so, if he really wanted to.'[83]

Baldwin seems to have succeeded admirably in his task. In South Wales, in Radnor, he met Rhys ap Gruffydd and Einion ab Einion Clud; Maelgwn ap Cadwallon in Cruker Castle; Morgan, son of Caradog ab Iestyn, in Margam; Rhys ap Gruffydd again, with his two sons, Maelgwn and Gruffydd, in Cardigan; and the third son of Rhys ap Gruffydd, Cynwrig, in a wood near Strata Florida. In North Wales he met Gruffydd ap Cynan in Towyn, and the next day his younger brother, Maredudd ap Cynan; and Rhodri ab Owain in Anglesey. In Powys he met Gruffydd ap Madog and Elise ap Madog. Some of these notables travelled with him for several days. Only Owain Cyfeiliog in Powys failed to put in an appearance, and him they excommunicated to encourage the others. Baldwin gave spirited and highly effective

81. *Itin.*, II.14.   82. ibid.
83. ibid., II.6.

25

sermons in Radnor, Hay-on-Wye, Llanddew, Abergavenny, Usk Castle, [Newport],[84] Llandaff, Swansea, Haverfordwest, Cardigan, Lampeter, beside a wood near Strata Florida, Llanbadarn Fawr, [at the bridge near Llanfair], Nefyn, on the seashore in Anglesey, [Rhuddlan Castle], Chester and Shrewsbury. About three thousand men of military age, most of them Welsh, were signed with the Cross.[85] Among these must be numbered quite a few local robbers, highwaymen and murderers;[86] and to them must be added a dozen archers, English or Norman, from St Clears, who had just killed a young Welshman.[87] Other folk, too old to go on a crusade, gave money.[88]

Peter de Leia, Bishop of St David's, who travelled with them all the way from Hereford to his own cathedral, and then on to the River Dovey, took the Cross after the very first sermon in Radnor, being preceded in this by one person only, Gerald himself. William de Salso Marisco, Bishop of Llandaff, preached in Usk Castle, entertained them in Llandaff itself, and stayed with them until they left his diocese. John, Abbot of Whitland, and Seisyll, Abbot of Strata Florida, joined them in Lampeter, preached there, and travelled on with them into North Wales. In Bangor Bishop Gwion took the Cross, to the dismay of his flock. In Powys they found that Reiner, Bishop of St Asaph, had been preaching the Cross before they arrived. Gerald is at pains to state categorically that Archbishop Baldwin said Mass at the high altar in the cathedrals of Llandaff,[89] St David's,[90] Bangor[91] and St Asaph.[92] He was the first Archbishop of Canterbury to visit these cathedrals,[93] and it was part of his mission to make it quite clear that their four bishoprics must remain under the domination of Canterbury and that St David's could never become a metropolitan see.

84. In the places marked with square brackets Gerald does not say in so many words that Baldwin gave a sermon.
85. *Itin.*, II.13.   86. ibid., I.5.
87. ibid., I. 10.
88. E.g. Cador of Swansea, *Itin.*, I.8.
89. *Itin.*, I.7.   90. ibid., II.2.
91. ibid., II.6.   92. ibid., II.10.
93. ibid., I.1 and II.1. He had been in Wales before, in 1187.

2. Gerald's role :

In 1188 Gerald of Wales was still a canon of St David's and the Archdeacon of Brecon, with a house in Llanddew. He had been a student in Paris for nine years and a lecturer there for three. He was in his early forties and he had written two books. He spoke Latin fluently and presumably French, and no doubt he was competent in Welsh and English. He was a Geraldine and a close relation of the Welsh princely families. In his own estimation he was clearly the most talented scholar and churchman in Wales, and this opinion must have been shared by most of his contemporaries. Apart from his determination to become Bishop and then, if it were ever possible, Archbishop of St David's, he seemed the ideal person to be sent as Baldwin's close associate.

The part he played during these six weeks of zealous missionary activity, difficult public relations, and unremitting and hazardous travel over harsh terrain, is not as obvious as one might perhaps think. The Welsh bishops and abbots stayed close to Baldwin. He was rarely without the company of some Welsh prince or princeling. They were all most hospitable, except the canons of St David's,[94] but it is obvious that they were watching Baldwin's every move. Gerald's value as liaison-officer was immense, but occasionally he must have been an embarrassment. It was not easy for Baldwin, that modest and lowly-born ex-monk, a man of few words and extremely slow in his reactions, to cope with such a tempestuous personality as Rhys ap Gruffydd, Prince of South Wales; but through his mother Angharad Gerald was the Prince's first cousin once removed. On the other hand Gerald was the defeated rival and bitter critic of Bishop Peter de Leia, who stayed with Baldwin during the whole journey through South Wales. Gerald helped with the preaching. He addressed the assembled Welshmen at Haverfordwest, preached in St David's cathedral, as the Arch-

94. ibid., I.1, a passage added in 1197.

bishop had to leave early, and gave sermons in Cardigan, Lampeter and Shrewsbury.

On his own admission, Gerald was an extremely handsome man.[95] He had known Baldwin for a number of years and the Archbishop was very fond of him.[96] His conversation was brilliant and he must have been a gay travelling-companion. He was intrigued by every place they visited, and familiar with quite a few of them. His personal enthusiasms seem to have had no limit: local history, local topography, folklore, animals of all sorts, clothing, language, weapons and warfare, religious houses, food, weather, demoniacal possession, mountain scenery, forests covered by the sea, silver mines, quicksands, genealogies, music.[97] A witty exchange overheard between two monks who were laying table could set him roaring.[98] He held nothing more hilarious than that an Archdeacon of Shrewsbury called Peche (= Sin) and his Dean who was a Daiville or De Eyville (= Devil or Evil) should have under their jurisdiction both Malplace (= Bad Place) and Malpas (= Bad Pass).[99] Lifted out of himself by this endless flow of fascinating talk, even Archbishop Baldwin, that grave and simple man, so soon to die in misery and disillusion outside the grim walls of Acre, was inspired to try a little joke. 'Why is the nightingale wiser than the Archbishop?' he asked, mopping his brow and shaking a few pebbles out of his sandals. 'Because it has the sense never to visit Wales.'[100]

Then, of course, Gerald was already on the way to becoming a well-known author. If you were with him for more than two or three days and he thought that your interest was worth cultivating, he would present you with copies of his books and expect you to start reading them straightaway, asking you each morning how you were getting on.[101] If a horse fell into a quicksand, you could be sure that it was the one carrying his manuscripts.[102] If a golden oriole flew out of a bush, he made a note of it. If he

95. Cp. n. 80.   96. *Spec.*, II.33.
97. See pp. 42–4 for fuller treatment.
98. *Itin.*, I.8.   99. ibid., II.13.
100. ibid., II.6. I have paraphrased Baldwin's riddle.
101. ibid., I.2.   102. ibid., I.8.

saw a dog without a tail, he wrote the odd circumstance down. All this brilliant conversation, all these personal interests, all these things observed would go into the book which he was writing at the moment. How do you do, Master Gerald? Always scribble, scribble, I suppose. Before you knew where you were, he would have given a copy to Henry, Richard or John, princes who had little or no interest in literature, and then all your peccadilloes would be noised abroad.[103]

The language problem is an interesting one. Baldwin obviously knew no Welsh and he gave his sermons in Latin. One assumes that Gerald was a fluent Welsh-speaker and that the most important of all his functions would have been to translate. This was not so. When Baldwin preached the Cross, someone else interpreted, usually Alexander, Archdeacon of Bangor.[104] When Gerald himself preached at Haverfordwest, he went out of his way to avoid using Welsh. 'Many found it odd and some, indeed, thought it little short of miraculous that when I, the Archdeacon, preached the word of God, speaking first in Latin and then in French, those who could not understand a word of either language were just as much moved to tears as the others, rushing forward in equal numbers to receive the sign of the Cross.'[105] Did he really know any Welsh? Maybe he used it when speaking to the Welsh princes. If so, he was very careful to avoid admitting it.[106]

103. ibid., First Preface. Henry II laughed his head off over the story of the Archdeacon of Brecon and the Bishop of St Asaph threatening to excommunicate each other. See *De rebus*, I.7.

104. In Radnor, the sermon 'was explained to the Welsh by an interpreter' (*Itin.*, I.1). In Usk Castle, 'Alexander, Archdeacon of Bangor, acted as interpreter for the Welsh' (*Itin.*, I.5). On Anglesey 'Alexander, the local Archdeacon . . . acted as our interpreter' (*Itin.*, II.7). Elsewhere there is no mention of translation.

105. *Itin.*, I.11. Odd and miraculous it may have been, but it seems unnecessarily complicated. Gerald nowhere else mentions the language which he is using.

106. The few words of Welsh in *Itin.*, I.6, I.8, etc., are rather pathetic. There are two short sentences of Welsh in *Desc.*, I.12.

3. *The route followed:*

It is possible to establish in close detail the route which the
Archbishop followed. The dating is less sure, and presumably
less important. Gerald gives us two firm dates: they left Llanfair
and rode to Nefyn on the 'vigilia Paschae floridi', the day before
Palm Sunday = Saturday 9 April;[107] and they crossed the
River Dee and rode to Chester on the 'feria tertia ante Pascha',
Holy Thursday = 14 April.[108] There is one other date, less
firm: Baldwin and Gerald began their journey from Hereford on
an unspecified day, crossed the border and came to New Radnor
'circa jejunii caput', 'about the beginning of the Lenten fast',
that is soon after Ash Wednesday, which was 2 March.[109] The
problem is to decide how soon after. Ranulph de Glanville, the
Justiciar, rode into New Radnor with them. There is evidence
that Ranulph de Glanville was with Henry II in Clarendon on
Tuesday 1 March, and that on that day the King summoned
Archbishop Baldwin to speak to him.[110] Whether or not Baldwin
did speak to the King about the matter in hand on 1 March, or
later, or, indeed, much later, is not known. What is certain is that
Baldwin and Gerald set off together from Hereford. The distance

107. *Itin.*, II.6.
108. ibid., II.11.
109. ibid., I.1.
110. The evidence is Letter CCXL in the series *Epistolae Cantuarienses
1187–1199* (ed. William Stubbs, Rolls Series, 38.II, 1865, pp. 221–2), in
which the emissaries of the Convent of Christ Church, Canterbury, report
on their interview with Henry II concerning their quarrel with Archbishop
Baldwin. 'Apud Clarendone regem invenimus in die Lunae [= 29 February
1188]. Die Martis [= 1 March] locuti sumus cum eo coram Randulfo de
Glanvilla . . . jussit nos apud Wintoniam expectare, donec cum archiepiscopo
loqueretur, quem mandaverat.' The King would hardly have packed the
monks off to Winchester if he was hoping to speak to Baldwin later that same
day. I can only assume that he failed to contact Baldwin, who was already in
Hereford. Otherwise, as Bishop Stubbs remarks with some exaggeration: 'At
least a week must have elapsed after the 2nd of March before they left
Radnor' (op. cit., p. lxiv, n. 4), Baldwin and Gerald going forward and
Ranulph de Glanville turning back.

from Hereford to New Radnor by the modern road is some
twenty-six miles, by horse an easy day's journey which would
have left Baldwin fresh enough to preach that same night. The
distance from Clarendon to New Radnor by the modern road is
some 130 miles. If Ranulph de Glanville set off from Clarendon
early on the morning of 2 March he could have done the journey
in, at the least, three days. In that case he could have caught up
with Baldwin and Gerald either in Hereford on the evening of
3 March or near the Welsh border on the afternoon of 4 March
and so ridden with them into New Radnor early that evening.

On twenty-four occasions only, if Chester and Shrewsbury
are included, Gerald tells us where they spent the night. From
their leaving Hereford, probably on the morning of Friday 4
March, until their arrival in St David's, probably on the evening
of Thursday 24 March, their journey can be made to last
twenty-one days. From their return to Hereford, probably on
Saturday 23 April, working backwards to their departure from
St David's on an unspecified day, probably Monday 28 March,
it seems to have lasted twenty-seven days. Three days are
missing. One could argue, without evidence, for the inclusion of
these three days piecemeal in various places. Rather than do this,
I have made them stay three days in St David's, which seems
plausible enough.[111] The timetable would then have been:

Wednesday 2 March: Ash Wednesday.
Friday 4 March: They left Hereford.[112] They crossed the

111. Another solution, of course, is to make the whole journey begin three
days later. It is unlikely that they would have stayed only one night in St
David's. It is true that Baldwin was called away from St David's to meet
Prince Rhys in Cardigan, but he did not hurry on the way. He probably
spent one night in Llanhyver Castle, and Gerald caught up with him and
they spent a night in St Dogmael's. It looks almost as if they contrived
together that Gerald should preach in St David's. After all, they had already
passed some time in Prince Rhys' company.

112. Gerald does not say at this point that they started from Hereford. At
some time about 24 April they ended their journey in that city and he wrote:
'We thus described a full circle and returned once more to the place from
which we had begun this rather exhausting journey through Wales' (*Itin.*,
II.13).

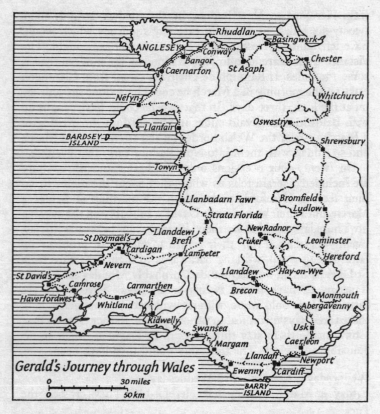

Gerald's Journey through Wales

0 ——————— 30 miles
0 ——————— 50 km

Welsh border [circa jejunii caput] and travelled with Ranulph
de Glanville to NEW RADNOR, where Baldwin preached and
where they presumably passed the night.

Saturday 5 March: That morning [in crastino vero mane] they
said Mass and Ranulph de Glanville left them and returned
to England They doubled back about two miles to CRUKER
CASTLE near OLD RADNOR. The youth Hector considered
taking the Cross. They presumably passed the night in Cruker
Castle.

Sunday 6 March: That morning [die sequente] Hector took the

Cross. That evening [circa vesperam] Maelgwn ap Cadwallon took the Cross. They presumably spent a second night in Cruker Castle.

Monday 7 March: They rode southwards, crossed the River Wye and a sermon was preached in HAY-ON-WYE, where they presumably passed the night. Baldwin was certainly in the castle.

Tuesday 8 March: That morning [mane] they rode towards Brecon, reached LLANDDEW, preached there and stayed the night, in the Bishop's palace or possibly in Gerald's archdeaconry.

Wednesday 9 March: They were in BRECON.

Thursday 10 March: They rode through Coed Grwyne, passed Llanthony on their left and reached ABERGAVENNY, where a sermon was preached. They presumably passed the night in the castle.

Friday 11 March: They rode to USK CASTLE, where Baldwin and William de Salso Marisco, Bishop of Llandaff, both preached. They presumably passed the night there.

Saturday 12 March: They left Monmouth far away on their left, rode through CAERLEON, crossed the River Usk three times and reached NEWPORT, where they spent the night.

Sunday 13 March: They preached in Newport and maybe passed a second night there.

Monday 14 March: They crossed the River Rhymney and came to CARDIFF. They probably stayed the night there.

Tuesday 15 March: That morning [in crastino] a sermon was preached in LLANDAFF. They remained there all day and spent the night with Bishop William.

Wednesday 16 March: That morning [mane] Baldwin said Mass in Llandaff cathedral and they left immediately. They passed EWENNY and came to MARGAM ABBEY. They probably stayed the night, the more so as Gerald praises Margam's hospitality.

Thursday 17 March: They forded the River Avon, followed the sea-shore, rowed across the River Neath and spent the night in SWANSEA CASTLE.

Friday 18 March: That morning [mane vero] Mass was said and a sermon was preached in Swansea. Cador came and went. That night [eadem nocte] the witty monks discussed the previous day's quicksands. They presumably spent a second night in Swansea.

Saturday 19 March: They crossed the River Loughor and the two Gwendraeth streams, and came to KIDWELLY CASTLE. Presumably they spent the night there.

Sunday 20 March: They rowed across the River Tywi, left Llanstephan and Laugharne on their left, and came to CARMARTHEN. Presumably they spent the night there.

Monday 21 March: They rode on to the monastery of WHIT-LAND. They obviously spent the night there, although Gerald does not say so.

Tuesday 22 March: That morning [in crastino], still in Whit-land, they signed the twelve archers of St Clears with the Cross. They traversed the River Taff and the two Cleddau streams, and so came to HAVERFORDWEST, where they presumably spent the night.

Wednesday 23 March: Baldwin and Gerald both preached in Haverfordwest. They probably spent a second night there.

Thursday 24 March: They rode twelve miles farther on to ST DAVID'S, passing through CAMROSE and along Newgale Sands. In St David's they were put up by Bishop Peter de Leia.

Friday 25 March:

Saturday 26 March: } Three full days in St David's?

Sunday 27 March:

Monday 28 March: Early in the morning [summo diliculo, with no mention of the day] Baldwin said Mass in St David's cathedral, left Gerald to preach, and set off through Cemais to meet Rhys ap Gruffydd again in Cardigan. There is talk of Llanhyver Castle in NEVERN. Baldwin probably stayed the night there.

Tuesday 29 March: Gerald joined Baldwin in the monastery in ST DOGMAEL'S and they spent the night there.

Wednesday 30 March: The next morning [in crastino] they

rode the short distance to CARDIGAN. That night they were
put up by Rhys ap Gruffydd.

Thursday 31 March: Baldwin and Gerald both preached at the
bridgehead over the River Teifi, and the site of a chapel was
marked out on the turf. Presumably they spent a second night
in Cardigan.

Friday 1 April: They left Cardigan Castle, crossed the River
Teifi and rode to LAMPETER. They spent the night there,
although Gerald does not say so.

Saturday 2 April: The next morning [in crastino] Baldwin,
Gerald, John, Abbot of Whitland, and Seisyll, Abbot of
Strata Florida, all preached in Lampeter. That same night
[ea nocte] they reached STRATA FLORIDA, where they stayed
for a while to repose themselves [moram fecimus].

Sunday 3 April: ⎫
Monday 4 April: ⎬ I will assume that they stayed three full days
Tuesday 5 April: ⎭ in Strata Florida.

Wednesday 6 April: They resumed their journey, stopping to
preach in the open air to Rhys ap Gruffydd and his three
sons. They rode through LLANDDEWI BREFI and reached
LLANBADARN FAWR, where they spent the night.

Thursday 7 April: The next morning [mane] they preached in
Llanbadarn Fawr. They rowed across the River Dovey,
entered North Wales and journeyed on to TOWYN, where they
spent the night.

Friday 8 April: Early the next morning [in crastino vero, mane]
Gruffydd ap Cynan met them. That same day [eodem die]
they were ferried across the River Mawddach and reached
LLANFAIR, where they spent the night.

Saturday 9 April: They crossed Traeth Mawr and Traeth
Bychan, and rode on to NEFYN, where they spent the night,
this being the 'vigilia videlicet Paschae floridi', the Saturday
before Palm Sunday.

Sunday 10 April: The next morning [in crastino] Baldwin
preached in Nefyn. They rode through CAERNARFON to
BANGOR, where they spent the night with Bishop Gwion.

Monday 11 April: The next morning [in crastino] Baldwin

said Mass in Bangor cathedral. They then crossed to ANGLE-
SEY. Baldwin, Alexander, Archdeacon of Bangor, and
Seisyll, Abbot of Strata Florida, all three preached. They
returned to Bangor.

Tuesday 12 April: They crossed the River Conway and came
to RHUDDLAN CASTLE, where they were put up by David ab
Owain.

Wednesday 13 April: In the morning [mane] they preached.
They rode on to ST ASAPH, where Baldwin said Mass. They
went straight on to BASINGWERK ABBEY, where they spent
the night.

Thursday 14 April: Holy Thursday, 'feria tertia ante Pascha'.
This next morning [in crastino] they crossed the River Dee
and rode to CHESTER.

Friday 15 April: ⎫ Good Friday. They spent Easter in
Saturday 16 April: ⎬ Easter Saturday. Chester
Sunday 17 April: ⎭ Easter Sunday. Baldwin preached.

Monday 18 April: They rode past WHITCHURCH ABBEY and
came to OSWESTRY, where they were put up by William
FitzAlan.

Tuesday 19 April: They travelled on to SHREWSBURY.

Wednesday 20 April: ⎫ They stayed a few days [diebus aliquot]
Thursday 21 April: ⎬ to rest in Shrewsbury. It could not have
Friday 22 April: ⎭ been less than three. Both Baldwin and
Gerald preached.

Saturday 23 April: They rode over WENLOCK EDGE past
BROMFIELD PRIORY and LUDLOW CASTLE, through LEO-
MINSTER and so came once more to HEREFORD.

4. *The three versions of* The Journey through Wales:

There can be no doubt that Gerald kept a diary as he rode
through Wales with Archbishop Baldwin. It may have been
little more than a list of places visited, people met and sermons
delivered, with perhaps rough notes on local topics which were
worth writing up. Only once does he go wrong on the route

followed, and that is in a sentence added twenty-six years later.[113]

As soon as the journey was over, he set about writing the first draft of his book. He had many other preoccupations. He was revising *The Topography of Ireland* and *The Conquest of Ireland*. In the spring of 1189 he crossed to France, under the impression that he was to fulfil his vow and go on the Third Crusade with Henry II, and after his death with Richard, but by midsummer he was unexpectedly back in Dover again. He had his day-to-day affairs to see to.

There are three manuscript copies of the first version of *The Journey through Wales*:

R.   British Library, Bib. Reg. 13B.VIII. Late twelfth or early thirteenth century.
B.   Bodleian Library, Rawlinson B.188. Early thirteenth century.
F.   Cambridge University Library, Ff.1.27. Late thirteenth or early fourteenth century.

None is the autograph of Gerald. F is simply an accurate copy of R. All three lack the First Preface, although it appears, down to the quotation from Juvenal, at the end of the text in B, with the dedication 'Guillelmo Eliensi episcopo', i.e. for William de Longchamp, Bishop of Ely, 1190–96,[114] instead of 'For Stephen, Archbishop of Canterbury'. They have the Second Preface, without, of course, the words 'Praefatio Secunda' and the reference to Stephen. The passages concerning William de Braose in *Itin.*, I.2, are far more trenchantly worded than they were to be later. A large part of what was to form the second and third versions had not yet been written;[115] and all in all the book

113. *Itin.*, II.6, where he puts the River Dysynni between the River Mawddach and the Traeth Mawr, and the River Artro between the Traeth Mawr and the Traeth Bychan.
114. By the time Gerald came to write *The Life of Geoffrey, Archbishop of York*, William de Longchamp had become for him the 'belua multiformis', the 'monster of all iniquities' (*V.G.*, II.19).
115. For a list of the main additions made in the second and third versions see Appendix I, pp. 275–7.

was still much more what it professed to be, an account of a seven-week-long preaching mission in Wales. This first version is thought to have been composed in the spring or summer of 1191.[116]

The second version[117] of *The Journey through Wales* is contained in one manuscript only and that a very late one:

Hc. British Library, Harleian 359. Sixteenth century.

The First Preface is there in its entirety, with the dedication 'Hugoni Lincolniensi episcopo magister Giraldus Kambrensis', i.e. for Hugh, Bishop of Lincoln, 1186–1200, instead of 'For Stephen, Archbishop of Canterbury', and the consequent change, 'Hugo Lincolniensis episcope', towards the end. The Second Preface is there, but with the words 'per te, vir inclite, Stephane Cantuariensis archiepiscope' not yet written. There is a most important addition in which Gerald tells how the canons of St David's tried to persuade Rhys ap Gruffydd to prevent Baldwin from carrying out his mission to Wales and above all from visiting St David's itself (*Itin.*, I.1). He is much more kind to William de Braose, and there is a new passage concerning his piety. Then there is a considerable number of accretions which greatly confuse the narrative-line of the book, but which are of interest to the modern reader.[118] This second version was probably written about 1197.[119]

116. It cannot have been written before the death of Baldwin on 19 November 1190, or after the downfall of William de Longchamp in October 1191.

117. In manuscripts V and N of *The Description of Wales* that book is dedicated to Hubert, Archbishop of Canterbury, and not yet to Stephen, with the consequent statement in the first paragraph of the First Preface that Gerald had previously dedicated *The Journey through Wales* to Hubert. Hubert Walter became Archbishop on 30 May 1193. No copy of *The Journey through Wales* with this dedication exists. Is this yet another version, between the first and the second? It is much more likely that Gerald simply took a copy of the first version and replaced the name of William de Longchamp by that of a new dedicatee, Hubert, Archbishop of Canterbury.

118. See Appendix I, pp. 275–7.

119. It contains allusions to historical events which took place in 1194. As we have seen, Gerald was in Lincoln from 1196 to 1198. He would no doubt

INTRODUCTION

The third version is contained in three manuscripts:

D. British Library, Domitian A.1. Mid thirteenth century.
Rd. British Library, Bib. Reg. 13B.XII. Late sixteenth century. Two copies.
P. Phillipps, 6914. Thirteenth century.

It is this version which is dedicated to Stephen Langton, Archbishop of Canterbury, 1207–28. It again contains a great amount of new material. A few of the additions are relevant to the journey and the preaching: a half-sentence elaborating the description of how Gerald took the Cross in Radnor (*Itin.*, I.1); an additional sentence on Gerald's preaching in Haverfordwest, and how he spoke in Latin and French (*Itin.*, I.11); the faulty description of the crossing of the Rivers Dysynni and Artro (*Itin.*, II.6); and the deathbed vision of Archbishop Richard, with the passage about Thomas Becket (*Itin.*, II.14). There are many other additions less germane to the issue.[120] This third and last version was probably written in 1214.[121]

---

have offered a copy of his book to Saint Hugh fairly soon but not immediately after his arrival.

120. See Appendix I, pp. 275–7.

121. Stephen Langton returned to England and took possession of his archbishopric in July 1213. The dedication addressed to him had first been written for Hugh, Bishop of Lincoln, and it would not be applicable to Stephen until some months at least after his arrival in England. Geoffrey of Llanthony is mentioned as the most recent Bishop of St David's in *Itin.*, II.1. He died at the end of 1214. His successor, Iorwerth, of Tally, was consecrated on 21 June 1215. The third version was probably completed before Geoffrey's death and certainly before Iorwerth's consecration. It may well have been presented to Stephen Langton when Gerald met him in Guildford in the autumn of 1215.

5. ' . . . *cum notabilibus suis*' :

One assumes that the chapter-headings are by Gerald himself.[122] Whether they are or not, with very few exceptions these headings end with the words 'with such additional details as are worth recording'.[123] We are, in short, warned from the very beginning of the 1191 version that Gerald does not propose to limit himself to Baldwin's rhetorical activities. In effect, a considerable part of *The Journey through Wales* has nothing to do with Baldwin at all, being a series of disquisitions upon such matters of local interest as caught Gerald's fancy as he rode along, were related to him during the candle-lit evenings or occurred to him later. If we are concerned only with Baldwin's mission and the preaching of the Third Crusade in Wales, this is a fundamental weakness in the book. If, as is more likely, we are interested in a more general way in the state of Wales at the end of the twelfth century, it is one of the book's chief attractions.

Like many authors, Gerald constantly re-wrote his books. The three different versions of *The Journey through Wales* have been discussed on pp. 36-9. It is the third version, Gerald's final revision, which we are reading. Quite a deal of the extraneous material was added after the writing of the first version. If we consider at this point the major changes which he made down the years, we shall see how the book evolved and, conversely, we shall establish how much of it did begin life as a day-to-day diary of Baldwin's journey.

In Appendix I on pp. 275-7 I have listed the twenty-two additions made in Version II and the nineteen additions made in Version III.[124] They are of greatly varying length and any mathematical analysis would be valueless. The importance of the

122. In all three manuscripts of the first version they are listed at the beginning, and they are in their place at the head of each chapter. This, of course, proves nothing.

123. The chapter-headings of *Itin.*, II.13 and II.14, lack these words. *Itin.*, I.6 has 'cum partium illarum notabilibus'.

124. I have omitted additions or changes of one or two words only with no particular significance.

change of dedication in the First Preface is discussed on pp. 37–9. There are two quotations from Gerald's earlier books, on Saint Patrick's horn from *The Topography of Ireland*,[125] and on Henry II's visit to St David's in 1172 from *The Conquest of Ireland*.[126] Thirteen of the additions describe various local prodigies and marvels. Three are nature notes on dogs and beavers. Six are historical anecdotes about William de Braose, Henry II, Owain Gwynedd, Richard I, a nameless Cistercian abbot and Robert de Belesme. Two are historical lists of the monarchs reigning in 1188 and of the princes of South and North Wales. One contains quotations from two books in the New Testament. One is a vague and negative remark about deeds of violence done in the Black Mountains. One consists of three additional sentences on the salubrious air of Llanthony. Three more contain interesting references to historical events which occurred after Version I was finished: Rhys ap Gruffydd's adventures in Llanhyver Castle in 1191–4, the sons of Owain ap Gruffydd and events which happened in 1194, and how Geoffrey of Llanthony became Bishop of St David's in 1203.

This leaves us with eight additions in the revised versions of 1197 and 1214 which really deal with the matter in hand. At the very beginning of his book Gerald adds the information that certain canons of St David's did their utmost to persuade Rhys ap Gruffydd to put an end to Baldwin's journey when it had hardly started and above all to prevent him from visiting St David's.[127] Gerald's own position was equivocal. He was a canon of St David's, and he was the leader of the movement for freeing the see from the jurisdiction of Canterbury. On the other hand he was proposing to ride to St David's at Baldwin's side and to preach the Cross in the cathedral as Baldwin's representative. At their fifth stop, in Brecon, Gerald presented a copy of *The Topography of Ireland* to Baldwin and the gift was greatly appreciated.[128] He stresses the fact, which we knew already, that, of all those who took the Cross as the result of the Archbishop's preaching, he himself was the first to stand up, and he did so

125. *Itin.*, I. 2. 126. ibid., II.1.
127. *Itin.*, I.1. 128. ibid., I.2.

41

only after mature reflection.[129] He makes clear to us that when he preached so eloquently in Haverfordwest, he spoke first in Latin and then in French.[130] Then come the two small topographical additions, the joke about the quicksands along the sea-shore between the River Avon and the River Neath,[131] and the muddle about the River Dysynni and the River Artro.[132] Finally there are the two additions to the word-portrait of Archbishop Baldwin: the rebuke by Pope Urban III[133] and the condemnation of both Baldwin and his predecessor Archbishop Richard for their failure to press home the advantage gained by Thomas Becket.[134]

There is an interesting piece of re-writing to observe. Bk I, ch. 4 of *The Journey through Wales* contains an account of the activities of William de Braose, Lord of Abergavenny and of Brecon. When he was at home in his archdeaconry in Llanddew, Gerald lived almost in the shadow of Brecon Castle. Version I had been highly critical of William. This was obviously an unwise move, and in Version II Gerald toned down what he had written and added an admiring passage. William quarrelled with John in 1207 and finally died in exile in Corbeuil on 9 August 1211. In Version III Gerald was thus able to return to his earlier criticism, but he chose not to do so in detail.

When all these later accretions and re-writings have been cleared away, it is obvious that Gerald had been every whit as discursive in his method of composition in the 1191 text of his book as he was to be in the additions made in Versions II and III. In effect, in the 13 +. 14 chapters of Version I there are no fewer than 129 of these digressions from the real matter in hand, some of them short, others very long. It can be argued that most of them are fair comment. It is agreeable that Gerald should have included attractive natural descriptions of the site of Llanthony Abbey, of his own birthplace in Manorbier and of the mountain-scenery of Snowdonia. Many of the places which they visited inspired him to expatiate upon historical events which had

129. ibid., I.1.
131. ibid., I.8.
133. ibid., II.14.
130. ibid., I.11.
132. ibid., II.6.
134. ibid.

occurred in the neighbourhood, local miracles and natural prodigies. Again this is interesting as long as it is kept under control. Sometimes, however, Gerald's comments are so numerous that we quite lose the thread of the narrative.[135] In the very long chapter on St David's, Baldwin is mentioned in one sentence only.[136] The chapter on Pembrokeshire has nothing to do with the journey at all.[137] Whatever attraction and interest this wandering method of composition may hold for the enquiring reader, it has weaknesses which are only too obvious. The miracle of the boy who stole pigeons from Saint David's church in Llanfaes[138] encouraged Gerald to add in Version III not dissimilar miracles in Bury St Edmunds, Howden and Winchcombe. The story of Owain ap Caradog's faithful hound[139] led to anecdotes of a dog in Antioch and an imprisoned king who was freed by his pack of hounds. From the freebooter of Haverfordwest Castle,[140] we move to the blind prisoner of Châteauroux. Stephen Wiriet and his poltergeist[141] open up a discussion of poltergeists in general, which in turn becomes a debate on why lightning strikes churches, illustrated by anecdotes of the possessed woman in Poitou and what Peter Abelard said to King Philippe I. Mention of the beavers in the River Teifi[142] becomes an essay on the habits, real and imagined, of those industrious animals. The bitch without a tail in Anglesey which bore tailless puppies encouraged Gerald to discuss the handing on to children of acquired physical peculiarities, and to tell stories of the knight Erchembald who had a scar beneath his nose, Alberic, Earl de Vere, who had a damaged eye, the man with a nervous tic, and even the queen who bore a black child because she had a painting of a Negro in her bedroom.[143]

Later on in this introduction I shall discuss the value of Gerald's encyclopaedic approach to the country in which he was

135. E.g. the journey through Hay-on-Wye, Llanddew and Brecon, *Itin.*, I.2; the journey through Llandaff, Ewenny and Margam Abbey, *Itin.*, I.7; the stay in Haverfordwest, *Itin.*, I.11; and the visit to Anglesey, *Itin.*, II.7.

136. *Itin.*, II.1. 137. ibid., I.12.
138. ibid., I.2. 139. ibid., I.7.
140. ibid., I. 11. 141. ibid., I. 12.
142. ibid., II.3. 143. ibid., II.7.

born.[144] For the moment we must agree that, however fascinating they may be, there are too many of these 'notabilia' and they detract from the artistic unity of his book.

6. *The editions :*

There have been five editions of the *Itinerarium Cambriae*. Only the last, that by the Rev. James F. Dimock in the Rolls Series, is of any value.

1585: David Powel. *Topographia Hiberniae, sive de Mirabilibus Hiberniae. Expugnatio Hiberniae. Itinerarium Cambriae, seu . . . Baldvini Cantuar. Archiepiscopi per Walliam legationis descriptio cum annotationibus D. Poveli.* London. The text of the *Itinerarium* is an amalgam of Versions I, II and III, with arbitrary omissions, e.g. the praise of Saint Thomas, II.14, pp. 206–7 ('The quarrel . . . a second time') and the deathbed vision of Archbishop Richard, II.14, pp. 207–8 ('When the martyr's first successor . . . the winnowing-fans').

1602: William Camden. *Anglica, Hibernica, Normannica, Cambrica, a veteribus scripta: ex quibus Asser Menevensis, Anonymus de vita Gulielmi Conquestoris, Thomas Walsingham, Thomas de la More, Gulielmus Gemiticensis, Giraldus Cambrensis: plerique nunc primum in lucem editi ex bibliotheca Gulielmi Camdeni.* Frankfurt. There is nothing *in lucem editum ex bibliotheca* about the *Itinerarium:* it is simply reprinted from David Powel.

1691: Henry Wharton. *Anglia Sacra, sive Collectio Historiarum . . . de Archiepiscopis et Episcopis Angliae, a prima fidei Christianae susceptione ad annum 1540; nunc primum in lucem editarum.* London. The *Itinerarium* is reprinted from Camden, who had reprinted it from Powel.

1804: Sir Richard Colt Hoare. *Itinerarium Cambriae, seu laboriosae Balduini Cantuariensis Archiepiscopi per Walliam legationis accurata descriptio autore S. Giraldo Cambrense. Cum*

144. See pp. 47–8.

annotationibus D. Poweli. London. This again is reprinted from Camden. Hoare has canonized Gerald.

1868: James F. Dimock. *Giraldi Cambrensis opera. Vol. VI. Itinerarium Kambriae et Descriptio Kambriae.* Rolls Series, London. This is a critical edition of Version III based on MS D, with full variants.

7. *The earlier translation:*

The *Itinerarium* has been translated into English only once before, but that translation has been printed three times.

1806: Sir Richard Colt Hoare. *The Itinerary of Archbishop Baldwin through Wales A.D. 1188 translated into English, and illustrated with views, annotations and a life of Giraldus by Sir R. Colt Hoare, Bart. Description of Wales, by Giraldus de Barri, with annotations by Sir R. C. Hoare.* 2 vols, London. This is an incorrect translation of Camden's faulty 1602 edition, itself reprinted from David Powel.

1847: *The Historical Works of Giraldus Cambrensis. Containing the Topography of Ireland and the History of the Conquest of Ireland, translated by T. Forester. The Itinerary through Wales, and the Description of Wales, translated by Sir R. C. Hoare. Revised and edited with additional notes by T. Wright.* Bohn's Antiquarian Library, London. The text of the *Itinerary* is a reprinting of Hoare's translation.

1908: *The Itinerary and Description of Wales. With an introduction by W. Llewelyn Williams.* Everyman's Library, London. The text of the *Itinerary* is yet another reprinting of Hoare.

8. *This translation:*

What follows at the end of this introduction is my own translation into modern English of the text of MS D of the third and last version of *The Journey through Wales*, the final revision which Gerald made in 1214 or thereabouts and which the Rev. James F. Dimock printed in 1868. I have also translated all the quotations, both prose and verse. For Welsh proper names I have consulted Sir John Lloyd, *A History of Wales*, 3rd edition, 1939, both for *The Journey through Wales* and *The Description of Wales*. For Welsh place-names I have followed *A Gazetteer of Welsh Place-names*, edited by Elwyn Davies, 1957. My book is a translation into English, and when a place-name has an accepted English form, e.g. Swansea, Brecon, the River Dovey, I have used it. Where I have failed to locate a quotation I have said so in the notes.

III. THE DESCRIPTION OF WALES

In some sense *The Description of Wales* stands in the same relation to *The Journey through Wales* as *The Topography of Ireland* does to *The Conquest of Ireland*. According to Gerald all four were his *œuvres de jeunesse*, his minor works, although he stresses that they had taken a long time to compose. His purpose in writing *The Description of Wales* was a simple straightforward one: he proposed to describe the Welsh people and Wales itself, his own country, to reveal in full the secrets of his native land, to rescue from oblivion recent happenings which had not been fully recorded elsewhere. His material is original and gathered from personal observation, although, indeed, Gildas had preceded him. Some critics might condemn it as humdrum and unworthy; but he offered it to posterity all the same as a gesture of gratitude to the land where he was born, and he hoped that it would give pleasure to his own relations and to his fellow-countrymen. He had no doubt that the book would bring him fame; it would certainly bring him neither wealth nor advancement.[145]

145. All these points are taken from the two Prefaces. See pp. 211-17.

1. *The shape and subject-matter :*

In intention at least *The Description of Wales* has a neat shape.
Book I, which is divided into eighteen chapters, has nothing but
good to say of the Welsh. Gerald's praise is unstinted: it is well-
informed and it covers a very wide field. First he describes the
natural features of Wales: its size and its essential division into
three parts, Gwynedd, Deheubarth and Powys; its cantrefs, the
royal palaces and the cathedral sees; its rivers and mountain-
ranges; its great fertility and its agricultural products. Inserted
into the first part of Book I is a genealogy of the Welsh princes,
showing that those of Deheubarth and Gwynedd all descend
from Rhodri Mawr. There is also a discussion of the name
Cambria. From this physical description of Wales, Gerald moves
on to a consideration of the Welsh people. They are bold, agile
and courageous. When they have to be they are frugal in their
eating habits, and they are modest in their dress. They are most
hospitable to strangers. They cut their hair short, care for their
teeth and shave their faces. They are a shrewd people. Gerald
praises their music-making, their wit, their readiness in repartee.
They are much given to prophecy and soothsaying. More than
anything else in the world they respect noble birth. He goes on to
describe how they live in wattled huts on the edge of the forest
and their rather haphazard methods of husbandry. They were
first converted to Christianity by Faganus and Duvianus.

Book II, with its ten chapters, shows the reverse side of the
medal, what Gerald calls the 'illaudabilia', the less praiseworthy
points, for as a serious historian he feels that he must not conceal
the truth, however unpalatable it may be. The Welsh are in-
constant and unstable, and they rarely keep their plighted word.
They live on plunder. In battle they appear ferocious at first, but
they soon turn in flight. They quarrel unceasingly among themselves, mainly over the possession of land. They are greedy and
they abuse the hospitality which is so readily offered. They
intermarry too closely; they hand on church benefices from father
to son; and, in the past at least, they were given to unnatural

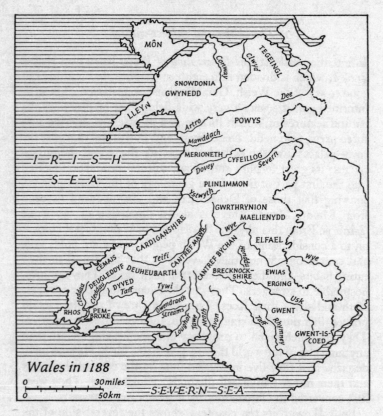

MÔN

Conway

Clwyd

TEGEINGL

SNOWDONIA
GWYNEDD

Dee

LLEYN

Artro

POWYS

Mawddach

MERIONETH

CYFEILLOG

Dovey

Severn

I—R—I—S—H
S—E—A

PLINLIMMON

Ystwyth

GWRTHRYNION
MAELIENYDD

Wye

CARDIGANSHIRE

ELFAEL

Teifi

CANTREF MAWR

Wye

CEMAIS

CANTREF BYCHAN

Honddu

EWIAS

DEUGLEDDYF

DEUHEUBARTH

BRECKNOCK-
SHIRE

Cleddau

Cleddau

DYVED
Taff

Tywi

ERGING

RHOS

PEM-
BROKE

Gwendraeth
Streams

Usk

GWENT

Loughor

Tawe

Neath

Avon

Taff

Rhymney

GWENT-IS-
COED

Wales in 1188

0   30 miles
0   50 km

S·E·V·E·R·N S·E·A

vice. The last three chapters of Book II are an extremely well-
informed and a curiously dispassionate analysis of the contemporary Welsh problem as Gerald saw it: 'How the Welsh
can be conquered', 'How Wales should be governed once it has
been conquered' and 'How the Welsh can best fight back and
keep up their resistance'. One can only say again that Gerald was
three quarters Anglo-Norman and only one quarter Welsh; that
he had few good words to say of the Norman invaders and none
at all of the English; and that the gall in which he so often
dipped his pen could be more bitter than any of this.

48

2. *The three versions of* The Description of Wales:

I have established that Gerald finished the first version of *The Journey through Wales* in the spring or summer of 1191. He seems to have begun writing *The Description of Wales* almost immediately. Once again the text exists in three redactions.

Of the first version of *The Description of Wales* no early copy now exists. The manuscripts used by James F. Dimock are:

V. British Library, Cotton, Vitellius C.X. Second half of fourteenth century.

N. British Library, Cotton, Nero D.VIII. 1376+, late fourteenth century, perhaps early fifteenth century.

Rc. British Library, Bib. Reg., 13C.III. Second half of fourteenth century.

In all probability V and N are independent copies of a common original, while Rc is a careless copy of V. There are many late copies. This first version was dedicated to Hubert, Archbishop of Canterbury. At some time Gerald seems to have presented a copy of it, possibly with no other change except the dedication itself, to Hugh, Bishop of Lincoln. This still existed in 1691, but it has since disappeared, no doubt in the fire which occurred in the library of Westminster Abbey in 1694. A feature of manuscripts V, N and Rc is that a whole folio from the Second Preface ('I have no doubt about it . . . to be praised by them')[146] was displaced in the lost copy from which they all derive and appears in error towards the beginning of Book II, ch. 7. Much more serious is the fact that they all three lack a very long sequence from the middle of Bk I, ch. 8, to the middle of Bk I, ch. 17 ('handfuls of arrows . . . or garden produce').[147] As we have seen, Gerald presented a copy of *The Journey through Wales* to Archbishop Hubert, who was consecrated on 30 May 1193.[148] It was after this that he gave Hubert a copy of *The Description of*

146. See pp. 216–17.
147. See pp. 234–52.
148. See p. 38, n. 117.

Wales.[149] In Bk I, ch. 3, he lists Dafydd ab Owain as Prince of North Wales, although he was expelled by his nephew Llywelyn ab Iorwerth in 1194.[150] The first version of *The Description of Wales* was therefore completed in 1193 or early in 1194.

Only one copy exists of the second version of *The Description of Wales*. It is one of the manuscripts already listed on p. 39 as containing the third version of *The Journey through Wales*:

D.   British Library, Domitian A.I. Mid thirteenth century.

It is this which forms the basis of Dimock's edition. Gerald presented the third version of *The Journey through Wales* to Archbishop Stephen Langton at the end of 1214 or the beginning of 1215. Soon afterwards he gave him this second version of *The Description of Wales*.[151] In the prologue to his book *The Rights and Privileges of the Church of St David's*, addressed to Stephen soon after 1215, Gerald says that he has already given him *The Description of Wales*. The date of this second version must therefore be early 1215.

There is one other manuscript:

Rd.   British Library, Bib. Reg. 13B.XII. Late sixteenth century.

Dimock lists this as a second copy of Version II, but it seems more sensible to call it Version III. At some moment, presumably after 1215, Gerald took a copy of Version II, read it through a last time and made four final changes.[152] The manuscript which he held in his hand has not come down to us, and more is the pity, for the corrections would be in his own handwriting; but what we have is a very late copy of a lost original.

---

149. See the First Preface of *The Description of Wales*, p. 211. This statement refers both to the first version given to Hubert and to the second version given to Stephen Langton.

150. See p. 222.

151. See the First Preface of *The Description of Wales*, p. 211.

152. See *Giraldi Cambrensis opera*, Rolls Series, Vol. VI, p. xxix.

3. *The changes made in the second and third versions* :

These are fewer than the ones made in the two later versions of *The Journey through Wales*.

Version II of *The Description of Wales* differs from Version I in thirteen points.[153] Of these six consist of additional supporting quotations, which are of no particular interest to us today.[154] The etymological explanation of the word 'cantref' and mention of the Rivers Dysynni and Artro are factual statements.[155] The two sentences on the marcher-lords simply reinforce what has gone before. On the contrary, Gerald's description of how the Welsh used to go fishing in coracles makes fascinating reading, the more so as it obviously comes from personal experience. Maximus is the Maximianus of Geoffrey of Monmouth,[156] who took the story from the *De excidio Britanniae* of Gildas.[157] Gerald went on to mention Gildas in the next paragraph, which is also an addition, but, of course, there is no Arthur there. The last change is the most striking of all, not for what was added, which is a repetition, but for what was cut out, which was Gerald's solution for the Welsh problem: 'Indeed, it may well be thought preferable to eject the entire population which lives

153. See Appendix II on pp. 278–9.

154. The three quotations about beavers from Cicero, Juvenal and Saint Bernard (*Desc.*, I.5, p. 229) form part of the long passage repeated from *The Journey through Wales*, Bk II, ch. 3, pp. 174–7. They had not been there in Versions I and II of Gerald's earlier book, but were added in Version III.

155. Once again we catch Gerald at work. The faulty statement about the Rivers Dysynni and Artro was not there in Versions I and II of *The Journey through Wales*, Bk II, ch. 6, p. 183. Gerald added it when he was preparing Version III in 1214. At almost the same time he was writing Version II of *The Description of Wales* and he again added the two rivers, this time quite felicitously. One could be romantic enough to imagine that items iii and iv in the additions to Version II of *The Description of Wales* were made on the same day as the two parallel additions to Version III of *The Journey through Wales*, but a few minutes later.

156. *Historia Regum Britanniae*, V. 9. See *The History of the Kings of Britain* in the Penguin Classics series, pp. 134–44.

157. §§. 13–14.

there now, so that Wales can be colonized anew. The present inhabitants are virtually ungovernable, and there are some who think that it would be far safer and more sensible to turn this rough and impenetrable country into an unpopulated forest area and game preserve.'[158]

The four changes in Version III have only a modest interest for us. Gerald had ascribed to Seneca a quotation from Cicero, only to have his doubts and to write instead 'a certain moral philosopher'. In two places he brought his Welsh history up to date, to include the expulsion of Dafydd ab Owain and the death of Prince Rhys. The neat turn of phrase about Maximus is no more than a grace note. All this is Gerald at the extreme end of his life turning the pages of one of his favourite books and making a final revision.

4. The editions :

In print the *Descriptio Cambriae* has had a curious but not unexpected history. There have been five editions:

1585: David Powel. *Topographia Hiberniae,*[159] etc. This book, already described as the first printed edition of the *Itinerarium Cambriae*, also contains the first edition of the *Descriptio Cambriae*. It is not clear which manuscript or manuscripts Powel used, but he took great liberties with the text. Book II displeased him and he simply left it out, pretending that it did not exist.

1602: William Camden. *Anglica, Hibernica,* etc. Book I of the *Descriptio* is reprinted verbatim from Powel. Book II is again ignored.

1691: Henry Wharton. *Anglia Sacra,* etc. Wharton reprinted Camden's text of Book I of the *Descriptio*, with minor unjustified changes. He then published for the first time the text

158. This passage is in MSS V and N, i.e. the two copies of Version I. It is printed in Dimock's edition, p. 225, n. 4.
159. See pp. 44–5 for the full titles of these books.

of Book II. For this he used the lost Westminster Abbey manuscript of Version I and MS D of Version II, forming an arbitrary amalgam, with changes and omissions.

1804: Sir Richard Colt Hoare. *Itinerarium Cambriae*, etc. The text of the *Descriptio* is that of Wharton, with one or two small changes.

1868: James F. Dimock. *Giraldi Cambrensis opera*. Vol. VI. *Itinerarium Kambriae et Descriptio Kambriae*. Rolls Series, London. As for the *Itinerarium*, this is a critical edition based on MS D, with full variants.

5. *The earlier translation:*

In 1806 Sir Richard Colt Hoare published his translation of *The Journey through Wales* and *The Description of Wales*. Book I of *The Description of Wales* is based on his own reprinting of Wharton's faulty Latin text, taken from Camden, taken in turn from Powel. Book II is based on Hoare's reprinting of Wharton's far from perfect first edition of 1691. In 1847 Hoare's translation was reprinted in Bohn's Antiquarian Library. In 1908 it was again reprinted in Everyman's Library.

6. *This translation:*

What follows in its place in this book is a translation of MS D of *The Description of Wales* as printed by Dimock. It does not include the four small changes in MS Rd, but these are set out in Appendix II on p. 279, and discussed on pp. 50 and 52.

IV. GERALD THE HISTORIAN

The Journey through Wales does not purport to be a history book. In the First Preface Gerald presents himself to us as one who finds pleasure in the liberal arts, as the aspirant man of letters, as

one of the new masters of the Latin tongue. His aim is to write
and speak Latin really well, to use language in an elegant way,
and his dream is that by doing so he may gain eternal fame and
please generations as yet unborn. In his Second Preface he is
much more explicit:

> This little work is like a highly polished mirror. In it I have portrayed
> the pathless places which we trod, named each mountain torrent and
> each purling spring, recorded the witty things we said, set down the
> hazards of our journey and our various travails, included an account
> of such noteworthy events as occurred in those parts, some in our
> own times, others long ago, with much natural description and re-
> markable excursions into natural history, adding at the end a word-
> picture of the country itself.[160]

There will, then, be a place for history, and no inconsiderable
one at that, but it must remain subservient to the main thread of
the narrative.

The truth is that *The Journey through Wales* provides us with
quite a comprehensive history of events in that country in the
twelfth century. These happenings are not presented in chrono-
logical sequence, but in the geographical order of each day's
journey, and this is bewildering to the reader. They are much
more full for South Wales than for the territory north of the River
Dovey, and even in the South Gerald has more to say about the
history of certain localities than of others, Brecknockshire,
Pembroke and St David's, for instance. A great number of these
events are introduced by the words 'nostro tempore', and one
does not know whether to translate this as 'in our own time' or
'in my own lifetime', but wherever the circumstances demand it
Gerald harks back to the reigns of Stephen, Henry I, William
Rufus and even William the Conqueror.[161] In effect, as my
notes to the text will show, quite a full account of the political
history of South Wales in the twelfth century and quite a comprehensive picture of the personalities involved [162] could be prepared using *The Journey through Wales* as one's only book of

160. See pp. 64–70.
161. He mentions Matilda once only (*Itin.*, I.2).
162. Eventually Gerald came to know everyone: Pope Innocent III, Henry
II, Richard I, John, Rhys ap Gruffydd, Owain Cyfeiliog, not to mention his

reference. It would be much less complete for Gwynedd and very thin for Powys. His main and almost only professed source of information seems to have been personal enquiry. Gildas and Nennius are never mentioned. There are frequent memories of the Triads, and quite a number of borrowings from Geoffrey of Monmouth, a writer for whom Gerald expresses great contempt. What is quite extraordinary is the accuracy of the detail. In the succeeding versions of both *The Journey through Wales* and *The Description of Wales* he does his utmost to keep up to date. Occasionally he makes a mistake. In the relevant portions of *The History of Wales* Sir John Lloyd refers constantly to Gerald's two books, and only on the rarest occasions does he find fault with their factual material.

The *Itinerary of Wales* is of high value for the study of Welsh history at the end of the twelfth century; accurate in its facts, genial in spirit and crowded with a wealth of gay and animated figures which move briskly across the scene, it pictures for us the Wales of Rhys ap Gruffydd, the native home of fierce but devoted tribesmen, the adopted home of haughty knights and grasping clerics, with a vividness and force not easily to be matched .
The perambulation of Wales by Baldwin and Giraldus in 1188 affords the opportunity of a political survey of the country at this period, and it is especially convenient to be able to make such a survey in this year, the last but one of Henry's long reign, before the disturbance which was brought about by his death. It reveals a Wales very largely in Welsh hands, especially in the north, ruled over, indeed, for the the most part by a large number of chieftains of no great force or ability, but with one towering figure among them in the person of the Lord Rhys.[163]

If his facts are for the most part firm, in his judgements and opinions Gerald is most certainly not to be relied on. This is very obvious in his more polemical writings, where he so often has a cause to plead, but even in *The Journey through Wales* the

---

own grandmother Nest, Archbishops Baldwin, Hubert Walter, Stephen Langton, Bishops Hugh of Lincoln, Peter de Leia of St David's, William de Longchamp of Ely. What a book of personalities he could have written in his old age, and what an opportunity he missed! The portraits are there, of course, but one has to dig for them.
163. op. cit., p. 564.

reader must be constantly on the alert. Not only does his presentation of Archbishop Baldwin,[164] his uncle Bishop David FitzGerald and William de Braose, to take three examples, differ widely from that of modern historians, but his picture of this last is deliberately changed and changed again in the succeeding versions of the text. Support is given to the narrative by the innumerable quotations, but these may well prove tedious to the modern reader. The books from which longer passages are most freely copied are Gerald's own two writings on Ireland.

In the First Preface to *The Description of Wales* Gerald again concentrates on the form of his writing, on his literary talent and the flowers of his rhetoric, seeing himself, too, as a painter, rich in precious colours, the master of his art.[165] Then he turns to the matter. At the back of his mind he has 'some major work', 'the composition of a great masterpiece upon a theme both sacred and sublime',[166] but while waiting for that to fructify, he has decided to write the history of his own country, a subject humble enough in all conscience compared with that of the *Iliad*, the *Thebaid* or the *Aeneid*, but then, what would you, he was born late in the day. In the Second Preface he gives us Cicero's definition: 'History is the recording of past events, the testimony of the ages, the light of truth, a living memory, a guide for conduct and a reminder of what happened long ago.'[167]

The difficulties which face the historian are very great: there is the research-work to be done, the establishment of the truth in all its detail; then one must order one's facts, ensure a correct balance, put events in proper sequence and exclude irrelevancies. When all this is achieved, there still remains 'the difficult problem of deciding what words to use and how best to express what you want to say'.[168] In *The Description of Wales* Gerald first treats physical geography; then he turns to social and economic history. What he offers us is a most detailed picture of the day-to-day existence of the ordinary Welshman in the

164. See, for example, D. Knowles, *The Monastic Order in England*, 1950, pp. 316–22.
165. See pp. 211–12. 166. See p. 213.
167. *De oratore*, II.9. See p. 217.
168. See p. 216.

twelfth century: his wattled hut on the edge of the forest; his unwillingness to plan an orchard or even plant a vegetable-garden; his methods of ploughing, reaping and fishing; his clothes; what he eats and his behaviour at table; how he cuts his hair, shaves his face and cleans his teeth; his wife's hairstyle; what he has to say for himself, his love of part-singing and his music-making; the family's communal bed, the bed-clothes, and what they all wear when they clamber into it. There is talk now of Gildas and a pretence of learned sources, but all this is lived material. With great simplicity of style and a loving attention to each domestic circumstance, Gerald describes all that he has seen and experienced in his travels through the countryside. He cannot end his book without summing up on the Welsh problem. Now he loses all his homely warmth. Coldly and dispassionately, as in a disputation, the case is weighed, first for and then against. For a non-military man he shows an extraordinary command of military strategy and tactics, not to mention military logistics; but this, of course, was the great debating-point, the subject on which he must have heard his father and his brothers lay down the law as long as he could remember anything. With his final ringing sentence no Welshman could quarrel: 'Whatever else may come to pass, I do not think that on the Day of Direst Judgement any race other than the Welsh, or any other language, will give answer to the Supreme Judge of all from this small corner of the earth.'[169] Characteristically Gerald does not speak these words himself but reports them as having been said by an old man of Pencader in 1163.

V. GERALD THE ARTIST

The Journey through Wales and *The Description of Wales* form natural counterparts to each other in that both books set out to describe that country and its people as they were in 1188, and that through them both shines clear the luminous personality of their author. The differences between the two books are equally obvious. As Sir John Lloyd has written in the memorable page

169. *Desc.*, II.10.

57

already quoted, in *The Journey through Wales* Gerald 'mingles in the crowd, catches its accents, is borne along by its changing passions, and thus becomes a very mirror of that fighting, chaffering, praying age'. In *The Description of Wales* 'there is a broader and more philosophical outlook, a complete survey taken from the Olympian heights of a scholar's lofty seclusion . . .'[170]

There is an air of spontaneity, of day-to-day reportage about *The Journey through Wales*. It is as if after each day of their travelling Gerald sat down to record succinctly just what he and Baldwin had achieved during the last twenty-four hours, and then to enliven his diary by describing all that they had seen, the places through which they had passed, the historical events, some of national importance but others of only ephemeral interest, which had occurred there over the last hundred years, the local anecdotage and folk-tales, the personalities whom they had met, the sites which they had visited or seen afar off or discussed in casual conversation as they rode along, the geography and natural history and scenic beauty of the region. We seem to be reading the travel-talk of Gerald and Baldwin, or rather all the interesting things which Gerald had felt inspired to say that day to his distinguished but taciturn companion, for the Archbishop is portrayed throughout as a receptive listener who had little or nothing to contribute himself. All this is discursive and anecdotal in the extreme, to the point that in some chapters the journey itself and its elevated purpose are not mentioned at all, and yet when the book is read from cover to cover it forms a total and satisfying whole. The freshness and spontaneity are, of course, in some measure contrived, for, as we have seen, over the years Gerald was constantly adding to what he had written.

Both books centre on the personality of Gerald himself, for it is on him that the limelight unceasingly plays. This is true even of the sermons delivered and of the exhortations given, for, as Thomas Jones so neatly puts it, Baldwin 'preached' but Gerald 'proclaimed the word of God with grace'.[171] In his other books, with all the harassments and disappointments of life to

170. J. E. Lloyd, *A History of Wales*, p. 564.
171. Thomas Jones, *Gerallt Gymro*, p. 65.

embitter him, he appears less amiable, but in *The Journey through Wales* he is a good companion. In 1188 he was just over forty and in the very prime of life. By nature he was ebullient, categorical, never at a loss for a word. As he tells us elsewhere, Alexander, Archdeacon of Bangor, was also an excellent conversationalist: the two Archdeacons together must have been a constant source of entertainment for Baldwin. Gerald's interests were universal and his knowledge encyclopaedic. Some of his descriptions of natural scenery are beautiful in the extreme: the hills around Llanthony Prima, the rugged promontory of St David's, the vast snowbound panoramas of Snowdonia. Where his personal affections are involved, for his birthplace at Manorbier, for example, he becomes quite lyrical. His convictions are very strong, and he expresses them unequivocally. His characters are painted with firm black and white strokes, and he recounts historical events sharply and clearly. He delights in a good yarn, especially if it has a touch of the macabre. His tales of children are quite lovingly told. As Thomas Jones again says, he has this talent 'that he tells a story as a story'.[172] He is in turn witty and gently humorous. One cannot deny that it is all spasmodic and inconsequential; and yet it has its central thread, for day followed day and the journey went on.

The Description of Wales is a colder and more deliberate book. Sir John Lloyd implies that it was written in an ivory tower, and ivory towers are notorious for their poor plumbing and inadequate heating. It contains fewer learned quotations than *The Journey through Wales*; and by its nature it has fewer anecdotes and no meanderings. What warmth it later generates, and in the middle it becomes very warm indeed, results from its being in large part a social study.

Whatever his other linguistic accomplishments, the language which Gerald loved best was clearly Latin: to this he was devoted and in this he was a nonpareil, inordinately proud of his skill and fluency. He has none of the economy, the conciseness of the great classical writers. His vocabulary is rich and florid; his clauses are bound together by a profusion of qualifying devices, conjunctions, adjectives, adverbs. The style is that of the

172. ibid., p. 57.

accomplished raconteur, the composer of cultured travelogues. It is studded with every imaginable figure of speech: personification, rhetorical questions, striking comparisons, metaphors and antitheses, alliteration, proverbial sayings, aphorisms, puns, exaggerations, understatements, short staccato sentences, long periodic developments. Gerald has a natural discursiveness and he is much given to repeating himself. What he has to say is over-weighted by etymological debates and never-ending quotations: but for all that his style flows on like one of the rivers of Wales which he describes so eloquently.

VI. SHORT BIBLIOGRAPHY

1. The Latin text of the Itinerarium Cambriae *and the* Descriptio Cambriae:

1868: James F. Dimock, *Giraldi Cambrensis opera*, Volume VI, Rolls Series, London.
For details of the earlier editions see pp. 44–5 and p. 52–3.

2. The earlier translation of each of the two works:

See pp. 45 and 53 for details.

3. Selected critical works:

1889: Henry Owen, *Gerald the Welshman*, London.
1902: A. G. Little, 'Giraldus Cambrensis', in *Mediaeval Wales*, London.
1920: W. S. Davies, *The Book of Invectives of Giraldus Cambrensis*, forming Vol. XXX of *Y Cymmrodor*, Introduction, pp. 1–74.
1928: F. M. Powicke, 'Gerald of Wales', in *Bulletin of the John Rylands Library*, Vol. XII, No. 2, Manchester.
1937: H. E. Butler, *The Autobiography of Giraldus Cambrensis*, edited and translated by, London.

1942: Robin Flower, 'Richard Davies, William Cecil and Giraldus Cambrensis', in *The National Library of Wales Journal*, Volume III, Nos 1 and 2, Aberystwyth.

1946–7: J. C. Davies, 'Giraldus Cambrensis, 1146–1946', in *Archaeologia Cambrensis*, Vol. XCIX, pp. 85–108 and pp. 256–80.

1947: Thomas Jones, *Gerallt Gymro. Gerald the Welshman*, Cardiff.

1949: Thomas Jones, 'Llên-Gwerin yn "Nheithlyfr" Gerallt Gymro', in *Mân Us*, pp. 35–45, Cardiff.

1949–50: Thomas Jones, 'Gerald the Welshman's *Itinerary through Wales* and *Description of Wales*: An Appreciation and Analysis', in *The National Library of Wales Journal*, Vol. VI, pp. 117–48 and pp. 197–222.

1969–72: Michael Richter, 'Giraldus Cambrensis: The Growth of the Welsh Nation', in *The National Library of Wales Journal*, Vol. XVI (1969–70), pp. 193–252 and Vol. XVII (1971–72), pp. 1–50.

1973: Michael Richter, 'Gerald of Wales: A Reassessment on the 750th Anniversary of His Death', in *Traditio*, Vol. XXIX, pp. 379–90.

1974: David Walker, 'Gerald of Wales: A Review of Recent Work', in *The Journal of the Historical Society of the Church in Wales*, Vol. XXIV, pp. 13–26.

4. *Books of general reference:*

1939: Sir John Lloyd, *A History of Wales from the Earliest Times to the Edwardian Conquest*, 3rd edition, London.

1957: Elwyn Davies, ed., *A Gazetteer of Welsh Place-names*, Cardiff.

VII. ACKNOWLEDGEMENTS

Professor A. O. H. Jarman of the University College of Cardiff, my friend for many years, lent me his copy of the *Gazetteer* of

Elwyn Davies and helped me with the two Welsh proverbs on
p. 240. Mr Thorlac Turville-Petre gave me references for the
three English proverbs on the next page. Miss Lowri Penrhyn
Jones took me through the article 'Llên-Gwerin yn "Nheithlyfr"
Gerallt Gymro' by Thomas Jones, another old friend, now, alas,
dead. Mr Robin Gwyndaf, Assistant Keeper of the Welsh Folk
Museum, St Fagans, located two English translations of Elidyr's
visit to fairyland. For the fourth time Mrs Betty Radice has been
my Egeria. I am grateful to them all.

VIII. LIST OF GERALD'S EXTANT WRITINGS

The references in brackets are to the texts printed in the eight
volumes of *Giraldi Cambrensis Opera*, ed. J. S. Brewer, J. F.
Dimock and G. F. Warner, Rolls series, 1861-91.

Top. Hib.	*Topographia Hibernica* (V, pp. 3-204)
Exp. Hib.	*Expugnatio Hibernica* (V, pp. 207-411)
Itin.	*Itinerarium Kambriae* (VI, pp. 3-152)
Desc.	*Descriptio Kambriae* (VI, pp. 155-227)
Gemma	*Gemma Ecclesiastica* (II, pp. 1-364)
V.G.	*De vita Galfridi Archiepiscopi Eboracensis* (IV, pp. 357-431)
Invect.	*De invectionibus* (I, pp. 123-96; II, pp. 3-96)
Symb. Elect.	*Symbolum Electorum* (I, pp. 197-395)
Spec.	*Speculum Ecclesiae* (IV, pp. 1-354)
De rebus	*De rebus a se gestis* (I, pp. 1-122)
De iure	*De iure et statu Menevensis Ecclesiae* (III, pp. 101-373)
V.S.D.	*De vita Sancti Davidis Archiepiscope Menevensis* (III, pp. 377-404)
V.S.R.	*Vita Sancti Remigii* (VII, pp. 1-80)
V.S.H.	*Vita Sancti Hugonis* (VII, pp. 83-147)
V.D.	*Vita Davidis II Episcopi Menevensis* (III, pp. 431-4)
De princ.	*Liber de Principis instructione* (VIII, pp. 3-329)
V.S.E.	*Vita Sancti Ethelberti* (III, pp. 407-30)

THE JOURNEY THROUGH WALES

FOR STEPHEN, ARCHBISHOP OF CANTERBURY,[1]
THE FIRST PREFACE TO GERALD'S ITINERARY.[2]

Just as in our daily habits we are affected by new circumstances and by fresh ideas, so are the minds of men influenced by their various life-patterns. There are, so the satirist tells us,

> A thousand kinds of men, each differing in desire:
> Each has his own intent, each burns with different fire.[3]

As we read in the comedy:

> That's how it is: Nature upholds
> As many views as men: and each to his own view holds.[4]

Conditioned as they are by their different social backgrounds, men will devote themselves to pursuits of the most varied kinds. Young soldiers delight in bearing arms and waging war; lawyers take pleasure in putting on their gowns and arguing cases; others strive anxiously to accumulate riches and see wealth as the supreme good. Some study Galen,[5] others give all their time to Justinian.[6] Those who aspire to honours frequent the court, and, as their reputations wax and wane, so their ambition, which is insatiable, can only leave them disillusioned.

1. As explained in the Introduction, p. 39, this dedication to Stephen Langton, Cardinal Archbishop of Canterbury 1207–28, is that of Version III. Version I lacks the First Preface, but MS B has the beginning of it, which is not in its place but added later on, with a dedication to William de Longchamp, Bishop of Ely. Version II has the First Preface, in full and in its proper place, with a dedication to Hugh, Bishop of Lincoln.

2. For itinerary Gerald uses the Greek word 'odoporion'.

3. Persius, *Satires*, V.52–3.

4. Terence, *Phormio*, II.4.14, quoted from memory ('capita' for 'homines', 'suus' for 'suos', 'cuique' for 'quoique').

5. Galen, i.e. medicine.   6. Justinian, i.e. the law.

Some, indeed, but very few, find pleasure in the liberal arts. Among their number we can wonder at the logicians, who, when they have made some small progress, are so delighted with their studies that we watch them 'pass their latter years in the mazy labyrinths of dialectics with as much joy as if they were bearing down upon the rocks where once of old the Sirens sang'.[7]

Among so many different sorts and conditions of men, where are the divine poets? Where are the worthy souls who preach morality? Where are the masters of the Latin tongue? Who nowadays in his writings, whether they be poetry or history, can hope to add new lustre to the art of letters? Who in our time, I ask, is building up a system of ethics, or, held firm for ever in the works he writes, recording for eternity deeds which are nobly done? In earlier times the man of letters stood on the topmost step in the hall of fame. Now those who devote themselves to study, which is toppled deep in ruin, or so it seems, and sunk in disrepute, are no longer there to be emulated, they earn no respect, on the contrary they are disliked and despised.

> By destiny all things have rushed
> From bad to worse, and in decline are backwards pushed.[8]

'Happy indeed, would be the arts', wrote Quintilian, 'if artists alone could be their judge';[9] but, as Apollinaris adds, 'It is a natural principle, deep rooted in the mind of man, that those who are ignorant of the arts are the first to condemn artists.'[10]

I return to my earlier argument. Which have brought greater benefit to humanity, the arms of Marius, or the poems of Virgilius Maro?[11] The weapons borne by Marius have long ago

7. Aulus Gellius, *Noctes Atticae*, XVI.8, quoted from memory (sentence reformed).

8. Virgil, *Georgics*, I.199–200 ('fato' for 'fatis').

9. Gerald writes 'ut ait Fabius': this is presumably Quintilian's *Institutio Oratoria*, but I cannot trace the quotation.

10. Sidonius Apollinaris, *Epistolae*, V.10, quoted from memory ('naturaliter enim' for 'simul et naturali vitio', 'ignorant' for 'non intelligunt', 'contemnant' for 'non mirentur').

11. Caius Marius, 157–86 BC, seven times consul. This is a typical pun on 'arma Mariana' and 'carmina Maroniana'.

rusted away; but the fame of Maro, who wrote the *Aeneid*, lives for all time. Although in his day literature was held in high honour by the leaders of the state, who were, moreover, themselves authors, we nevertheless find the poet writing:

Faced with the War-god's weapons, our songs are no more strong
Than the doves of Jove's Dodona which the north wind blows along.[12]

Can you hesitate for a moment to say which has proved the better and the more profitable, the works of Saint Jerome,[13] or the riches of Croesus?[14] Where today can you see the silver of Croesus still shining bright, where does his gold now glitter? The poor coenobite's learning still illumines the world, and shows us which path to follow. However great he may have been, it is true that Jerome suffered insults and beatings in Rome at the hands of those who hated him, and that in the end he was driven to cross the sea and seek a refuge for his studies in the solitude of Bethlehem.

It appears then, from what I have said, that this distinction can be made: wealth and violence seem to sustain us in this life, but after death they avail us nothing; on the contrary, the pursuit of letters brings us little except dislike as long as we live, but once we are dead our fame is immortal. Like a last will and testament, what we have written down in black ink is only of importance when we ourselves no longer exist. As one poet wrote:

So envy feeds on the living, but after our death it dies down:
Only then can the honour we merit keep fresh our fame and renown.[15]

Another said much the same thing:

Though jealousy still spreads o'er me its melancholy pall,
Once dead I shall be honoured: envy, like night, must fall.[16]

12. Virgil, *Bucolics*, IX.11–13, quoted from memory (much rewritten).
13. Saint Jerome, AD c. 347–c. 420, the most learned of the Latin fathers.
14 Croesus, King of Lydia, reigned c. 560–c. 546 BC, whose wealth was proverbial.
15. Ovid, *Amores*, I.15.39.
16. Statius, *Thebaid*, XII.818–19 ('denique' for 'mox tibi').

65

Those who strive with such ingenuity to acquire polished speech and a correct style, when all that they are really doing is to saturate themselves in what others have said and written before them, have, it is true, little reason to pride themselves on their own inventive faculties. To be sure, men who really speak or write well, using language in an elegant way, as, for example, it is heard in the many cases argued so eloquently in law in the vast body of our jurisprudence, stand out as worthy of the highest praise. For myself I would have said that those who can string sentences together in a pleasing way are much to be admired, not the listeners merely, not those who have occasion to repeat what is written by others, but the actual writers.[17] You will find that the language of royal courts and that of the schools have many points in common, designed as they both are first to attract your attention and then to hold it. There is no doubt at all that a skill in dialectic is of the greatest use, a shrewd assembling and appreciation, as it were, of all the other arts and sciences, but only when employed with the control and moderation which become perfect by practice. In itself courtly language is not all that necessary, except for suave sycophants and men of great ambition. If you seek advancement at court, ambition lures you on and holds you in its snare, it will not let you get away alive, it will not let you leave the court, unless, of course, it is really satisfied. If, on the other hand, your labour is in vain, you will stay just one more year, and then another year after that, and so ad infinitum, wasting your time together with your substance, throwing away the days of your life, which can never be regained, and that is the greatest loss of all. You can see that life at court is just like a game of dice, for as the poet says:

> The coaxing dice attract the gambler's greedy hand:
> He may not have lost already, but he loses in the end.[18]

Make one small change in this and you can say in the same way:

17. This does not mean much, but Gerald wanted to contrast 'auditores' and 'recitatores' with 'repertores'.
18. Ovid, *Ars Amatoria*, I.451–2 ('dum' for 'et').

The court with its attractions grips tight his greedy hands:
If he's not done so already, he wastes the time he spends.

It is worth adding, or so I think, that playing dice and frequenting the court are similar in the prizes which they offer: neither leads to contentment, both reward with complete impartiality the worthy and the unworthy.

Since, among so many different sorts and conditions of men,

Each follows his own desire,[19]

and since

Our hearts are plagued with varying whims,[20]

my own particular choice is the pursuit of letters, by which I hope to please generations yet unborn. Life here below lasts a brief moment and is always in a state of flux. It is, then, a pleasant thought that one's name will live for ever and that, having won the right to eternal fame, one will always be praised and honoured. It is a sure indication of an elevated mind to strive to achieve something which, even if it produces only hostility in this life, will ensure one's lasting glory after death. Authors, and particularly poets, aspire to immortality. This does not mean that they refuse material rewards, if they are offered. As the poet asks:

What room is there then for talent, save in the bravest hearts
Which scorn all domestic problems and live on poetic arts,
Sustained by our lord Apollo and Bacchus the god of wine?[21]

I completely wasted my time when I wrote my *Topography of Ireland* for Henry II, King of the English, and the companion volume, my *Vaticinal History*, for Richard of Poitou, his son and successor in vice, although I would prefer not to have to say it.[22]

19. Virgil, *Bucolics*, II.65.
20. I cannot trace this quotation.
21. Juvenal, *Satires*, 7.63–5 ('est' added). After this quotation ends the portion of the First Preface which is added at the conclusion of MS B of Version I. See Introduction, p. 37.
22. Gerald had completed *The Topography of Ireland* by the spring of 1188, for he gave a copy of it to Archbishop Baldwin in Llanddew in the March of

Both these princes had little or no interest in literature, and both were much preoccupied with other matters. It is to you, Stephen, Archbishop of Canterbury,[23] a man of great renown, equally at home in the pursuit of letters and in the practice of religion, that I have dedicated this present far from negligible work about Wild Wales, composed in a learned style and divided into two separate parts. Virtue ever calls to virtue, spurning vice: and so I hope that you will receive, with the same pleasure as if it had been written about you, all that I have set down in this little book about your predecessor but one, a venerable man who became Archbishop of Canterbury. It is to you, too, that I propose to dedicate another opusculum, *How to Bring Up a Prince*, when, with God to lead me on and if my own life is spared, I bring it to completion.[24] My only proviso is that, in some moment of relaxation from your never-ending pre-occupations of prayer and worldly affairs, you accept the charge of actually reading it when you can find time. I have decided to offer to you, for your enjoyment, these fruits of my labours, and others, too, each in its proper order. Even if my major writings do not interest you, I hope that these smaller works may do so: interest you, I repeat, so that they may at one and the same time win me some reward at your hands and express my gratitude to you for it.

You are much less entangled than others in family ties and commitments, so that, when you have rewards to distribute, which task you perform with great skill and munificence, instead of concentrating on your own relations and those closely connected with you, you can remember the men who are really

---

that year (*Itin.*, I.2). The Second Preface of that work is addressed to Henry II. Gerald usually calls *The Conquest of Ireland* by this name, *The Vaticinal History*, because Book III, of which we have only the Preface, was to have contained the Prophecies of Merlin. The work is dedicated to Richard of Poitou and so must have been finished before the death of Henry II on 6 July 1189, when Richard the Lion Heart became King of England.

23. Hugh, Bishop of Lincoln, in Version II. This part of the First Preface is not in Version I.

24. *How to Bring Up a Prince* seems to have been begun c. 1190, but it was not finished until 1216.

worth encouragement, because they have served the cause of literature. In the great quarrel which has lasted so long between the ecclesiastical and the secular authorities, in you the Church in England has found a firm and faithful friend; and it has found few others. You are about the only churchman of our time who has been promoted according to the rules, and you are a remarkable example of a man who holds the rank of bishop only after having been elected in accordance with canonical law.

However, it is not by standing cap in hand that I have tried to please you, not by placing a cushion for you to sit on, by pulling a feather out of the said cushion lest it irk you, by flicking off you a particle of dust which was not there anyway.[25] You are completely hemmed in by flatterers of this sort. It is by writing literary compositions for you that I have tried to give you pleasure. You are a famous personality, known to everyone, one of that small band of individuals who really count. Your own natural talent, developed to the full by the efforts which you have made, has showered on you almost every honour which an archbishop can dare to accept. If your prayers and your administrative duties leave you no time to read what I have written, or if perchance I fail to please you by what I have done, then, indeed, the esteem in which literature once was held really has vanished, and my work must be left to posterity, in the hope that one day such honours may return.

SECOND PREFACE[26]

Deeds which are known to have been done in a praiseworthy spirit of devotion should receive all the publicity that is due to them. Enthusiasm which is deferred from day to day soon withers away completely. Whatever talent we may possess will disappear if we are too lazy to use it. If it lies idle, the sword will soon be coated over with rust.

25. This is a memory of Ovid, *Ars Amatoria*, I.149–51.
26. As Version I lacks the First Preface, except for that portion of it which is added at the end of MS B, it naturally also lacks these two words.

In a pool which is stagnant the water is foul.[27]

Rather than let my pen rust away through disuse, I have decided to commit to writing the holy mission which Baldwin, Archbishop of Canterbury, made to Wales. This little work is like a highly polished mirror. In it I have portrayed the pathless places which we trod, named each mountain torrent and each purling spring, recorded the witty things we said, set down the hazards of our journey and our various travails, included an account of such noteworthy events as occurred in those parts, some in our own times, others long ago, with much natural description and remarkable excursions into natural history, adding at the end a word-picture of the country itself. Stephen, Archbishop of Canterbury, man of great renown, all this I dedicate through you to ages yet to come. I cannot let all the effort which has been made be forgotten, simply because I am too lazy to set it down, or all the commendation which is due disappear in silence.

27. Ovid, *Epistolae ex Ponto*, I.5.6 ('et capiunt' for 'ut capiant').

HERE BEGIN THE CHAPTER-HEADINGS.

[Book I]

1. Book I describes the journey through Hereford and Radnor, with such additional details as are worth recording.[28]
2. The journey through Hay-on-Wye and Brecknockshire.
3. Ewias and Llanthony.
4. The journey through Coed Grwyne and Abergavenny.
5. Our journey takes us past Usk Castle and through Caerleon.
6. Our journey through Newport and Cardiff.
7. The see of Llandaff and Margam Abbey.
8. How we crossed the Rivers Avon and Neath, and then passed through Swansea and Gower.
9. How we crossed the River Loughor and the two Gwendraeth streams; and what happened at Kidwelly.
10. How we crossed the River Tywi in a boat. Carmarthen and the monastery of Whitland.
11. Haverfordwest and Rhos.
12. Pembrokeshire.
13. Our journey through Camrose and Newgale as far as St David's.

[Book II]

1. Book II describes the see of St David's.
2. Our journey through Cemais and our stay in St Dogmael's monastery.
3. The River Teifi, Cardiganshire and Newcastle Emlyn.

28. As explained on p. 40 of the Introduction, the words 'cum notabilibus suis' appear at the end of all but three of the chapter-headings of both Book I and Book II. I have translated them this once only.

4. Our journey through Lampeter, the Abbey of Strata Florida, Llanddewi Brefi and the church of Saint Padarn the Great.
5. How we crossed the River Dovey in boats and so came to the territory of the sons of Cynan.
6. How we crossed the Traeth Mawr and the Traeth Bychan. Nefyn, Caernarfon and Bangor.
7. The island of Anglesey or Mona.
8. How we crossed the River Conway in a boat. Dinas Emrys.
9. The mountains of Snowdonia.
10. How we travelled through Degannwy, Rhuddlan and the cathedral town of Llanelwy or St Asaph. The quicksand and Coleshill.
11. How we crossed the River Dee. Chester.
12. How we journeyed through Whitchurch, Oswestry, Powys and Shrewsbury.
13. Our journey over Wenlock Edge, through Bromfield, Ludlow Castle and Leominster, and so back to Hereford.
14. A description of Baldwin, Archbishop of Canterbury.

Here begins the Journey of Gerald the Welshman
and the difficult mission to Wales carried out by Baldwin,
Archbishop of Canterbury.

BOOK I

Chapter 1[29]
The journey through Hereford and Radnor, with such additional details as are worth recording.

In the year AD 1188, Baldwin, Archbishop of Canterbury, crossed the borders of Herefordshire and entered Wales. He was a man whom everyone respected, for he was well known for his learning and his piety. It was in the service of the Cross, from whence cometh our salvation, that he had undertaken this journey from England to Wales. At that time Urban III was Pope,[30] Frederick King of the Germans and Holy Roman Emperor,[31] and Isaac Emperor of Constantinople.[32] Philippe, son of Louis, was then reigning in France,[33] Henry II in England, William in Sicily,[34] Béla in Hungary[35] and Guy in Palestine.[36] In this very same year God in His judgement, which is never unjust but sometimes difficult to understand, permitted Saladin, the leader of the Egyptians and of the men of Damascus, to win a victory in pitched battle and so seize the kingdom of Jerusalem.[37]

29. The chapters are numbered in the list of chapter-headings printed on pp. 71–2, but they are not numbered at the beginning of each individual chapter.

30. Pope Urban III died on 19 October 1187. He was succeeded by Gregory VIII, who died on 17 December 1187. Clement III was Pope in 1188 and should have been listed here. He died in 1191.

31. Frederick Barbarossa became King of the Germans in 1152 and Holy Roman Emperor in 1155. He died in 1190.

32. Isaac Angelus became Emperor of Constantinople in 1185. He was deposed in 1195.

33. Philippe Auguste reigned over France from 1180 to 1223.

34. William II, a descendant of Roger Guiscard, reigned over Sicily from 1166 to 1189.

35. Béla III reigned over Hungary from 1174 to 1196.

36. Guy of Lusignan was crowned King of Jerusalem in 1186.

37. After his defeat of the Templars and Hospitallers at Tiberias in May of

74

Soon after Ash Wednesday Baldwin reached Radnor.[38] Ranulph de Glanville went with him as far as this town: he was a most important person, a member of the King's Privy Council and Chief Justiciar of the whole kingdom.[39] In Radnor Baldwin was met by Rhys ap Gruffydd, Prince of South Wales,[40] and by other nobles from those parts. The Archbishop delivered a public sermon on the taking of the Cross, and this was explained to the Welsh by an interpreter. I myself, who have written these words, was the first to stand up. I threw myself at the holy man's feet and devoutly took the sign of the Cross. It was the urgent admonition given some time before by the King which inspired me to give this example to the others, and the persuasion and oft-repeated promises of the Archbishop and the Chief Justiciar, who never tired of repeating the King's words. I acted of my own free will, after anxiously talking the matter over time and time again, in view of the insult and injury being done at this moment to the Cross of Christ. In so doing I gave strong encouragement to the others and an added incentive to what they had just been told. Peter de Leia, the Cluniac monk who was Bishop of St David's,[41] followed my example and did what I had

that year, and of the united Christian army at Hittin in July, Saladin entered Jerusalem on 2 October 1187.

38. In my Introduction, pp. 30–31, I have suggested that Archbishop Baldwin and Gerald left Hereford on Friday, 4 March, and that they rode to New Radnor in one day, arriving there early that evening. The Latin words 'circa jejunii caput' make this acceptable enough. On the other hand, as I have agreed on p. 31, n. 111, the first part of the journey, from Hereford to St David's, could conceivably be moved forward by as much as three days.

39. Ranulph de Glanville, to whom the *Tractatus de legibus et consuetudinibus regni Angliae* is sometimes ascribed, had been Chief Justiciar and Henry II's principal adviser since 1180. He went on the Third Crusade and died at Acre in 1190.

40. Since the death of Owain Gwynedd in 1170, Rhys ap Gruffydd ap Rhys, known as the Lord Rhys, who ruled over South Wales, had been the outstanding leader of the Welsh people. He was the son of Gruffydd ap Rhys ap Tewdwr and the nephew of Nest. Gerald was thus his first cousin once removed. Rhys ap Gruffydd died in 1197.

41. Peter de Leia, Prior of Much Wenlock, became Bishop of St David's on 7 November 1176. He did not go on the Third Crusade. He died in 1198. He had, of course, been Gerald's successful rival in the election of 1176. In

done. Next came Einion, son of Einion Clud, prince of Elfael,[42] and many others, too. Einion rose to his feet and said to Rhys, who was present and whose daughter he had married: 'My lord and father, with your permission I hasten to avenge the injury done to God the Father Almighty.' Rhys himself went home quite determined to make the holy journey as soon as the Archbishop should have entered his own territory. The result was that for nearly a fortnight he applied himself with great energy to all the preparations necessary for so long a journey, collecting pack-animals and sumpter-saddles, persuading other men to go with him and raising funds. Then his wife, Gwenllian, daughter of Madog,[43] one of the princes of Powys, who was moreover his fourth cousin, a regrettable circumstance which happens so often in this country, put a sudden stop to his noble intentions by playing upon his weakness and exercising her womanly charms. As Solomon says, 'A man's heart deviseth his way: but the Lord directeth his steps.'[44] Only a short time before the day which he had chosen for his departure, as Rhys stood chatting with his men about the sermon which he had heard, a young man called Gruffydd, a distinguished member of his own family who afterwards took the Cross himself, is reported to have said to him: 'What man of spirit can hesitate for a moment to undertake this journey when, among the many hazards involved, none could be more unfortunate, none could cause greater distress, than the prospect of coming back alive?'

As soon as he returned home, certain of the canons of St David's, who had just taken the precaution of gaining the approval and support of the leading men of his court, went to see Rhys. Jealous of the interests of their own church, they used every argument they could think of to persuade him to refuse to

---

The Journey through Wales Gerald speaks kindly of him, e.g. *Itin.*, I.13. It is very odd that he never mentions Peter's efforts to rebuild the cathedral in St David's.

42. Einion ab Einion Clud succeeded his father as Prince of Elfael in 1177. He died in 1191.

43. Gwenllian was daughter of Madog ap Maredudd, Prince of Powys.

44. Proverbs, 16.9.

allow the Archbishop of Canterbury to continue his journey into
the interior of Wales, and more especially, for until then such a
thing had been quite unheard of, to visit St David's itself, the
metropolitan see of the country. If he were to proceed, so they
said not once but many times, great harm and damage would be
done to the standing of the metropolitan see, and only with the
greatest difficulty would it be able to recover its former position.[45]
I can assure you that they pressed these arguments most
forcibly upon the prince, but they failed to convince him. He was
a man so open in his own behaviour and of such great natural
kindness that he realized that a rebuff of this sort would greatly
wound the Archbishop's feelings.

Mass was celebrated early the next morning and then Ranulph
de Glanville returned to England. We ourselves journeyed on to
Cruker Castle, which is about two miles from Radnor. There a
robust and courageous young man, called Hector, had a talk
with the Archbishop about taking the Cross. 'If I had provisions
for just one day's journey,' said he, 'I would agree to do what
you ask, for I could go without food on the second day.' The
following morning the Archbishop signed him with the Cross.
That same evening as twilight fell there arrived Maelgwn ap
Cadwallon, Prince of Maelienydd.[46] The Archbishop spoke to
him, briefly but to the point, and he, too, was signed with the
Cross, despite the fears and lamentations of his family.

At this point I must tell you what happened, in the reign of
Henry I, King of the English, to the castellan of Radnor castle,
in the territory of Builth, which is not far away, being adjacent
to his own lands, which he himself had conquered. He had gone
into the church of Saint Afan, called Llanafan in Welsh, and
there he had spent the night with his dogs, which was a foolish
and irreverent thing to do. He got up at first light, as hunters are
wont to do, but he found that all his dogs had gone mad and that he
himself was blind. He had lost his sight completely and he had

45. St David's had never been an archbishopric. Cp. p. 159, n. 255, for a
full discussion.
46. Maelgwn ap Cadwallon, Prince of Maelienydd, succeeded his father in
1179. He died in 1197.

to grope his way out with his hand. From that day onwards he passed his days in tedium and darkness. Then he conceived the happy idea of having himself led all the way to Jerusalem, for he did not wish to allow his spiritual light to be extinguished as his eyes had been. Surrounded by a group of his friends, he had himself armed and, sitting on a strong warhorse, he was conducted by his men to where the war was being fought. He charged forward in the front line, but was immediately struck down by a blow from a sword and so ended his life with honour.

About this time another event worth recording occurred in Gwrthrynion, which is only a few furlongs from this same spot. Einion, the son-in-law of Rhys, ruled over that region.[47] He was much addicted to hunting and one day, as he was driving the game from his coverts, an attendant of his, who was carrying a bow, shot a doe as she came leaping out. Despite her sex she was found to have horns with twelve tines and to be much heavier than a doe, both round her haunches and elsewhere. This was considered to be a very strange thing, and the head and horns of the unnatural beast were sent off to Henry II, King of the English. The event was made all the more extraordinary, because the man who, by an unfortunate accident, had shot the proscribed animal with his arrow immediately began to feel ill and lost the sight of his right eye. At the same time he suffered a stroke, and he remained feeble-minded and impotent until the day of his death.

A staff which once belonged to Saint Curig, or so it is said, can be seen in the church of Saint Germanus in this same district of Gwrthrynion. It is completely encased in gold and silver, and the top part has the rough shape of a cross. Its miraculous power has been proved in all manner of cases, but it is particularly efficacious in smoothing away and pressing the pus from glandular swellings and gross tumours which grow so often on the human body. All those who suffer from such vexatious afflictions will be restored to health if they go to the staff in faith and offer an oblation of one penny. It happened in our time that a person with a tumour handed a halfpenny to the

47. Einion ab Einion Clud, Prince of Elfael.

78

crosier: the result was that only one half of his swelling went down. Soon afterwards he completed his oblation by offering the staff a second halfpenny, whereupon he was immediately cured. Another man came to the staff and promised faithfully that he would give a penny at some later date. He was cured, but on the appointed date he failed to pay. To his consternation his tumour swelled up again. His sin was pardoned, for he trebled the oblation and in great fear and trembling had the faith to pay threepence, with the happy result that he was completely restored to health.

In the church at Glascwm, in Elfael, there is a handbell which has most miraculous powers. It is supposed to have belonged to Saint David and it is called a 'bangu'. In an attempt to liberate him, a certain woman took this handbell to her husband, who was chained up in the castle of Rhaiadr Gwy, in Gwrthrynion, which castle Rhys ap Gruffydd had built in our time. The keepers of the castle not only refused to set the man free, but they even seized the bell. That same night God took vengeance on them, for the whole town was burned down, except the wall on which the handbell hung.

In our time, in the town of Llywel, in Brecknockshire, the local church was burned down in an enemy raid. Everything was destroyed, inside and out, except the box in which the consecrated host was kept.

On the night when Henry I, King of the English, died,[48] it happened in the Elfael district, which is separated from Hay by the River Wye, that two large pools suddenly burst their banks, one of them natural and the other artificial. The artificial pool rushed precipitously down the valleys, as one would expect, and was soon empty; but, remarkably enough, the natural lake reformed itself, with all its fish and whatever else lived in it, in a certain valley not more than two miles away.

In Normandy, a few days before the death of Henry II,[49] all the fish, and they were very numerous, in a certain pool some five miles distant from Séez, near the castle of Exmes, fought

48. Henry I died at Lyons-la-Forêt in Normandy on 1 December 1135.
49. Henry II died at Chinon in Touraine on 6th July 1189.

together so violently in the night, some in the water and some even leaping in the air, that the noise which they made attracted to the spot a vast crowd of local people. So deadly was the battle waged by these fish that in the morning scarcely one was found alive in the pool. By this extraordinary prodigy the self-destruction of a great number of fish foretold the death of one particular man.

Wales recalls with horror the great number of terrible disasters which, as the result of the miserable desire to seize possession of land, have occurred in our time, among blood-brothers and close relations, between the Wye and the Severn, that is in Maelienydd, Elfael and Gwrthrynion.

Chapter 2
The journey through Hay-on-Wye and Brecknockshire.

We crossed the River Wye and made our way into Brecknockshire. After the sermon which was given in Hay, we saw a great number of men who wanted to take the Cross come running towards the castle where the Archbishop was, leaving their cloaks behind in the hands of the wives and friends who had tried to hold them back.

Early the next morning we began our journey towards Brecon. The word of the Lord was preached in Llanddew, and there we spent the night.[50] Brecon, which is the castle and chief town of the district, is called Aberhonddu, for it is situated where the River Honddu flows into the Usk. In the Welsh language 'aber' means where one river joins another. Llanddew means the Church of God. While we were in Brecon, I, Gerald, the Archdeacon of the place, presented to the Archbishop a copy of my own far from negligible work called *The Topography of Ireland*. The Archbishop received it graciously and read a portion of it with close

50. As Archdeacon of Brecon Gerald had a house which he greatly loved in Llanddew. Cp. *Itin.*, I.3. By the mid sixteenth century, according to John Leland, the Bishops' Palace had become 'no thing but an onsemeli ruine' and Gerald's archdeaconry had 'fallen douen for the more part' (*Itinerary*, V, p. 72).

attention each day during the journey, or else had it read to him. When he returned to England he read the remainder of the book in the presence of his retainers.

I thought that it would be useful to include at this point certain important events which have happened in this region during our own lifetime. A short time before in the great war in which the sons of Iestin ap Gwrgant ravaged the whole neighbourhood,[51] the extensive lake from which the River Llynfi flows, pouring its waters into the River Wye opposite Glasbury, was found to be bright green. Certain elderly folk who lived in the area were asked what this signified. They replied that the water had become discoloured in the same way a short while before the devastation caused by Hywel ap Maredudd.[52]

About the same time a certain priest called Hugh, who served the chapel of Saint Nicholas in Brecon Castle, dreamed that he saw a venerable old man standing beside him. 'Take this message', said the venerable old man, 'to your master William de Braose, who has had the effrontery to keep for his own use the property granted long ago to the chapel of Saint Nicholas for charitable purposes.[53] "What is not surrendered to Christ is removed by taxation. What you refuse to a priest you will hand over to a godless soldier." ' This happened once, twice and a third time. In the end the chaplain travelled to Llanddew to see the local Archdeacon, who was none other than the author of this book. He described the vision to the Archdeacon and repeated the message, which he had remembered exactly, although he had not heard the words before. The Archdeacon

51. Iestin ap Gwrgant was Prince of Glamorgan from 1081 onwards. He was deposed, became a religious and died in the priory of Llangenydd in Gower. His sons were Caradog, Gruffydd, Goronwy and Rhys.

52. This seems to have been in 1136.

53. William de Braose, d. 1211, was the descendant and heir of the William de Braose, near Falaise, who received great estates in England at the Conquest. The family held Bramber Castle and the rape of Bramber in Sussex. This William's mother was Bertha, second daughter of Milo FitzWalter, Earl of Hereford, d. 1143 (cp. p. 89, n. 77), and through her he inherited the vast Welsh possessions of her grandfather, Bernard de Neufmarché (cp. p. 88, n. 74). He was the castellan of Brecon Castle. Llanddew was only a mile or so away from Brecon.

immediately recognized it as a quotation from Saint Augustine.[54] He showed the chaplain where it was to be found in his writings and explained what it meant. Saint Augustine was criticizing those who refused to pay tithes and rents and other church dues. What he threatened in this passage certainly happened very soon to the person in question.

We have undoubtedly seen in our own lifetime and proved it to be true that the great leaders who seize the possessions of the Church squander all the treasure that they have acquired and hand over to mercenary soldiers what they should have left in the hands of their priests. This is particularly true of Henry II, King of the English, the reigning monarch, who has indulged in this malpractice more than most people, showing that a little leaven leaveneth the whole lump [55] and that worse evils always follow when this sort of thing is done.

This man William de Braose was much to be condemned for what he did, and, indeed, for other misdeeds of a like nature; but nothing that is human can be perfect and, as the Emperor said, to know everything and yet not to sin is an attribute of the Godhead rather than of man.[56] There is one thing, however, which I have thought worthy of being recorded about him, that whenever he spoke he always mentioned God first. 'In the name of God let such and such be done,' he would say. 'In God's name let this or that be carried out.' 'If it should please God,' or 'If God grant it,' or 'By the grace of God it shall be so.' We learn from Saint Paul that everything ought always to be committed and commended to God in this way. In the Acts of the Apostles, when Paul said goodbye to the brethren, we read: 'But I will return again unto you, if God will.' [57] In the same way Saint James says in his epistle, 'If the Lord will, we shall live,' [58] showing that such expressions should be included in every plan for the future, everything being commended in this way to God's will and ordinance. William de Braose was a rich and powerful man. As such he had occasion to send letters all over the place;

---

54. I cannot trace this quotation.   55. I Corinthians 5.6.
56. This is presumably Marcus Aurelius, but I cannot trace the quotation.
57. Acts, 18.21.   58. James, 4.15.

and it was his habit to overload them, or perhaps I should say to honour them,[59] with words which asked the favour of God's indulgence in this way, to the point that it became quite boring not only to his scribes but also to the recipients when they had the letters read aloud to them. However, each year he used to give a gold coin to each of his scribes, over and above their salary, for having ended each of his letters with a plea for God's assistance. He was exceedingly devout: and to what I have written may be added the fact that when he was on a journey and he saw a cross or a church, even if he were in the midst of a conversation with someone, a commoner, or even a person in high place, he would immediately begin to pray. Only when he had finished his prayer would he resume his conversation again after the interruption.[60] When he met young boys on his travels, he would bid them good day, and so encourage them to give him a kind word in return; in this way, when his salutation was answered, he received a blessing from these simple innocents. His wife, Matilda de Saint Valery, had exactly the same habits.[61] She was, I say, a prudent and chaste woman, well equipped to rule her household, as highly skilled in preserving her property within doors as in increasing it out of doors. I can only hope that, as a reward for their devout lives, they have both been granted eternal glory, just as they enjoyed grace and felicity here below.

It happened in this same neighbourhood that a boy tried to steal some young pigeons from a nest in Saint David's church in Llanfaes.[62] His hand stuck fast to the stone on which he was leaning, this being no doubt a miraculous punishment inflicted by the Saint, who was protecting the birds of his own church. For three days and nights the boy, accompanied by his parents

59. Gerald is making a pun on 'onerare' and 'honorare'.

60. As we have seen, William de Braose died in 1211. These verbs 'if he were', 'he would begin', 'would he resume' are in the present tense in Versions I and II. Gerald altered them in Version III. There are other similar changes of tense in this passage.

61. Matilda de Saint Valery, an arrogant woman, was largely responsible for her husband's fall from royal favour in 1206. She was imprisoned with her eldest son William in Windsor Castle by John, and there they both starved to death.   62. Llanfaes is in Brecknockshire.

and his friends, offered vigils, fasts and prayers at the church altar. On the third day, by God's intervention, the power which held his hand fast was loosened and he was released from the miraculous force which bound him there to the stone. I myself saw this same boy, then no longer young but become an old man living in Newbury in England, for so the years had passed, when he appeared before David II, Bishop of St David's,[63] and confirmed that these events really had occurred, the reason for this being, of course, that they had taken place in that Bishop's own diocese. The stone is preserved to this day among the relics of the church in question, with the marks of the boy's fingers pressed into the flint as though in wax and clearly visible.

In our own lifetime a miracle very similar to this happened in Bury St Edmunds. A poor woman used to visit the Saint's shrine, ostensibly to pay her devotions. She came not to give, but to take away. It was her habit to steal the gold and silver offered by others. The way she took it was extremely clever, for she would kiss it, suck it into her lips as she did so, and then carry it away hidden in her mouth. One day as she was actually doing this, such being her custom, her lips and tongue stuck fast to the altar. She was caught in the act by divine intervention, and she spat out the piece of silver which she had in her mouth. A great crowd of people came running to gape at this, some of them Jews and some of them Christians. There she remained, fixed and motionless, for the greater part of the day, so that the miracle was clear for all to see and there could be no doubt about it in anyone's mind.

In the north of England, just across the Humber, in Howden church, the parson's *belle amie* sat herself down without thinking on the wooden tomb of Saint Osana,[64] the sister of King Osred,[65]

63. This was David FitzGerald, Gerald's uncle, Bishop of St David's from 1148 to 1176. He was in constant dispute with his canons and spent much of his time in England.

64. Saint Osana has a paragraph as 'Sancta Osana, soror Osredi Regis' in *Acta Sanctorum Iunii tomus tertius*, 16–19, ed. Godefroi Henschen et aliis, Antwerp, 1701, p. 551. Her day is 18 June. The learned Jesuit fathers do not record this rather homely miracle.

65. King Osred ruled over Northumbria from 705 to 716. He is mentioned several times in Bede, *Ecclesiastical History*, V.20, 22, 24.

which jutted out in an open space as if it were a seat. When she wanted to get up, her backside stuck tight to the wood and she was unable to wrench herself free. The people came running. They cut away her clothing until she was quite naked and kept beating her hard with lashes until the blood flowed. She wept bitterly and prayed for forgiveness. In view of her repentance and the penalty which she had paid, she was freed by divine intervention and allowed to go home.

In our days another great miracle has caused quite a stir. This had to do with the psalter of Quendrada, the sister of Saint Kenelm,[66] at whose instigation he was murdered. In Winchcombe,[67] on the vigil of Saint Kenelm, when, at the invitation of the monks, a great crowd of women from the neighbourhood had congregated for the celebrations, as their custom was, the assistant cellarer had intercourse with one of them inside the precincts of the monastery. The next day he had the audacity to carry this psalter in the procession of the relics of the saints. When the solemn procession was over, he made his way back to the choir. The psalter stuck to his hands and he could not put it down. He was greatly astonished and confounded by what had happened. Then he remembered the crime which he had committed the previous evening. He confessed his sin and did penance. His repentance was sincere enough, and he was helped by the prayers of his fellow-monks. In the end, by divine intervention, he was able to free himself from the psalter and so was liberated. The book in question is held in great veneration in the monastery, for, when the dead body of Kenelm was carried out and the crowd shouted: 'He is God's martyr! There is no doubt about it! He is the martyr of God!' Quendrada, who was guilty of her brother's murder and had it very much on her conscience, replied: 'He is indeed God's martyr, as truly as my eyes are resting on this psalter!' By chance she was reading the psalter at the moment. Thereupon, by divine intervention, her

66. Saint Kenelm, infant son and successor of Cenwulf, King of Mercia, was murdered in a wood at Clent, Worcestershire, in 821, by his sister Cwenthryth, here called Quendrada. His feast-day is 17 July.

67. Winchcombe Abbey was founded by Cenwulf, King of Mercia, in 798 and dedicated in 811 by Wulfred, Archbishop of Canterbury.

85

two eyes were torn from her head and fell plop on the open book, where you can still see the marks of her blood to this day.

I must tell you what they say about a torque which is supposed to have belonged to Saint Cynog.[68] From its weight, texture and colour one would think that it was gold. It is made of four sections, as you can see from the joins, wrought together artificially by a series of weldings and divided in the middle by a dog's head, which stands erect with its teeth bared. The local inhabitants consider this to be a most potent relic, and no one would dare to break a promise which he had made when it was held in front of him. On the torque there is the mark of a mighty blow, as if someone had hit it with an iron hammer. A certain man, or so they say, tried to break the collar, for the sake of the gold. He was punished by God, for he immediately lost the sight of both eyes. To his life's end he lingered on in darkness.

Saint Patrick's horn is a similar cause of wonder. It is made of bronze, not of gold, and it was brought into these parts quite recently from Spain. Its miraculous power was first revealed in this neighbourhood, as a terrible example to one and all, when a foolish priest called Bernard was ill-advised enough to blow it, as I have explained in my *Topography of Ireland*:[69]

In Wales, and this has been a great source of wonder to me, I have seen a bearer at a funeral with a bronze horn, supposed to have belonged to Saint Patrick, which he was wearing round his neck as if it were a relic. He maintained that, out of respect for the Saint, no one had ever dared to blow it. He held the horn out so that the people who congregated there might kiss it, as they do in Ireland. Thereupon a certain priest, called Bernard, snatched it from his hands. He placed the end of the horn in his mouth, blew into the metal and began to

68. Saint Cynog, one of the many sons of Brychan, from whom Breck-nockshire or Brycheiniog is supposed to have taken its name, suffered martyrdom and was buried in the church at Merthyr Cynog. Gerald has obviously examined this torque.

69. Cp. *The Topography of Ireland*, III.34. See Professor R. P. C. Hanson, *St Patrick: His Origins and Career*, London, 1968, and his article in *Nottingham Mediaeval Studies*, Vol. XV (1971), pp. 3–26, 'English Translation of the "Confession" and the "Letter to Coroticus" of Saint Patrick'. Saint Patrick lived from c. 390 to c. 460.

sound it. Immediately, with all those people watching him, the horn-blower became paralysed in the mouth, and suffered a second afflic-tion, too. Until then he had been remarkable for the ready flow of his eloquence and much given to disparaging and denouncing other people, but now he immediately lost all power of speaking. His organs of speech were damaged to such an extent that from this day forward he had a marked impediment. Secondly, he became so lethargic that he forgot everything he had ever known, and even had great difficulty in remembering what his name was. His memory deteriorated to such an extent that I have frequently seen him strug-gling to call to mind once more the psalms which he formerly knew so well by heart; and I have been amazed to watch him striving to remember his letters, with which he was once so familiar, as if he were some old schoolmaster in his dotage. Because of his foolish deed he left home and made his way to Ireland to visit Saint Patrick. His health improved, but he never recovered fully.

The common people, and the clergy, too, not only in Ireland and Scotland, but also in Wales, have such a reverence for portable bells, staffs crooked at the top and encased in gold, silver or bronze, and other similar relics of the saints, that they are more afraid of swearing oaths upon them and then breaking their word than they are upon the Gospels. The reason is that, from some occult power with which they are gifted as if by God, and from the vengeance of the particular saint in whose sight they are particularly pleasing, those who scorn them are pun-ished severely, and those who break their word live to rue the day.[70]

Another remarkable thing which I must tell you about Saint Patrick's horn is that, if you hold the larger end to your ear, you will hear a sweet melody being played, as if you had left a harp uncovered and the breeze blew gently on it, making a soft reverberation.

In our lifetime another thing happened in this region about which I must tell you. A wild sow, which had by chance been suckled by a bitch remarkable for its acute sense of smell, lying tight-pressed against its dugs, became, when fully grown, so

70. This paragraph is a free rendering of *The Topography* of *Ireland*, III.33.

extraordinarily skilled in the pursuit of game that in following a scent it was considered far superior to the Molossian hounds, which started with a natural advantage and then were trained by man.[71] This argument can be applied not only to the brute beast, but also to man himself, for they are both greatly influenced by the dam whose milk they suck.

In the same region and almost at the same time a remarkable event occurred. A certain knight, name Gilbert, surname Hagurnell, after a long and unremitting anguish, which lasted three years, and the most severe pains as of a woman in labour, at length gave birth to a calf, an event which was witnessed by a great crowd of onlookers. Perhaps it was a portent of some unusual calamity yet to come. It was more probably a punishment exacted for some unnatural act of vice.

It appears from ancient yet authentic records kept in these parts that while Saint Illtyd was living as a hermit at Llanhamlach,[72] the mare which used to carry his provisions to him became gravid after being covered by a stag, and gave birth to a creature which could run very fast, its front part being like that of a horse and its haunches resembling those of a deer.

This county [of Brecknock] is divided into three cantrefs.[73] Bernard de Neufmarché was the first Norman to seize possession of it from the suzerainty of the Welsh.[74] He married Nest, the daughter of Nest, herself daughter of Gruffydd ap Llywelyn, who for so long had oppressed all Wales by his tyranny. She took her name Nest from her mother, but the English changed it

71. The hounds of the Molossi, a people of Epirus, were famous in antiquity.

72. Saint Illtyd or Illtud was Abbot of the monastery at Llanilltud Fawr, now Llantwit Major, where according to the legend both Samson, Bishop of Dol, and Gildas had received their training. He lived as a hermit, first at Oystermouth and later at Llanhamlach. He died c. 540.

73. The three cantrefs of Brycheiniog were Cantref Selyf, Cantref Tewdos and Cantref Einon, named after the three sons of Einon ap Gruffydd ab Elise.

74. Bernard de Neufmarché or Newmarch witnessed a charter executed by William the Conqueror in 1086-7 in favour of Battle Abbey, signing 'Bernardus de Novo Mercato'. He captured Brecknockshire from Bleddyn ap Maernarch c. 1092. He seems to have held the territory until c. 1125.

and called her Agnes.[75] Bernard had children by her, among them a distinguished knight called Mahel, who lost his paternal inheritance by an injustice, as I shall tell you. His mother broke her marriage vow and fell in love with a certain knight, with whom she committed adultery. This became known, and her son Mahel assaulted her lover one night when he was returning from his mother. He gave him a severe beating, mutilated him and packed him off in great disgrace. The mother, disturbed by the remarkable uproar which ensued, and greatly grieved in her woman's heart, was filled with a burning desire for revenge. She fled to Henry I, King of the English, and told him that her son Mahel was not Bernard's child, but the offspring of another man with whom she had been in love and with whom she had had secret and illicit intercourse. This she maintained rather from malice than because it was true, confirming it by an oath which she swore in person before the whole court. As a result of this oath, which was really perjury, King Henry, who was swayed more by prejudice than by reason, gave Nest's elder daughter,[76] whom she accepted as Bernard's child, in marriage to a distinguished young knight of his own family, Milo FitzWalter, constable of Gloucester, adding the lands of Brecknock as a marriage portion. Later on Milo was made Earl of Hereford by Matilda, Empress of Rome and daughter of Henry I.[77] By his wife Milo became the father of a distinguished family, among them five sons, all of them famous knights, Roger, Walter, Henry, William and Mahel.[78] Each of them succeeded to their father's inheritance, except William, yet they all died without

75. Nest, or Agnes, was the daughter of Osbern FitzRichard. Her mother, also called Nest, was the daughter of Gruffydd ap Llywelyn ap Seisyll, Prince of North Wales, who was killed in 1063, during the Welsh campaign of Harold and Tostig.

76. This daughter was Sybil and she married Milo FitzWalter in 1121.

77. The Empress Matilda landed at Arundel on 30 September 1139. She revived the Earldom of Hereford for Milo FitzWalter in 1141. Milo was accidentally shot on 24 December 1143 while hunting in the Forest of Dean.

78. Roger died in 1155. Walter was last heard of in 1159. Henry was killed in Gwent by Seisyll ap Dyfnwal in 1175. William did not live to succeed. As described on p. 91, Mahel was killed in 1175 in Bronllys Castle when a stone fell on his head during a fire.

issue; and every one of them, by some extraordinary act of vengeance or by some fatal misfortune, came to an untimely end. So this woman, at great loss to her personal modesty, and with the sacrifice of all decorum and self-respect, by this one shameful act deprived both her son of his inheritance and herself of her honour. She did this to reap revenge and to satisfy her anger, yet by her action she deviated not a whit from her womanly nature.

It is not to be wondered at if a woman bears malice, for this comes to her naturally. We read in Ecclesiastes: 'One man among a thousand have I found: but a woman among all those have I not found.'[79] Similarly we read in Ecclesiasticus: 'There is no head above the head of a serpent; and there is no wrath above the wrath of a woman';[80] and again in the same book: 'All wickedness is but little to the wickedness of a woman.'[81] Just as we may gather gooseberries from among the thorns[82] or pick prickly pears from cactus plants, so, when he is describing the nature of woman, Cicero says: 'It may well happen that men will be guilty of one sinful deed in an attempt to gain some personal advantage; but women will not hesitate to commit every crime in the calendar simply to satisfy a passing whim.'[83] Talking about women, Juvenal says: 'No one is bolder than they are when they are caught in the act: from their very sense of guilt, they lose their temper and become incensed';[84] and again, 'A woman is never more implacable than when her sense of shame is egging her on';[85] and yet again, 'No one enjoys revenge more than a woman.'[86]

Mahel, the youngest[87] of these five brothers, all of them sons

---

79. Ecclesiastes, 7.28.   80. Ecclesiasticus, 25.15.
81. Ecclésiasticus, 25.19. Gerald writes 'hominis malitia' for 'omnis malitia', thus giving additional point to the sentence.
82. The text reads 'ut de spinis uvas ... colligamus'. The Italian for gooseberry is still 'uva spina'.
83. 'Tullius ait': but I cannot trace this quotation.
84. Juvenal, *Satires*, 6.284-5.
85. Juvenal, *Satires*, 10.328-9.
86. Juvenal, *Satires*, 13.191-2 (words reversed and 'quia' for 'quod').
87. Gerald writes 'penultimus' for 'ultimus'.

of Earl Milo, was the last in the line of inheritance. He was even more notorious than the others for his inhuman cruelty. He was so intent upon doing harm to David II, Bishop of St David's, and to everything and everybody under his control, both lands and retainers, that David was forced to abandon his jurisdiction over the whole of Brecknockshire and to go into exile, first to other parts of his diocese and then to England.[88] Meanwhile, one day when Mahel was being entertained as a guest by Walter de Clifford in the castle of Bronllys, it happened that the building was burned down by accident.[89] Mahel was struck on the head by a stone which fell from the main tower and he received a mortal blow. He immediately sent messengers to the Bishop to ask him to come back at full speed. 'O father!' he lamented, 'holy Bishop, your saint has exacted a most cruel revenge! He has not waited for me to repent, miserable sinner that I am. Instead he has lost no time at all in causing my death and destruction!' He ended his tyrannical behaviour and his life together, repeatedly bewailing his fate with tears and lamentation. He died in misery before the first year of his rule was completed.

In ancient times a man called Brychan was the nobly born and powerful ruler of this county of Brecknock. Indeed, it is from him that it is called Brycheiniog.[90] The Welsh annals bear witness to

88. David II, Bishop of St David's, was, of course, David FitzGerald, Gerald's uncle. He suffered severe persecution from Mahel, the youngest son of Milo FitzWalter, and he was constantly at loggerheads with his chapter.

89. This is Walter de Clifford, d. c. 1190, son of Richard FitzPons. Bronllys Castle was burned in 1175. Walter was the father of Fair Rosamond, mistress of Henry II. Gerald seems to have been one of the first to have condemned this relationship: '[Rex], qui adulter antea fuerat occultus, effectus postea manifestus, non mundi quidem rosa juxta falsam et frivolam nominis impositionem, sed immundi verius rosa vocata palam et impudenter abutendo . . .' (Until then the King had kept his adultery secret, but it later became common knowledge, for, from her being Fair Rosamond in the every-day and indeed quite unwarranted sense of the word, he was really debasing her into what she came to be called quite openly and shamelessly, that tart Rosie) (*De Princ.*, II.4).

90. Brychan is a shadowy figure who ruled over Brycheiniog in the second half of the fifth century AD, giving his name to the territory. Cp. Rachel

the fact that he had twenty-four daughters. From their youth upwards they were all dedicated to the religious life, and they ended their days blissfully in this state of sanctity. There are still many churches in Wales which have the honour of being named after them. One is on the top of a hill in Brecknockshire, not far from the main castle of Brecon. It is called the church of Saint Eluned, after the name of the saintly virgin who on that spot refused the hand of an earthly ruler and married instead the King Eternal, thus triumphing in an ecstasy of self-denial.[91] Each year on the first day of August her feast-day is celebrated with great solemnity in this same place. On that day great crowds of ordinary folk assemble there from far and wide. Thanks to the merits of this blessed virgin, those who are suffering from maladies of any sort recover the health for which they pray. It seems to me that it is well worth my going into details of what happens almost every year at this feast of the virgin Eluned. You can see young men and maidens, some in the church itself, some in the churchyard and others in the dance which threads its way round the graves. They sing traditional songs, all of a sudden they collapse on the ground, and then those who, until now, have followed their leader peacefully as if in a trance, leap in the air as if seized by frenzy. In full view of the crowds they mime with their hands and feet whatever work they have done contrary to the commandment on sabbath days. You can see one man putting his hand to an [imaginary] plough, another goading on his oxen with a stick, and all as they go singing country airs, to lighten the tedium of their labour. This man is imitating a cobbler at his bench, that man over there is miming a tanner at his work. Here you see a girl pretending that

Bromwich, *Trioedd Ynys Prydein*, Triads 70, 81, 81.C.18 and 96, especially 81.C.18 for 'The Offspring of Brychan Brycheiniog'.

91. Saint Eluned is variously spelt Almedha (by Gerald), Elevetha, Elyned, Aled, Tayled, etc. The chapel which marked the site of her martyrdom was apparently still standing in 1698. Gerald must obviously have seen the folk-ceremonies which took place there on her feast-day, which was 1 August, Lammas Day. In William Worcestre's *Itineraries*, ed. J. H. Harvey, *Oxford Medieval Texts*, 1969, p. 63, she appears as Adwenhelye.

she has a distaff in her hand, drawing out the thread with her hands, stretching it at arm's length, and then winding it back onto the spindle; another, as she trips along, fits the woof to the warp; a third tosses her shuttle, now this way, now that, from one hand to the other, and, with jerky gestures of her tiny tool, seems for all the world to be weaving cloth from the thread which she has prepared. When all is over, they enter the church. They are led up to the altar and there, as they make their oblation, you will be surprised to see them awaken from their trance and recover their normal composure. God in His mercy desireth not the death of a sinner, but rather that he may turn from his wickedness: and so, by taking part in these festivities, many men at once see and feel in their hearts the remission of their sins, and are absolved and pardoned.

This region produces a great amount of corn. If there is ever a shortage, supplies are quickly brought in from the neighbouring parts of England. There is ample pasture and plenty of woodland, the first full of cattle, the second teeming with wild animals. There is no lack of freshwater fish, both in the Usk and the Wye. Salmon and trout are fished from these rivers, but the Wye has more salmon and the Usk more trout. In winter salmon are in season in the Wye, but in summer they abound in the Usk. The Wye is particularly rich in grayling, an excellent fish which some call umber. They are very common round Milan, and Saint Ambrose praises them highly in his writings. 'There is no other fish so attractive to look at,' he says, 'so delicate in its flavour, so delightful to eat.'[92] Brecknock Mere, also called Clamosus, a broad expanse of water which is very well known,[93] supplies plenty of pike, perch, excellent trout, tench and mud-loving eels for the local inhabitants.

I cannot miss the opportunity of telling you about an event which happened there shortly before our time. In the days of Henry I, King of the English, Gruffydd, son of Rhys ap

92. Saint Ambrose, *Exameron*, V.2, quoted from memory. Ambrose was writing of the thymallus. Cp. Isidore of Seville, *Etymologiae*, XII.6.
93. Brecknock Mere, which Gerald calls Clamosus, is also known as Llangors Lake.

Tewdwr,[94] was lord of a commote, that is the quarter of a cantref,[95] in Cantref Mawr, called Caeo,[96] which he held in tenure from the King. It was considered equal in importance and repute to South Wales, which the Welsh call Deheubarth, that is Right-Hand Wales.[97] One day Gruffydd, who was returning home from the King's court, passed by this lake which, it being the cold winter season, was covered with waterfowl of one sort and another. He was accompanied by Milo, Earl of Hereford and Lord of Brecknock,[98] and by Payn FitzJohn,[99] who then held Ewias, both of them secretaries and Privy Councillors of the King, and men of great importance. Earl Milo was chaffing Gruffydd about his claim to noble blood. His remarks were not meant to be taken seriously, for he was trying to be funny. 'There is an old saying in Wales,' he went on, 'that, if the rightful ruler of the land comes to this lake and orders the birds there to sing, they all burst into song.' Gruffydd had more wit than wealth, for, although he had not inherited much property, he was ambitious enough and second to none in self-

94. Gruffydd ap Rhys ap Tewdwr, d. 1137, was the brother of Nest and thus a great-uncle of Gerald.

95. According to Sir John Lloyd, Wales was originally divided into a series of 'gwlads' or 'tuds', that is countries or tribes of free tribesmen. Later on a smaller and more precise geographical and judicial unit became necessary, and this was the 'cantref' or 'hundred hamlets' < 'can' 'tref', as explained by Gerald, *Desc.*, I.4, p. 223. Later still, towards the end of the eleventh century, an even smaller unit was adopted, the 'commote' or 'neighbourhood' < 'cymwd'; cp. what Gerald writes here: 'kemmoti, id est, quartae partis cantaredi'. 'The leading feature of the commote is its court, for the trial of disputes among the free tribesmen, and this is sometimes called the court of the commote or the cantref... In the laws, it is the commote which appears as the living and active body, the references to the cantref being for the most part perfunctory, with a smack of antiquity about them' (Sir John Lloyd *The History of Wales*, pp. 300–301).

96. Caeo was in the upper valley of the River Cothi, according to Gerald in Cantref Mawr, but really in Cantref Bychan.

97. Deheubarth, or Deheubarth Kymry, Right-Hand Wales, in Latin 'dextralis pars Britanniae', was originally the whole of South Wales, but it came to mean South Wales less Gwent and Morgannwg.

98. Milo FitzWalter died in 1143.

99. Payn FitzJohn died in 1137. Milo's eldest son Roger married Payn's eldest daughter Cecilia.

esteem. 'Well,' he answered, 'you now rule the country, so you had better be the first to speak to them.' The waterfowl took no notice at all of Milo. Then Payn spoke to them, but again they took no notice. Gruffydd saw that his two companions would insist that he should address the birds in his turn. He got off his horse, knelt down facing the east, and then, as if he were about to fight a battle, he fell forward face to the ground and lay there flat. Then he raised his eyes and hands to heaven and prayed devoutly to God. When his prayer was finished, he stood up, marked his face and his forehead with the sign of the Cross and said in a loud clear voice: 'Almighty and omnipotent God, Jesus Christ our Lord, show Your miraculous power to us here today. If You have ordained that I should descend in direct line from the five princes of Wales, make these birds declare it in Your name.' Immediately all the birds, each according to his kind, beat the water with their wings and began to sing with one accord and to proclaim him master. Everyone present was dumbfounded and astonished. Earl Milo and Payn FitzJohn hurried back to the King's court. They were greatly impressed by what had happened and gave the King a detailed account of it. He listened to what they had to say and then replied: 'By the death of Christ,' for that was his favourite oath, 'I am not the slightest bit surprised. It is we who hold the power, and so we are free to commit acts of violence and injustice against these people, and yet we know full well that it is they who are the rightful heirs to the land.'

The local inhabitants will assure you that the lake has many miraculous properties. As I have already told you, it sometimes turns bright green, and in our days it has been known to become scarlet, not all over, but as if blood were flowing along certain currents and eddies. What is more, those who live there sometimes observe it to be completely covered with buildings or rich pasture-lands, or adorned with gardens and orchards. In the winter months, when it is covered with ice, and when the surface is frozen over with a smooth and slippery coat, it emits a horrible groaning sound, like the lowing of a vast herd of cattle all driven together in one place. It is possible, of course, that this is

95

caused by the cracking of the ice and the sudden violent eruption of enclosed pockets of air through vents imperceptible to the eye.

Except to the north, the region is sheltered on all sides by lofty mountains: to the west by Cantref Bychan; to the south by a range of hills the chief of which is Cadair Arthur, or Arthur's Chair, so called from two peaks which rise up in the form of a throne.[100] This summit is a very lofty spot and most difficult of access, so that in the minds of simple folk it is thought to have belonged to Arthur, the greatest and most distinguished King of the Britons.[101] On the topmost point of this mountain a spring of water bubbles forth. Its deep basin is square in shape and like a well, but no stream ever runs from it. Trout are said to be found there from time to time. As the region is protected by these high mountains to the south, the air is cooler there and the sun less fierce, so that the climate is most temperate and unusually healthy. To the east stretch the Black Mountains of Talgarth and Ewias. The natives of these parts are much given to implacable quarrels and never-ending disputes. They spend their time fighting each other and shed their blood freely in internecine feuds. I leave it to others to tell you about the inhuman crimes which have been committed there in our own lifetime: marriages most cruelly brought about, inflicted rather than contracted, only to be cut short by separation and bloodshed, and many other savage acts of violence.

Chapter 3
Ewias and Llanthony.

In the deep vale of Ewias, which is shut in on all sides by a circle of lofty mountains and which is no more than three arrow-shots in width, there stands the abbey church of Saint John the Baptist. It is roofed in with sheets of lead and built of squared stones, which are admirably suited to the nature of the place. This church is constructed on the very spot where once there stood the humble chapel of Saint David, the Archbishop, which

100. Cadair Arthur is now called Brecon Beacons or Bannau Brycheiniog.
101. Gerald had been reading Geoffrey of Monmouth.

was adorned with woodland moss and wreathed about with ivy. It is a site most suited to the practice of religion and better chosen for canonical discipline than that of any of the other monasteries in the whole Island of Britain. It was originally founded by two hermits, in honour of the eremetical way of life, in solitude and far removed from the bustle of everyday existence, and built on the bank of the Honddu, in a deep recess where that river flows along the vale. It is from the Honddu that it takes the name Llanhonddu, for 'llan' means a place dedicated to religion. This derivation may seem far-fetched, for the real name of the place in Welsh is Nant Honddu. 'Nant' means a stream of running water: and in the Welsh language the place is still today called Llanddewi Nant Honddu by the local inhabitants, that is the church of David on the River Honddu. The English have corrupted the name to Llanthony, whereas it ought to be called either Nant Honddu with an *N* and a *t*, that is the Honddu stream, or else Llanhonddu with an *L* but no *t*, that is the church on the Honddu. It rains a lot there because of the mountains, the winds blow strong, and in winter it is always capped with clouds. The climate is temperate and healthy, the air soothing and clement, if somewhat heavy, and illness is rare. When, sadly afflicted and worn out by long labour in their daughter house, the monks are brought back, as it were, to their mother's breasts, they are soon restored to the health for which they yearn, for this is their salubrious cure, this is their sole asylum and retreat.[102] As I have explained in my *Topography of Ireland*,[103] the farther one travels to the east, the more the sky above seems to be pure and limpid, but this is only because the wind which blows it clear is harsher and more piercing. On the contrary, as one goes farther westward and northwestward, the air in those parts produces a climate which may well be more cloudy and more thick, but it is certainly more temperate and healthy. As

102. Gerald obviously knew Llanthony Abbey very well. One even wonders if he were there as a boy before going to St Peter's Abbey in Gloucester, or if he came there for a change of air during his time in Gloucester. The daughter house in Gloucester was Llanthony Secunda.

103. *The Topography of Ireland*, I.37.

they sit in their cloisters in this monastery, breathing the fresh air, the monks gaze up at distant prospects which rise above their own lofty roof-tops, and there they see, as far as any eye can reach, mountain-peaks which rise to meet the sky and often enough herds of wild deer which are grazing on their summits. Even on a clear day, the sun's round ball is not visible above these lofty mountain-tops until the hour of prime, or maybe just before. This was formerly a happy, a delightful spot, most suited to the life of contemplation, a place from its first founding fruitful and to itself sufficient. Once it was free, but it has since been reduced to servitude, through the boundless extravagance of the English, its own reputation for rich living, uncontrolled ambition, the ever-growing vice of ingratitude, the negligence of its prelates and its patrons and, far worse than all of these, the fact that the daughter house, become a step-daughter, has odiously and enviously supplanted its own mother.

In my opinion it is a fact worthy of remark that all the priors who did harm to the establishment about which I am telling you were punished by God when their moment came to die. Prior William,[104] who was the first to despoil the house of its herds and stores, was deposed in the end and expelled by the brothers, with the result that he was held unworthy to be buried with the other priors. Clement[105] seemed to be attached to the place, and he spent much of his time there in study and prayer. All the same he followed the example of the priest Eli,[106] in that he made no attempt to reprove the brothers or to restrain them when they plundered the house and committed other outrages. In the end he died from a paralytic stroke. Prior Roger[107] did even more damage than his predecessors. He did not even try to disguise the fact that he was busy stealing every single thing which they had left behind. He stripped the church of all its books, orna-

104. William of Wycombe, fourth Prior of Llanthony Prima, 1137–c. 1150, resigned in the end and retired to Frome.
105. Clement of Gloucester, fifth Prior of Llanthony Prima, c. 1150–74?
106. I Samuel 2.
107. Roger of Norwich, sixth Prior of Llanthony Prima, 1174?–c. 1189. Clearly none of these three was a Welshman.

ments and charters. Long before his death he became paralysed. He resigned from his appointment, but he lingered on from day to day as a very sick man. Some short time later he died without recovering his health.

In the reign of Henry I, King of the English, at a time when the mother church was renowned both for its affluence and its practice of religion – two things which you rarely find united – and when the daughter church which was to rival it had not yet been founded – and how I wish that it had never come into being at all! – Llanthony's fame as a religious house attracted a visit from Roger, Bishop of Salisbury, who was then the Chief Minister of the realm and second only to the King himself.[108] To encourage virtue, albeit in another, is a virtue in itself; and it is no small proof of goodness to be able to inspire in someone else a detestation of vices, even if you have not been able to avoid them yourself. The Bishop spent some time admiring the natural amenities of the site, the lonely life being led there by the community and the day-to-day activities of the brothers, who were devoting themselves to the service of God, as befits holy men, observing the Rule, never complaining, never quarrelling. He was greatly impressed by all this. He went back to the King and told him all that he had seen which he considered worthy of report. He spent the greater part of the day in praising the place and then finished his panegyric with these words: 'What more can I say?' he asked. 'The entire treasure of the King and his realm would not be sufficient to build such a cloister.' When he had held the minds of the King and his whole court in suspense for a long time by this assertion, he finally explained the enigma by revealing that what he really meant was the circle of mountains which enclosed the monastery on all sides.

A certain knight called William had been the first to discover this place and to see its possibilities, together with a priest called Ernisius, who was with him at the time.[109] They had perhaps

108. Roger, Bishop of Salisbury, Henry I's Justiciar in function if not in name, held the commote of Cydweli from 1106 onwards. Cp. p. 137, n. 209.

109. William de Laci, a Norman knight, was joined by Ernisius, chaplain to Queen Matilda, in 1103.

heard the statement of Jerome, as it is written in *The Lives of the Fathers*, to the effect that, as it had increased in riches, the Church of Christ had decreased in virtue, its vices growing as its wealth became greater.[110] They made a habit of beseeching God, in all devotion and with everyone listening to them, that this place which they had chosen might never be embarrassed with great possessions. They were greatly distressed when it began to be endowed with land and church benefices, first by the donations of Hugh de Lacy, its original lord and master,[111] and then by the gifts of other faithful men. In their desire for poverty, they refused many offers of manors and churches in these early years. Situated as they were in the wilderness, they refused to permit the overgrown recesses of the valley, where it widened out into an impenetrable wood, ever to be cleared or levelled off to make an open meadow, for they had no wish to abandon their eremitical mode of life. In the end it started acquiring wealth and endowments at tremendous speed. There followed a period of unrest and warfare, during which the daughter house, so soon to become the rival of its mother, came into being in Gloucester, under the patronage of Milo, Earl of Hereford.[112] By divine providence, and through the virtues and prayers of these holy men, both of whose bodies lie buried beside the high altar, the mother house continued in that laudable state of poverty which it had always affected, whereas the daughter rejoiced in a vast superfluity of wealth and possessions. Let the bustling and active take up their residence then in Gloucester, leaving this other foundation for men of contemplation. There in Gloucester men strive for earthly possessions, but here in Llanthony let them rather turn their minds towards the promise of eternal bliss. There let them enjoy the company of mortal men, but here let

110. Does Gerald mean the *De Viris Illustribus*? I cannot trace the quotation.

111. After his brother Roger's unsuccessful revolt in 1095, Hugh de Laci was given Ewias by William Rufus. Hugh died in 1115 and Ewias then passed to Payn FitzJohn. Cp. p. 94, n. 99.

112. The Priory of Llanthony Secunda by Gloucester was founded by Milo FitzWalter, Earl of Hereford, in 1136 and the new church was dedicated in 1137.

them prefer the concourse of the angels. There let the great men of this world be entertained, but here let Christ's poor and needy seek relief. There, I say, let them keep up their clamour about the affairs and the pretences of this world, while here the brothers continue to mutter over their books and whisper over their prayers. There let wealth grow ever greater, wealth the prime cause and creator of vice, and of all the cares which follow in its train; but here in Llanthony let the golden mean continue to flourish, and moderation, the mother of all virtues.

In both the houses, in Gloucester and here, too, the canonical Rule instituted by Augustine is still observed, for nowadays this order is to be preferred to all the others.[113] In its original state of poverty the Rule of Saint Benedict[114] was wholly admirable; but later on the order accumulated vast wealth through the fervent charity of great numbers of benefactors, and this was increased by the bounty of the faithful, with the result that, under cover of a most regrettable dispensation, gluttony and indulgence ended in corruption. The Cistercian order,[115] which derived from the Benedictines, clung tenaciously to its original vows of poverty and holiness, and, in its first beginnings, it, too, was much to be praised and commended; but there again ambition, the blind mother of all our ills, which sets no limit to our aspirations, crept up and took possession of it. As Seneca maintains: 'Too much success simply makes us greedy for more: and we are never so temperate in our desires that they can be satisfied with what we actually have. From big things we move forward to even bigger ones; and once we have achieved the unexpected we set our hopes upon what is completely unreasonable.'[116] Ovid says exactly the same:

113. The Augustinian Canons came into being after the Roman synods of 1059 and 1063, and by 1150 the Rule of Saint Augustine was recognized all over Europe.

114. This was the Rule of Saint Benedict of Nursia, who lived c. 480–c. 547.

115. The Cistercians or White Monks, as distinct from the Benedictines or Black Monks, took their name from Cîteaux in Burgundy. The founders of the order moved to Cîteaux in 1098 as a break-away group from the Benedictines of Molesme.

116. Seneca, *De Clementia*, I.1 ('amplectuntur' for 'complectuntur').

Our minds soon lose control when things go all our way:
When we enjoy success, we end in disarray.[117]

In another place he says:

Our wealth has grown so great and yet our greed grows greater:
However much we have, still more we'll covet later.[118]

In his *Odes*, Horace tells us:

However great our wealth may wax,
It seems too small, still something lacks.[119]

He had previously said:

We've money in plenty: with it comes care;
We're always greedy for more than our share.[120]

Then he goes on:

Seek much; much lacks. Far happier he
Whom God has succoured sparingly.[121]

Lucan has the same message for us:

The poor man's life is carefree and safe his humble home
Where, bringing bribes undreamed-of, the Gods have not yet come.[122]

Petronius says:

Unhappy Tantalus cannot slake his thirst, or feed
On the evasive fruit, however great his need.
Such is the rich man's fate: for all that he has seized,
His mouth is ever parched, his hunger unappeased.[123]

Those mountain-heights abound in horses and wild game, those woods are richly stocked with pigs, the shady groves with goats, the pasture-lands with sheep, the meadows with cattle, the

117. Ovid, *Ars Amatoria*, II.437–8.
118. Ovid, *Fasti*, I.211–12 ('petunt' for 'volunt').
119. Horace, *Odes*, III.24.62–4.
120. Horace, *Odes*, III.16.17–18.
121. Horace, *Odes*, III.16.42–4.
122. Lucan, *Pharsalia*, V.527–9.
123. Petronius, *Satires*, 82.35–8 ('nec poma fugacia' for 'poma aut pendentia'; 'late qui tenet' for 'cernens qui timet', but this latter is an acceptable variant).

farms with ploughs. All the things and creatures which I have mentioned are there in great abundance, and yet we are so insatiable in our wicked desires that each in its turn seems insufficient for our needs. We occupy each other's territory, we move boundary-fences, we invade each other's plots of land. Our market-places are piled high with goods for sale, and yet our courts are kept busy with legal cases, the palaces of our kings re-echo with complaints. This is what we read in Isaiah: 'Woe unto them that join house to house, that lay field to field, till there be no place, that they may be placed alone in the midst of the earth.' [124]

If the prophet inveighs in this way against those who occupy their lands right up to the boundary, what would he say about the men who trespass far beyond? From these and other causes it has come about that the fine lustre of true religious faith has been transmuted into tarnished dross, and evil habits lie there hid beneath a fair exterior. Their inner faith, I say,

> Which once was starry white, is now the opposite. [125]

Concerning these men the Scripture seems to be fulfilled: 'Beware of false prophets, which come to you in sheep's clothing, but inwardly they are ravening wolves.' [126]

I am inclined to think that the lust for possessions, so noisily acclaimed the whole world over, springs in this case from good intentions. The monks of the Cistercian order, who are in fact extremely abstemious, busy themselves unceasingly to provide hospitality for all and sundry, offering limitless charity to pilgrims and the needy. They do not live as others do on fixed incomes, but on the sweat of their brows and their own good management. That is why they are so anxious to acquire land from the proceeds of which they can meet the demands of hospitality. They are constantly on the lookout for rich lands and broad pastures. If only they would occasionally call to mind what Solomon had to say on the subject, this might remove from their

124. Isaiah, 5.8.
125. Ovid, *Metamorphoses*, II.541 ('Qui' for 'Cui').
126. Matthew, 7.15.

holy order the damnable stigma of ambition: 'Whoso bringeth an offering of the goods of the poor, doth as one that killeth the son before his father's eyes.'[127] Gregory said: 'Putting things to good use can never justify the fact that they have been wrongly acquired.'[128] Ambrose said the same: 'He who takes wrongly so that he may give to others does more harm than good.'[129] These men seem to be saying with the Apostle: 'Let us do evil, that good may come.'[130] It is written: 'Compassion should be of such a nature that men may welcome it, instead of being repelled by it; it should purge away your sins, instead of being an offence before the Lord; it should spring from your own unaided efforts, instead of depending upon someone else's charity.'[131] Solomon said: 'Honour the Lord with thy substance.'[132] What shall they answer who seize other men's goods, and have then given it away in alms? They will say: 'O Lord! In thy name we have done charitable deeds, we have fed the poor, we have clothed the naked, we have received the stranger at our gate.' The Lord will answer: 'You speak of what you have given away, but you do not mention the fact that you have stolen it in the first place. You are mindful of those whom you have fed, but you have forgotten those whom you have destroyed.'

I have thought it relevant to include here an exemplum found in the answer which Richard, King of the English, made to Fulk, a virtuous and holy man, through whose agency God has wrought many unquestionable miracles in the kingdom of the French in our own days.[133] This saintly man had been talking

127. Ecclesiasticus, 34.24, quoted from memory.
128. I cannot trace this quotation.
129. I cannot trace this quotation.
130. Romans, 3.8.
131. I cannot trace this quotation.
132. Proverbs, 3.9.

133. This witty anecdote is repeated by Raphael Holinshed, *Chronicles of England, Scotland and Ireland*. He spoils it by being far too long-winded. 'Hereof it came, that on a time whiles he soiourned in France about his warres, which he hold against K. Philip, there came vnto him a French préest whose name was Fulco, who required the K. in any wise to put from him thrée abhominable daughters which he had, and to bestow them in marriage, least God punished him for them. Thou liest hypocrite (said the

to the King for some time. 'You have three daughters,' he said, 'and, as long as they remain with you, you will never receive the grace of God. Their names are Superbia, Luxuria and Cupiditas.' For a moment the King did not know what to answer. Then he replied: 'I have already given these daughters of mine away in marriage. Pride I gave to the Templars, Lechery I gave to the Black Monks[134] and Covetousness to the White Monks.'[135]

It is an extraordinary circumstance, indeed, I have always felt it to be a miracle, concerning this place Llanthony, that although the lofty mountain-tops which shut it in on all sides are formed, not of stones and rocks, but rather of soft earth covered with grass, blocks of marble are frequently to be found there. These are commonly called free-stones, because they are easily split and can be polished with iron tools. The church is built of them and very attractive they make it. They have this remarkable property, that you can search until you are quite exhausted and collect all these free-stones, until none is left and no more could possibly be found, and then, three or four days later, you can look again and there they all are, just as numerous as before, easy to find if you look and there for you to take.

As far as the Cluniacs[136] and the Cistercians are concerned,

---

king) to thy verie face, for all the world knoweth that I haue not one daughter. I lie not (said the préest) for thou hast thrée daughters, one of them is called pride, the second couetousnesse, and the third lecherie. With that the king called to him his lords & barons, and said to them; "This hypocrite heere had required me to marrie awaie my thrée daughters, which (as he saith) I cherish, nourish, foster and mainteine, that is to say pride, couetousnesse, and lecherie. And now that I haue found out necessarie & fit husbands for them, I will doo it with effect, and seeke no more delaies. I therefore bequeath my pride to the high minded templers and hospitallers, which are so proud as Lucifer himselfe. My couetousnesse I give vnto the white moonks, otherwise called of the Cisteuux order, for they couet the divell and all. My lecherie I commit to the prelates of the church, who haue most pleasure and felicitie therein."' (ed. of 1807, Vol. II, p. 271).

134. The Benedictines.
135. The Cistercians.
136. The Cluniacs took their name from the Burgundian Abbey of Cluny, founded near Mâcon as a reformed house by William the Pious, Duke of Aquitaine.

what follows is a fair appraisal of the two orders. Give the Cluniacs today a tract of land covered with marvellous buildings, endow them with ample revenues and enrich the place with vast possessions: before you can turn round it will all be ruined and reduced to poverty. On the other hand, settle the Cistercians in some barren retreat which is hidden away in an overgrown forest: a year or two later you will find splendid churches there and fine monastic buildings, with a great amount of property and all the wealth you can imagine. Their contrasting ways of life and their different objectives are the root causes of this distinction, or so it seems to me. I mean offence to neither, but I can only say what I think. The Cistercians pride themselves on their sobriety, parsimony and planning for the future; whereas the Cluniacs suffer from greed, gluttony and intemperance. The Cistercians all gather together and congregate in one place, like so many bees, agreeing with each other in all things: they share a common purse and what it holds is spent frugally. As against this, whatever they have collected and put together over a period, usually from the devout offerings of the faithful, the Cluniacs squander each in his own way and divert to improper uses. The welfare of the community suffers as a result, for each individual has his own expenses and all consult their own interests. As Sallust says: 'By careful planning small beginnings grow to great; disagree among yourselves and vast wealth will soon be dissipated.'[137] What is more, rather than forgo a single one of the ten or thirteen courses to which they claim the right by custom, even in a time of famine, the Cluniacs will allow the lands and wealthy manors of their monastery to be distrained, and suffer the poor to collapse in heaps outside their very gates and die of hunger for want of Christian charity. The Cistercians, on the other hand, differ completely in their determination to do good. Rather than see a single poor and needy man suffer seriously from neglect they would give up both the simple dishes with which they satisfy their hunger.

In our times an attempt has been made to perfect the statutes of the Cistercians and to remove any possible cause of criticism.

137. Sallust, *Jugurtha*, 10 ('vero' added).

A clause has been added to their Rule which makes it clear that no manors or farmlands shall ever again be purchased by the order. They must be satisfied with those properties which are made over to them unconditionally and donated to them free of charge.[138]

The Augustinian canons are more content than any of the others with a humble and modest mode of life. They may not be wholly successful in this, but as far as they can they hold in check the urges of ambition. They dwell among secular people, but they avoid as far as possible the temptations of this world. They are certainly in no way notorious for gluttony or drunkenness, and the possibility of incurring public criticism for lechery or evil-living fills them with dread and shame. All this will be considered at greater length in a book which, if God permits, I propose to write about the religious orders.[139]

In this most temperate area I myself have been appointed to a post of some importance, to use the jargon with which we are all so familiar, but it affords me no great promise of wealth and certainly no expectation of ever playing my part in the tragic pomps and ceremonies of this world. I occupy a tiny dwelling-house not far from the principal castle of Brecknockshire and, indeed, adjacent to it.[140] This is convenient enough for my studies and my work, and here I pass my time in a sort of happy-go-lucky mediocrity. The house gives me pleasure and it is conducive to thoughts of the next world. I would not change it for all the riches of Croesus.[141] I certainly prefer it beyond all measure to the perishable and transitory things of this world. Now I must return to my story.

138. The success of the Cistercians and their vast acquisitions of land had made their original statutes out of date. See D. Knowles, *The Monastic Order in England*, 1950, pp. 348 ff., for the need for reform.

139. This book was never written.

140. This was Gerald's archdeaconry at Llanddew.

141. Croesus, King of Lydia, reigned 560–46 BC, whose wealth was proverbial.

Chapter 4
The journey through Coed Grwyne and Abergavenny.

From Llanddew we made our way along the rugged pass of Coed Grwyne or Grwyne Wood, by a narrow trackway overgrown with trees. On our left we passed by the noble monastery of Llanthony in its great circle of mountains. The castle of Abergavenny takes it name from its situation at the confluence of the River Gavenny and the Usk.

A short time after the death of Henry I, King of the English, it happened that Richard de Clare, a nobleman of high birth who, in addition to the Clare estates, held Cardiganshire in South Wales, passed this way on a journey from England to Wales.[142] He was accompanied by a large force of men-at-arms led by Brian de Wallingford, then overlord of this area,[143] who was acting as his guide through the pass. When they reached the entrance to the wood, Richard de Clare sent back Brian and his men, and rode unarmed into the forest, although this was much against Brian's wishes and, indeed, against his express advice. Richard was foolish enough to imagine that the trackway was safe. Ahead of him went a singer to announce his coming and a fiddler who accompanied the singer on his instrument. From then onwards things happened very quickly. The Welsh had prepared an ambush for Richard. All of a sudden Iorwerth, the brother of Morgan of Caerleon,[144] and others of their family, rushed out from where they were hidden in the thickets, cut down Richard de Clare and most of his men, and made off with their baggage which they had seized in this savage way.

142. Richard FitzGilbert, ruler of Cardiganshire, was ambushed and murdered in Coed Grwyne on 15 April 1136. He was the son of Gilbert FitzRichard. The family took its name from the manor of Clare in Suffolk.

143. Brian FitzCount, a natural son of Count Alan of Brittany, was ruler of Upper Gwent at that time.

144. This was Iorwerth ab Owain ap Caradog. His brother, Morgan ab Owain, ruled over Gwynllwg and Caerleon. In 1158 Morgan was ambushed and murdered by Ifor ap Meurig, known as Ifor Bach, whereupon Iorwerth succeeded him.

Just how ill-advised and foolhardy it is to be so presumptuous is made only too obvious by disasters of this sort. We learn to be careful about the future and to exercise caution even when all seems to be going well. To rush on regardless is simply false bravado. It is at once rash and inconsiderate to take no heed at all of the advice given by those who are trying to help us.

A sermon was given at Abergavenny and many took the Cross. A certain nobleman of those parts, called Arthenus, came in great humility to meet the Archbishop, who was in a hurry to reach Usk Castle. Arthenus apologized for not having arrived sooner. When the Archbishop asked him if he would take the Cross, he answered: 'I cannot take such a step without consulting my friends.' 'Ought you not to discuss the matter with your wife?' asked the Archbishop. Arthenus looked down at the ground and replied with some embarrassment: 'This is man's work which we are considering. There is no point in asking the advice of a woman.' Thereupon he took the Cross from the Archbishop without waiting any longer.

I leave it to others to tell the story of the bloodthirsty outrages which have been committed one after another in these parts in our own lifetime, sometimes by the local inhabitants at the expense of those in command of the castles, and then, the other way round, the vindictive retaliations of the castle-governors against the locals. Ranulf Poer, Sheriff of Herefordshire, was the person responsible for the most recent terrifying atrocities committed here with such inhuman slaughter in our own times, although Henry II, King of the English, was the real instigator. I have thought it better not to relate them in detail, lest they serve to encourage other equally infamous men.[145] Occasionally

145. Gerald is referring, with some circumspection, to the Massacre of Abergavenny in 1175. As mentioned on p. 89, n. 78, Henry, the third son of Milo FitzWalter, Earl of Hereford, was killed by Seisyll ap Dyfnwal in 1175. William, the fourth son, did not live to succeed. Mahel, the fifth son, was killed a little later in 1175 in Bronllys Castle, when a stone fell on his head during a fire. There was no other male heir, and Brecknockshire and Upper Gwent passed to William de Braose through his mother, Bertha, who was another child of Milo FitzWalter. William de Braose decided to avenge the death of his uncle Henry. On a pretext he summoned Seisyll ap Dyfnwal, his

some temporary advantage may seem to ensue from an evil action; yet, though the punishment of wickedness may be deferred, it must in the end be weighed in the scales of the Just Avenger, and so cannot be avoided altogether, perhaps in our own time, perhaps in the years to come. As the poet said:

> Ill-gotten gains can only bring unhappiness.[146]

After seven years of peace and tranquillity over all this area, the sons and grandsons of those who had been murdered grew to man's estate and from being boys became fully-grown adults.[147] Burning with revenge, they concealed themselves with a strong force of soldiery in the overgrown ditches of Abergavenny Castle, which they had occupied when the castellan was away. The previous day one of their number, a man called Seisyll the son of Eudas, had said to the constable, as if he were warning him, but apparently more for a joke and a laugh than seriously: 'That is where we shall climb in tonight.' As he spoke he pointed to one of the corners of the wall, where it seemed to be lower than elsewhere. Sometimes

> We joke and joking tell the truth;[148]

and similarly it is a fact that

> From those who hate us we can often learn the truth.[149]

The constable and his household stayed on guard all night, refusing to take off their armour and remaining on the alert until first light. In the end, tired out by their vigil and feeling safe now

---

son Geoffrey and a number of other Welshmen from Gwent to Abergavenny Castle, and there they were murdered out of hand. At the same time William de Braose's retainers ravaged Seisyll's lands, killed his son Cadwaladr and captured his wife. In this passage Gerald implicates Ranulf Poer, Sheriff of Herefordshire, and holds Henry II as ultimately responsible. In Version I of *The Journey through Wales* he had given a more detailed account of the massacre.

146. Ovid, *Amores*, I.10.48.
147. This was in 1182.
148. Horace, *Satires*, I.1.24–5 ('ridendo' for 'ridentem', 'quis' for 'quid').
149. Ovid, *Metamorphoses*, IV.428.

that day had dawned, they all retired to bed. Thereupon their enemies dragged the scaling-ladders which they had prepared to the precise corner of the walls which Seisyll had pointed out. The constable and his wife were captured and so were most of their men. A few escaped, finding refuge in the master tower. The Welsh occupied the castle and burned the whole place down. God in His justice thus decreed that the original crime should be punished on the very spot where it had been committed.

Some short time after the capture of Abergavenny Castle, Ranulf Poer, the Sheriff of Herefordshire, was busy building another strong-point at Dingestow near Monmouth.[150] With him he had a squad of men from Hereford. One night

Aurora, as she left Tithonus' saffron bed,[151]

was just beginning to drive away the shades of darkness, and dawn was breaking through, when Ranulf and his men were attacked by a band of young men from Gwent and the neighbourhood. These were the descendants of the murdered men, who had now grown up. This time Ranulf's troops were not caught off their guard and they were not taken unawares, for they were not without information of the imminent arrival of their enemies. On the contrary, they knew well what was planned, they were fully forewarned, they were armed and they were drawn up in battle array. They were forced to take refuge in the fortifications which they had built, and Ranulf Poer, nine of the leading captains from Herefordshire and quite a few other fighting-men died after being run through the body with lances. Ranulf received a number of serious wounds, any one of which would have put paid to him. In particular his throat was cut with a sword, all the veins and arteries being severed, so that he breathed out his soul with his dying gasp. It is a fact worthy of remark that, despite all this, he was able to make signs for a priest to come and he received him as he died. He was given this boon through the merit of his past life and because, or so it is believed, he had been in the habit of showing greater honour and respect to those chosen to follow Christ than to other folk. Be that as it may, he

150. This was later in 1182.   151. Virgil, *Georgics*, I.447.

made his confession and received Extreme Unction before he expired. It is often observed, and a great number of people bear witness to this, that those men who respect the priesthood more often than not do receive Extreme Unction before they die. The opposite is also true, and those who jeer at priests and bring false witness against them usually die without this consolation, as you can see for yourself.

William de Braose was not the instigator of the atrocity which I have preferred to pass over in silence. He was not the author of it, and, indeed, he played no part in it at all. If he was responsible in any way, it was because he did nothing to stop it. While the murder-squads were running berserk and carrying out the order which they had received, William was tossed into the moat at one of its deepest and sheerest points, this being part of the plan. He was pulled out and made captive by men who were his bitterest enemies. At that precise moment his own troops made a sally and, by divine intervention, he was rescued, not merely alive but completely unharmed. From this it is quite clear that he who does something unwillingly, or who merely permits it to happen, is guilty to a lesser degree and is punished less severely than he who not only plans a crime but also plays a part in it. This was obvious in the case of Christ's passion: Judas was hanged, the Jews were either killed or banished, Pilate was sent into exile. As for King Henry II, who agreed to this act of treachery and gave the order for it to be carried out, the manner of his death has since made it clear to what extent he was a man of sorrow and confusion. His ignominy was made the more obvious by the fact that he began his punishment in this world. The reason for it was this particular outrage and, with it, all the other crimes which he had committed during his ghastly career. If God gives me strength, I shall set all this out in my *How to Bring Up a Prince*.[152]

It is worth mentioning, or so I think, that the men of Gwent,

152. *How to Bring Up a Prince* seems to have been begun c. 1190, but it was not finished until 1216. This explains why Version I of *The Journey through Wales* has 'I have set all this out' (propalavimus) and Versions II and III have 'prolabimus'.

for that is what they are called, have much more experience of warfare, are more famous for their martial exploits and, in particular, are more skilled with the bow and arrow than those who come from other parts of Wales. I will give you a few examples to show just how true this is. In this capture by stratagem of Abergavenny Castle which I have just described to you, two men-at-arms were rushing across a bridge to take refuge in the tower which had been built on a great mound of earth. The Welsh shot at them from behind, and with the arrows which sped from their bows they actually penetrated the oak doorway of the tower, which was almost as thick as a man's palm. As a permanent reminder of the strength of their impact, the arrows have been left sticking in the door just where their iron heads struck. William de Braose also testifies that, in the war against the Welsh, one of his men-at-arms was struck by an arrow shot at him by a Welshman. It went right through his thigh, high up, where it was protected outside and inside the leg by his iron cuishes, and then through the skirt of his leather tunic; next it penetrated that part of the saddle which is called the alva or seat; and finally it lodged in his horse, driving in so deep that it killed the animal. An arrow pinned the thigh of another soldier to his saddle, although the tassets of his leather tunic were there to protect him outside and inside the leg. He tugged on the reins and pulled his horse round in a half-circle, whereupon another arrow, shot by the same bowman, hit him in exactly the same place in the other thigh. so that he was skewered to his horse on both sides. It is difficult to see what more you could do, even if you had a ballista. The bows they use are not made of horn, nor of sapwood, nor yet of yew. The Welsh carve their bows out of the dwarf elm-trees in the forest. They are nothing much to look at, not even rubbed smooth, but left in a rough and unpolished state. Still, they are firm and strong. You could not shoot far with them; but they are powerful enough to inflict serious wounds in a close fight.

Now I must end this diversion and return to our journey.

Chapter 5
Our journey takes us past Usk Castle and through Caerleon.

In Usk Castle a large group of men was signed with the Cross. This was the result of the Archbishop's sermon and of an address by that good and honest man, William, Bishop of Llandaff,[153] who remained constantly at our side as long as we were in his diocese. Alexander, Archdeacon of Bangor, acted as interpreter for the Welsh.[154] To the great astonishment of everyone present, and it was, indeed, an extraordinary circumstance, some of the most notorious criminals of those parts were among those converted, robbers, highwaymen and murderers.

We went through Caerleon, passing far away on our left Monmouth Castle and the great Forest of Dean, which is across the Wye, but still on this side of the Severn, and which supplies Gloucester with venison and iron ore. We spent the night in Newport. We had to cross the River Usk three times. Caerleon is the modern name of the City of the Legions. In Welsh 'caer' means a city or encampment. The legions sent to this island by the Romans had the habit of wintering in this spot, and so it came to be called the City of the Legions. Caerleon is of unquestioned antiquity. It was constructed with great care by the Romans, the walls being built of brick. You can still see many vestiges of its one-time splendour. There are immense palaces, which, with the gilded gables of their roofs, once rivalled the magnificence of ancient Rome. They were set up in the first place by some of the most eminent men of the Roman state, and they were therefore embellished with every architectural conceit. There is a lofty tower, and beside it remarkable hot baths, the remains of temples and an amphitheatre. All this is enclosed

153. William de Salso Marisco, Bishop of Llandaff, had been consecrated by Baldwin himself in 1185. He died in 1191 and the bishopric was offered to Gerald. He sounds more ordinary in English as William Saltmarsh. He had been Abbot of St Augustine's, Bristol.

154. Alexander, Archdeacon of Bangor, had stayed with Archbishop Thomas during his exile, 1164–70. His Welsh name was Cuhelyn. Elsewhere Gerald calls him 'vir sermone facetus et facundus' (V.S.R., XXIX).

within impressive walls, parts of which still remain standing. Wherever you look, both within and without the circuit of these walls, you can see constructions dug deep into the earth, conduits for water, underground passages and air-vents. Most remarkable of all to my mind are the stoves, which once transmitted heat through narrow pipes inserted in the side-walls and which are built with extraordinary skill.[155]

Two men of noble birth, Julius and Aaron, suffered martyrdom there and were buried in the city. Each had a church named after him. Next to Albanus and Amphibalus, they were the most famous protomartyrs of Great Britain. In former times there were three fine churches in Caerleon. The first was named after Julius the martyr: this was graced by a choir of nuns dedicated to the service of God. The second was founded in the name of Saint Aaron, his comrade: this was noted for its distinguished chapter of canons. The third was famed far and wide as the metropolitan church for the whole of Wales. Amphibalus, who taught Saint Albanus and instructed him in the true faith, was born in this place. Caerleon is beautifully situated on the bank of the River Usk. When the tide comes in, ships sail right up to the city. It is surrounded by woods and meadows. It was here that the Roman legates came to seek audience at the great Arthur's famous court. Here, too, Archbishop Dyfrig handed over his supreme function to David of Menevia, for the metropolitan see was moved from Caerleon in accordance with the prophecy of Merlin Ambrosius: 'Menevia shall be dressed in the pall of the City of the Legions,' and so on.[156]

High above the water, and not far from Caerleon, there stands a rocky eminence which dominates the River Severn. In the English language it is called Goldcliff, the Golden Rock. When

155. Gerald obviously knew Caerleon well. Much of this is very reminiscent of Geoffrey of Monmouth. Cp. '. . . they had adorned the city with royal palaces, and by the gold-painted gables of its roofs it was a match for Rome' (The History of the Kings of Britain, IX.12, my translation, Penguin Classics).

156. Again there is clear evidence that Gerald had been reading The History of the Kings of Britain, IX.12–15. Merlin's prophecy is taken direct from VII.3. For Dyfrig, see p. 160.

the sun's rays strike it, the stone shines very bright and takes on a golden sheen.

> I could not ever think that quite without intent
> Dame Nature had such splendour to the high rocks lent,
> Or that so fair a flower could be without its fruit.[157]

If someone who was skilled in such work would only dig down into the mineral deposits and penetrate the very entrails of the earth, he might extract sweet honey from the stone and oil from the rock. Indeed, many of nature's riches still lie hidden from us, undiscovered as yet because we have given no attention to them, but the diligence and careful enquiry of later generations will no doubt reveal them. Sheer urgent necessity set our ancestors on the way of inventing certain of the amenities of human existence. In the same way zeal and industry have brought advantages to those who have come after, while their superior intellectual powers have made many things available to our contemporaries. That is what the poet meant, when he said that there were two reasons for discoveries of this sort:

> Hard work finds its reward,
> Unwelcome though it be, and need when times are hard.[158]

It is worth relating that in our days there lived in the neighbourhood of this City of the Legions a certain Welshman called Meilyr who could explain the occult and foretell the future.[159] He acquired his skill in the following way. One evening, and, to be precise, it was Palm Sunday, he happened to meet a girl whom he had loved for a long time. She was very beautiful, the spot was an attractive one, and it seemed too good an opportunity to be missed. He was enjoying himself in her arms and tasting her delights, when suddenly, instead of the beautiful girl, he found in his embrace a hairy creature, rough and shaggy, and, indeed, repulsive beyond words. As he stared at the monster his wits deserted him and he became quite mad. He remained in this

157. I cannot trace this quotation.
158. Virgil, *Georgics*, I.145–6.
159. According to Gerald, the soothsayer Meilyr died during the capture of Usk Castle by Richard of Clare, Earl of Pembroke, in 1174. Cp. p. 120.

condition for many years. Eventually he recovered his health in the church of St David's, thanks to the virtues of the saintly men of that place. All the same, he retained a very close and most remarkable familiarity with unclean spirits, being able to see them, recognizing them, talking to them and calling them each by his own name, so that with their help he could often prophesy the future. Just as they are, too, he was often mistaken about events in the distant future, or happenings far away in space; but he was less often wrong about matters nearer home or likely to occur within the coming year. He nearly always saw these spirits standing close beside him and near at hand. They would appear in the form of huntsmen, with horns hanging round their necks, but it was human souls which they were pursuing, not animals or wild beasts. He saw them most often and in greatest numbers outside monasteries and houses of religion. Wherever man is in revolt, there they deploy their full battalions, there they need their greatest strength. Whenever anyone told a lie in his presence, Meilyr was immediately aware of it, for he saw a demon dancing and exulting on the liar's tongue. Although he was completely illiterate, if he looked at a book which was incorrect, which contained some false statement, or which aimed at deceiving the reader, he immediately put his finger on the offending passage. If you asked him how he knew this, he said that a devil first pointed out the place with its finger. In the same way, and again with a demon to help him, whenever he went into the dormitory of a monastery, he would point to the bed of any false monk whose religion was a pretext and did not come from the heart. He maintained that the vice of gluttony and greed was sordid beyond words; the vice of lust and libidinousness was perhaps more pleasing to the eye, but it was really even more foul. When he was harassed beyond endurance by these unclean spirits, Saint John's Gospel was placed on his lap, and then they all vanished immediately, flying away like so many birds. If the Gospel were afterwards removed and the *History of the Kings of Britain* by Geoffrey of Monmouth put there in its place, just to see what would happen, the demons would alight all over his body, and on the book, too, staying there longer than usual and being even more demanding.[160] Barnabas, one remembers, or so we read in the stories told about him, used to place Saint Matthew's Gospel on people who were ill, and they were cured immediately.[161] It is clear from this, and so it is, indeed, from the account which I have just given to you, how much respect and reverence we owe to each of the books of the Gospel. It is equally clear that anyone who knowingly perjures himself on one of the Gospels deviates from the path of truth with great danger to himself and with the risk of eternal damnation.

To what has gone before I add the story of the downfall of Enoch, Abbot of Strata Marcella, which disaster is quite notorious and, indeed, well known to everyone in Wales.[162] Meilyr announced it to a great number of people on the very day following the night on which it happened. The date on which he made this announcement was noted carefully, and many who heard what he said remembered having done so: yet it was only eight days or so later that definite information arrived and that the affair became common knowledge. When they came to ask Meilyr how he learned of it, he said that the very next morning a demon visited him in the guise of a huntsman. This spirit told Meilyr the whole story, saying that the Abbot would be ruined, for he himself had persuaded him to run away from his monastery and take a nun with him. The demon was very pleased with his success and exulted over Enoch's downfall. Maybe this was allowed to happen so that the Abbot might be humiliated and reprimanded. It certainly seemed so from what happened subsequently, for Enoch soon came back, a much humbler man and so much chastened that he could hardly be said to have sinned at all. As Seneca wrote: 'Anyone who rises to his feet even stronger

160. Gerald rarely misses a chance of a gibe at Geoffrey of Monmouth. Here he calls Geoffrey's book 'Historia Britonum a Galfrido Arthuro tractata'.

161. Saint Barnabas the Apostle, not one of the Twelve.

162. The Cistercian Abbey of Strata Marcella was founded in 1170. Enoch was the first Abbot. He seems to have established a Cistercian nunnery at Llansantffraed-in-Elwell and then to have become involved with one of the nuns there. Gerald refers to the scandal again in *Gemma*, II.17, but there he calls the Abbot Enatus.

after a fall can hardly be said to have fallen at all.'[163] After he had denied Christ, Peter was stronger than ever. Paul was stronger after he had been persecuted and stoned: 'for where sin abounds, grace will much more abound'.[164] After her fall from grace, Mary Magdalene was stronger than before.

Meilyr revealed in confidence to Cynan, the good and saintly Abbot of Whitland,[165] his opinion of a certain woman whom he had been observing closely. Thereupon the holy man wept and confessed that he had lusted after her. He let himself be whipped by three of his monks, this being the punishment for incontinence. From his long experience of things and by natural intuition, drawing his conclusions from certain conjectural signs and from his knowledge of what has happened in the past, the Old Enemy can foretell the future with great skill. In the same way, and by taking note of the same revealing signs, he can insinuate himself into men's hearts, and sometimes discover the workings of their minds from exterior appearances.

About this same time an incubus frequented Nether Gwent. There he was in the habit of making love to a certain young woman. He often visited the place where she lived, and in his conversations with the local inhabitants he revealed many secret matters and events which had not yet occurred. Meilyr was questioned about this and he said that he knew the incubus well. He even said what his name was. He maintained that whenever war was imminent, or some great upset in a country, these incubuses were in the habit of visiting human beings. This was soon proved to be true: for shortly afterwards Hywel, the son of Iorwerth of Caerleon, attacked the neighbourhood and destroyed the whole area.[166] A little later Henry II, King of the English, captured the King of Scotland and so restored peace to his own

163. I cannot trace this quotation.

164. Romans, 5.20, freely quoted and with the tenses changed from the Vulgate.

165. The Cistercian Abbey of Whitland was founded in 1143 by Maredudd ap Maelgwn. It was re-founded in 1176. Cynan seems to have been Abbot c. 1165. He died in 1176, the year of the re-founding.

166. Hywel ab Iorwerth and his father captured Caerleon in 1173, and Hywel then ravaged the countryside as far as Chepstow. Cp. p. 203.

realm.[167] As a result Hywel had good reason to fear that Henry would be free to take vengeance on him for the war which he had waged. He was relieved of his anxiety by this statement made to him by Meilyr. 'Hywel,' said he, 'you need not fear the King's anger. In a short time he will have to turn his attention elsewhere. One of his cities, the noblest which he possesses across the Channel, is being besieged by the King of the French. He will be forced to put aside all other preoccupations and to cross the sea without losing a moment.' Three days later Hywel received the news that this had indeed come about, for the city of Rouen was being besieged.[168] Meilyr also prophesied long before the event the investment of Usk Castle, which Hywel had held for some time.[169] He forewarned Hywel, who occupied the castle, in the following way, saying that he himself would be wounded in the engagement, but not killed, for he would escape from the town alive. Only in this detail was he wrong, for Meilyr died soon afterwards from the wound which he had received. The Enemy knows how to favour his friends, but this is how he rewards them in the end.

It seems most odd to me, among all these other remarkable circumstances, that Meilyr was able to see these demons clearly with the eyes in his head. Spirits cannot be seen with our physical eyes, unless they themselves assume corporal substance. Given that they had assumed such corporal substance, and thus made themselves visible, how was it that they could not be seen by other individuals who were assuredly present and were standing quite near? Possibly they could be seen only by some supernatural sort of physical vision, rather like that in the Book of Daniel, when King Belshazzar saw the writing on the wall: 'Mene, Tekel, Peres', which means 'numbered, weighed,

167. William the Lion, King of Scotland, was taken prisoner near Alnwick on 13 July 1174. Later in the year he signed the ignominious Treaty of Falaise and so regained his freedom.

168. Henry II crossed to Normandy on 11 August 1174 and very soon raised the siege of Rouen by Louis VII.

169. Richard of Clare, Earl of Pembroke, captured Usk Castle in 1174, and the soothsayer Meilyr was apparently killed in the fighting.

divided'. That same night Belshazzar lost both his kingdom and his life.[170]

Wales knows only too well how, in this same neighbourhood and in our own times, through a blind lust for conquest and through a rupture of all the ties of common blood and family connection, evil example has spread far and wide throughout the land, and good faith has disappeared, to be replaced by shameful perfidy.

Chapter 6
Our journey through Newport and Cardiff.

At Newport, where the River Usk runs down from its source in Cantref Bychan and flows into the sea, many people were persuaded to take the Cross. We passed the River Rhymney and so came to Cardiff Castle, where it stands so nobly on the River Taff. A small stream known as Nant Pencarn winds through the district called Wentloog[171] in the Newport area. It is passable only at certain places and by certain fords, more because of the way in which it has hollowed out its bed and of the muddiness of the marshland which surrounds it than through the depth of its waters. In olden times there was a ford just at the point where the public highroad came out. It was called Rhyd Pencarn, which in Latin means 'vadum sub capite rupis' (the ford beneath the overhanging rock). The Welsh word 'rhyd' means 'vadum', 'pen' means 'caput' and 'carn' means 'rupes'. Merlin Silvester had occasion to mention the ford, and this is what he said about it: 'Whenever you see a strong man with a freckled face cross over Rhyd Pencarn on his way to lead an invasion of South Wales, you can be quite sure that the Welsh troops will be beaten.' It so happened in our own lifetime that Henry II, King of the English, took up arms against Rhys ap Gruffydd.[172] He was marching towards Carmarthen, along the

170. Daniel, 5.25–30.
171. Wentloog was originally Gwynllwg, so called from Gwynllyw, who once ruled the cantref.
172. This was in 1163.

coast-road which runs round the south of Wales. On the day when Henry was due to cross Nant Pencarn, the Welshmen of the older generation watched his approach to the ford with the closest attention. They knew that he was strong and they knew that he was freckled, and they had no doubt whatsoever that, if he succeeded in crossing the ford, the prophecy would indeed be fulfilled in his case. Now the old ford about which the prophecy had been made had not been used for many a long year. Henry rode swiftly along the road leading to the river and came to the other ford which is normally used today. To do the King honour and to show their pleasure at his coming, the buglers and trumpeters, who are called 'cornhiriez', from 'cornu' and 'hir', which means long, because they blow on long horns, began to sound their instruments on the opposite bank of the ford. Thereupon the horse on which the King was riding was so startled by this strange harsh noise that it took no notice of the spurs and refused to enter the water. Henry tugged on the reins and hurried off in a fit of rage to the old ford, which he crossed at full speed. The Welsh were sad at heart as they journeyed back home. Having watched Henry ride at full speed through the water, they were quite sure from what they had seen that their side would be beaten.[173]

In our own days an extraordinary event occurred in Cardiff Castle. William, Earl of Gloucester, son of Earl Robert, held the castle and with it the whole of Glamorgan, that is Morgan's Land, which he had inherited.[174] For some reason or other he had quarrelled with one of his feudal dependants, who was called Ivor Bach. This Ivor was a man of immense courage, but he was very short. According to Welsh law he possessed a strip of mountain and forestland. William was trying to take part or all of this away from him. At that time Cardiff Castle was fortified by a circle of very high walls, and these walls were guarded by a

173. In the event Rhys ap Gruffydd surrendered to Henry II at Pencader.
174. Robert, Earl of Gloucester, the illegitimate son of Henry I, died in 1147. The events of this paragraph took place in 1158. Ifor Bach is the Ifor ap Meurig who waylaid and murdered Morgan ab Owain earlier in that same year. Cp. p. 108.

huge squad of sentinels, at least one hundred and twenty men-at-arms and a great number of archers. What is more, the town was full of William's personal retainers. One night, in complete disregard of all these sentinels and security-forces, Ivor carried some ladders to the walls, clambered over them without being seen, seized hold of the Earl and his Countess,[175] with their small son, who was their only child, made off with them all three, and carried them into the woods. He refused to release them until he had recovered everything that had been taken from him unjustly, and a little more. As the poet warns us,

> Be mindful what you do when you insult the bold.
> They may be in your power, their silver and their gold
> Is yours to take: yet, so despoiled, they still bear arms.[176]

On his return from Ireland, on the first Saturday after Easter, Henry II, King of the English, spent the night in this same town of Cardiff.[177] He heard Mass on the Sunday morning. When the service was over, all those present left Saint Piran's chapel, except the King himself, who stayed behind at his devotions longer than usual. At length he too came out and made to mount his horse at the chapel door. A man stood there facing him, up on a baulk of wood which he was using as a platform. He was fair-haired, with a round tonsure, his face was emaciated, he was of more than average height and he seemed to be about forty years old. He wore a white habit, reaching down to his feet, which were bare. He had a girdle round his waist. He spoke to the King in English, saying 'God holde thee, cuning', which in Latin means 'Deus te custodiat, rex'. Then he went on in the same language: 'Christ salutes you, with His Holy Mother, John the Baptist and the Apostle Peter. They command you to prohibit strictly in all the lands under your sway every kind of buying and selling on Sundays, and not to permit any work whatsoever to be done anywhere on those days, except the

175. This was the Countess Hawise. Her son Robert never inherited, for he died in 1166.
176. I cannot trace this quotation.
177. This happened in 1172.

preparation of such food as is necessary for immediate con-
sumption, so that divine service may be performed and listened
to with due devotion. If you do this, all your undertakings will
meet with complete success, and you will live happily until the
end of your days.' The King turned to a soldier called Philip de
Mercros, who was holding his horse's rein, and said to him in
French: 'Ask this bumpkin if he has been dreaming.' The
soldier repeated the King's question to the man in English. He
answered in the same language: 'Whether I have dreamed it or
not, just consider what day this is.' He addressed these words to
the King, not to the interpreter. 'If you fail to do as I say,' he
went on, 'and if you do not soon amend your ways, before this
year is out you will hear such news of what you hold most dear
in all the world, and you will be so troubled by it, that it will
stay with you until the end of your life.' When the man had said
this, the King stuck his spurs into his horse and rode forward a
short way towards the gate. He had not gone eight steps when he
pulled on the reins. 'Call the good man back to me!' he cried.
The soldier about whom I have told you and a young lad called
William, who were left alone in the town with the King,
shouted to the man to come back. They could not find him in the
chapel. They looked for him in the hall and in all the inns, but
they could not find him anywhere. The King waited all alone for
a long time while the others were searching. They failed in their
attempt, and the King was very depressed and vexed because he
had not spoken at greater length with him. He rode off towards
Newport, across the bridge over the River Rhymney.[178] Just as
the man had threatened, so it happened before the year was out.
The following Lent[179] the King's three sons, Henry, the eldest,
and the two others, Richard of Poitou and Geoffrey of Brittany,
rebelled against him and deserted to Louis, King of the French.

178. This story is repeated in *De Princ.*, II.12. There 'Philippus de
Mercros' is called 'Philippus de Marceos' and Gerald says that he had the
details from him in person, 'qui etiam haec nobis vera relatione propalavit'.
Then he refers back to *The Journey through Wales*, 'sicut in Itinerario
scripsimus'.
179. 1173.

This caused the King greater uneasiness than he had ever experienced before. As the result of the behaviour of one of his sons, this was to last without any respite until he drew his final breath.[180] By the grace of God, who desireth not the death of a sinner, but rather that he may turn from his wickedness, and live, the King received many other warnings and reproofs, both at this time and as his death came nearer. He was impervious to advice and he took no notice whatsoever, being obstinate and obdurate by nature. If God permits I will explain all this at greater length in my book *How to Bring Up a Prince*.

Not far from Cardiff there is a small island just off the shore of the Severn Sea which the local inhabitants call Barry. It takes its name from Saint Baroc, who used to live there. His remains have been placed in a coffin, and they can be found there in an ivy-clad chapel. A noble family resident on the coast of South Wales has taken its name from the island, because it owns it and the neighbouring estates. Barry was first of all the family's fore-name, and then its surname became de Barry.[181]

It is an odd thing that in a rock by the sea where one first lands on the island there is a small crack. If you press your ear to it, you can hear a noise like that of blacksmiths at work, the blowing of bellows, the strokes of hammers and the harsh grinding of files on metal,

> ... iron bars being wrought
> In the Chalybes' mines and the fire in the furnace puffed hot.[182]

One could well imagine that a sound of this sort would come from the sea-waters rushing into hidden orifices beneath the island, but it is no less loud when the waves draw back, and it can be heard just as well when the shore is dry as when the tide is up.

180. Henry II died on 6 July 1189.
181. Gerald's father was William de Barry and his grandfather Odo de Barry.
182. Virgil, *Aeneid*, VIII.420–21, quoted from memory ('stridentesque' for 'striduntque', 'stricturas' for 'stricturae', 'anhelum' for 'anhelat').

Chapter 7
The see of Llandaff and Margam Abbey.

The next morning the Cross was preached in Llandaff. The English stood on one side and the Welsh on the other; and from each nation many took the Cross. That night we were put up by William, the local Bishop, who seemed a discreet and honest fellow.[183] The name Llandaff means the church on the River Taff, but the building itself is called Saint Teilo's, after a former Bishop of the diocese.[184] On the morning after that, Mass was celebrated by the Archbishop at the high altar in the cathedral. Then we set off immediately for the fine Cistercian monastery of Margam, passing by the cell of Ewenny on our way.[185] At that time Margam Abbey was ruled over by Abbot Cynan, a learned man and one discreet in his behaviour.[186] Of all the houses belonging to the Cistercian order in Wales this was by far the most renowned for alms and charity. As a result of the almost limitless liberality and most open-handed hospitality which it offered unceasingly to the needy and those in transit – and this you can accept as an undoubted and unquestioned fact – whenever a time of serious famine threatened, when corn grew scarce and all provisions failed, Margam's stocks were visibly increased

183. William de Salso Marisco. Cp. p. 114, n. 153.

184. Saint Teilo, a Celtic Saint of the sixth century who may well have founded a monastery at Llandeilo-fawr. His connection with Llandaff seems to have been legendary.

185. Ewenny Priory was founded in 1141 as a cell of St Peter's, Gloucester, following a donation by Maurice of London, who held Cydweli and Ogham. Sir Richard Colt Hoare records the existence of a tombstone there with the inscription: ICI GIST MORICE DE LUNDRES LE FVNDUR. DEU LI RENDE SUN LABUR. AM.

186. Margam Abbey was founded by Robert, Earl of Gloucester, in 1147. In c. 1165 the Abbot of the Cistercian Abbey of Whitland was a certain Cynan, and he died in 1176, cp. p. 119, n. 165. He witnessed a grant of land to Margam by William, Earl of Gloucester, the son of Robert. It is curious that both Abbots had the same name. What does Gerald mean by 'at that time' = 'tunc', which is added in Version III? Does he mean 1188? The adjective 'discretus' is a term of high praise for Gerald.

by God in His mercy, just as was the poor widow's cruse of oil when He spake by Elijah.[187]

At the time of its first foundation, or thereabouts, a certain young man of those parts, by birth a Welshman, kept making vociferous claims for certain lands which had been donated to the monastery, for he wanted to use them himself. He pressed his claims by various acts of violence, and eventually he was inspired by the Devil to set light to the best barn belonging to the monks, which was piled high at the time with corn. Then he lost his reason completely and careered about the countryside, quite distraught and raving mad. There seemed no likelihood that he would recover, and in the end his relations had to seize hold of him and tie him up. Soon afterwards he tore off the chains which bound him, overpowered his captors and escaped to the Abbey gateway, baying like a dog and shouting that, thanks to the monks, he was being burnt up inside. In a few days he died, still howling miserably.

Another untoward event occurred. A young man received a blow from someone or other in the refectory of the guest house. The following morning the man who had hit him was, by the wrath of God, killed by his enemies. His corpse lay stretched out in the very same spot in the refectory where he had offered insult to the holy house and its assembled inmates.

In our own times there was a serious famine. A vast crowd of poor and needy assembled daily outside the monastery gateway. The monks debated what they should do, and a boat was sent to Bristol in England to purchase enough corn to meet this demand upon their charity. The vessel was delayed by contrary winds and it did not return. Thereupon a miracle occurred. On the very day when provisions ran out completely, not only for the poor but even for the monks themselves, to the great surprise of one and all a field near the monastery was suddenly found to be ready for reaping, a month and more before the normal harvest-time and, indeed, before anyone else in the neighbourhood was even thinking of gathering a crop. Thus God in His mercy supplied the monks and the crowds of poor people with enough

187. Reference to I Kings 17, 10–16.

corn to keep them going until the autumn. By these miracles, and others of a similar nature, this house watched over by God began to be venerated and held in high esteem by a great number of people.

It also happened in our own lifetime, when the four sons of Caradog ap Iestin, who were the nephews of Prince Rhys by his sister, to wit Morgan, Maredudd, Owain and Cadwallon, were ruling in their father's stead over the lands which they were eventually to inherit, as is the custom among the Welsh, that, in a fit of jealousy and malice now reborn, which was worthy of Cain himself, Cadwallon murdered his brother Owain.[188] The wrath of God soon caught up with him. He was leading an assault on a certain castle, when a wall collapsed on top of him and he was crushed to pieces and killed. In the presence of many of his own and his brothers' troops he died a miserable death, and so paid the penalty which he deserved for the fratricidal crime which he had committed.

Another thing happened which is worth recording. This same Owain had a greyhound which was very tall and handsome, its coat being streaked with a variety of colours. It defended its master and in so doing was wounded in seven places, for it was shot through the body with arrows and prodded with spears. In return it bit and tore at Owain's assailants and those who were assassinating him. Its wounds healed, but they left scars. Later the dog was sent by William, Earl of Gloucester, to Henry II, King of the English, as evidence of this remarkable achievement.

Of all animals the dog is most attached to man. A dog recognizes its master and, if that master dies, it may itself refuse to go on living. In defence of its master a dog has the courage to face death. In short a dog is prepared to die both for its owners and with its owners. I have thought it worth while to insert here an anecdote related by Suetonius in his book *The Habits of Living*

188. Caradog ap Iestin married Gwladus, daughter of Gruffydd ap Rhys. He held the Rhwng Nedd ac Afan and was lord of the castle of Aberafan or Port Talbot. These sanguinary quarrels between his four sons seem to have occurred a little before 1175.

Creatures.[189] Saint Ambrose tells the same story in the *Hexameron.*[190]

They say that one evening just as twilight was falling a man who was out walking with his dog in a remote suburb of Antioch was murdered by a passing soldier, simply for the sake of what he had on him. Under cover of darkness the soldier escaped to another part of the city. The corpse lay there unburied. A great crowd of onlookers assembled, and the dog kept bewailing its master's death by whining pitiably. As if by chance the murderer returned and mingled with the crowd which had gathered. He went up to the body, as if he, too, were in mourning. By walking about among the bystanders as if he were on duty, he hoped to establish his innocence, for such is the low cunning of our human race. The dog stopped whining for a moment and rushed forward to avenge its master. It seized hold of the murderer and held him tight. As it did so it bayed lugubriously for its owner, and this made everyone burst into tears. It was accepted as some sort of evidence against the soldier that the dog should have picked him out from all those present and refused to let him go, the more so as he could not be considered innocent of the crime on the plea that the dog disliked him, or was jealous of him, or had been maltreated by him. The soldier denied most emphatically that he was the murderer, but suspicion that he had in fact killed the man was so great and it was being asserted so vehemently that they decided that the case must be tried by judicial combat. The two were brought together face to face in a field, with a vast mob gathered round them, the dog armed only with its teeth and the soldier holding a stick about a yard long. The dog won. The alleged murderer was conquered, and he died an ignominious death on the public gallows.

Pliny tells us, [191] and Solinus repeats the same story,[192] that a certain king, who was very keen on hunting, was captured by his enemies and locked up in prison. He had always been very kind to his hounds. In the end he was freed in the most extraordinary

189. Is there such a book by Suetonius? Can Gerald mean the lost *Pratum*?

190. Saint Ambrose, *Hexameron*, VI.4.24, quoted more or less accurately down to 'let him go', after which it is largely Gerald, but some of the words still come from Ambrose.

191. Pliny the Elder, *Historia Naturalis*, VIII.61.142, has a brief reference to the 200 dogs of a King of the Garamantes, which Gerald has worked up.

192. Solinus, *Collectanea rerum memorabilium*, XV.9.

way, and without any help whatsoever from his friends, by a local pack of dogs, which had chosen of their own free will to range the mountain slopes and woodland glades, issuing forth only to attack and savage human beings, and their herds and flocks.

To all that has gone before I must add what I myself have learnt about the habits of dogs from my own experience and my own observation. A dog trusts its nose rather than its eyes when it wants to recognize something, and this is especially true of its master, supposing that it has lost him for a short time in a crowd. When it has been separated from its owner or the man in charge of it and thinks that it has found him again, it first of all examines him with its eyes. Then it smells his clothes for surer evidence, as if nature had located in its nose the most infallible powers of judgement. A dog's tongue has healing powers, but that of a wolf can cause its death. If a dog is hurt, it can heal itself by licking the places, but a wolf's tongue only infects the wounds. If a dog has a bad place on its neck, or its head, or some other part of its body which it cannot reach with its tongue, it transfers the healing properties of its tongue to the wound with one of its hind feet and so heals itself.

Chapter 8
How we crossed the Rivers Avon and Neath, and then passed through Swansea and Gower.

We set out once more and, not far from Margam, where the twin hazards of a sandy shore and an incoming tide begin, we crossed the ford over the River Avon, not without being delayed for some time by the ebbing of the water. We hurried along the coast-road towards the River Neath, with Morgan, the eldest son of Caradog, as our guide and leader.[193] As we approached the Neath, which is the most dangerous and difficult of access of all the rivers of South Wales, on account of its quicksands,

193. This was Morgan ap Caradog ap Iestyn. He had succeeded to his father c. 1175.

which immediately engulf anything placed upon them, one of
our pack-horses, the only one possessed by the writer of these
lines, was almost sucked down into the abyss. With a number of
other animals it had followed the lower road, and now it was
jogging along in the middle of the group. In the end it was pulled
out with some difficulty, thanks to the efforts made by our
servants, who risked their lives in doing so, and not without
some damage done to my books and baggage. It was true that we
had Morgan, the prince of those parts, as our guide, but we
reached the river only after considerable danger and quite a few
upsets. Against the advice of our leader, our fear of the unusual
surface made us hurry across the quicksands, for

Terror gave us wings.[194]

As we came to realize before we won through, it is better to
advance more slowly and with great circumspection over such
dangerous terrain as this. We crossed the Neath in a boat and not
by a ford,[195] for the passages through the river change with every
monthly tide and they cannot be located at all after a heavy fall
of rain, when the waters are swollen with floods and inundations.
We passed Neath monastery on our right and so approached the
diocese of St David's. We had entered the diocese of Llandaff at
Abergavenny and it was here that we left it behind us.

In our own lifetime it happened that, when David II, Bishop of
St David's, was making this same journey,[196] he found the waters
of the ford across the River Neath disturbed by a fierce wind
which had blown in with the rising tide. A chaplain called
Rhydderch the Liar,[197] who lived in those parts and had con-
siderable experience in crossing the river, was asked by the
Bishop to undertake the dangerous task of locating the ford.
This priest mounted a large and powerful horse belonging to the
Bishop, which had been carefully chosen from among all the

194. Virgil, *Aeneid*, VIII.224.
195. According to Sir Richard Colt Hoare, this would have been by Breton
Ferry.
196. He was Gerald's uncle.
197. Gerald calls the chaplain Rederth Falsus.

THE JOURNEY THROUGH WALES

others for this purpose. He had recently been suspended from
his duties. He crossed the ford successfully, and then rode off at
full speed into the neighbouring woods. He could not be induced
to return until he was assured that he would be restored to his
chaplaincy and given a sum of money to compensate him for his
suspension. The Bishop received his horse back and Rhydderch
was authorized to say Mass again.

In this way we entered the province called Gower and spent the
night in the castle at Swansea, called in Welsh Abertawe, that is
the place where the River Tawe enters the sea. The local
inhabitants gathered together after Mass the next morning and
many were persuaded to take the Cross. An elderly man of those
parts called Cador went up to the Archbishop and addressed
him as follows: 'My lord, if I still had my former strength and
the full vigour of my lost youth, no demand upon my charity
could restrain me, no lack of zeal could deter me from undertaking what you preach. It is, alas, only too true that the weakness of old age and the ravages of time make it impossible for me
to gain in this way, however much I long to do so. To be sure,

> The years to come bring compensations with them, too,[198]

just as

> Those which have passed long since bear many joys away.[199]

If in my infirmity I am too weak to win merit in full measure, let
me still, by making a donation of one tenth of all that I possess,
gain of that grace at least a moiety.' As he said this Cador ran
forward and knelt at the Archbishop's feet, weeping as he did so.
In the Archbishop's hands he placed a tenth part of all his
worldly goods, for the service of the Cross, entreating him in
return for the remission of half the penance which he was
enjoining. When he had done this, he went off by himself for a
short while. Then he came back and made a further statement:
'My lord, if intention is really nine tenths of the deed, and if our
desire to do something is in a sense almost as praiseworthy as our
actually having done it, I ask you to remit the whole penance,

198. Horace, *Ars Poetica*, 175.   199. ibid., 176.

for my desire to undertake this journey is really genuine. If you
will remit it, I for my part will double my contribution and hand
over to you a second tenth of whatever remains to me of my
property.' The Archbishop smiled as he heard this. He put his
arms round Cador, for he could not but admire both his devoutness and his ingenuity.

That same night two monks, who were waiting on the Archbishop in his room, stood chatting together about the events of
the day and the dangers of the road. 'It's a hard country, this,'
said one. The other, who was a wit, replied: 'Not at all. Yesterday we found it far too soft.' One was referring to the barrenness
of the countryside, the other to the quicksands.

Somewhat before our own time an odd thing happened in
these parts.[200] The priest Elidyr always maintained that it was
he who was the person concerned. When he was a young
innocent only twelve years old and busy learning to read, he ran
away one day and hid under the hollow bank of some river or
other, for he had had more than enough of the harsh discipline
and frequent blows meted out by his teacher. As Solomon says:
'Learning's root is bitter, but the fruit it bears is sweet.'[201] Two
days passed and there he still lay hidden, with nothing at all to
eat. Then two tiny men appeared, no bigger than pigmies. 'If
you will come away with us,' they said, 'we will take you to a
land where all is playtime and pleasure.' The boy agreed to go.
He rose to his feet and followed them. They led him first

200. See Thomas Jones, 'Llên-gwerin yn "Nheithlyfr" Gerallt Gymro',
in *Mân Us*, Cardiff, 1949, pp. 35–45, for a re-telling of Gerald's folktales, and
especially Elidyr's story. One of my own undergraduates, Miss Lowri
Penrhyn Jones, remembers reading it in a Welsh story-book when she was a
child. I am told by Mr Robin Gwyndaf, Assistant Keeper of the Welsh Folk
Museum in St Fagans, that it also appears in W. Jenkyn Thomas, *The Welsh
Fairy Book*, 2nd edn, Univ. of Wales Press, 1952, pp. 42–9; and in Gwyn
Jones, *Welsh Legends and Folk-Tales*, Oxford Univ. Press, 1955, pp. 164–8.

201. This is a favourite reference of Gerald's. Here he wrongly ascribes it
to Solomon, i.e. Proverbs. In *The Topography of Ireland*, III.48, he gives the
correct reference to Saint Jerome, *Epistola ad Rusticum monachum* (*Saint
Jérôme, Lettres*, ed. Jérôme Labourt, Paris, 1961, Vol. VII, Letter CXXV,
p. 125): 'De amaro semine literarum dulces fructus capio.' It seems to be
rather a dim memory.

through a dark underground tunnel and then into a most attractive country, where there were lovely rivers and meadows, and delightful woodlands and plains. It was rather dark, because the sun did not shine there. The days were all overcast, as if by clouds, and the nights were pitch-black, for there was no moon nor stars. The boy was taken to see their king and presented to him, with all his court standing round. They were amazed to see him, and the king stared at him for a long time. Then he handed him over to his own son, who was still a child. All these men were very tiny, but beautifully made and well-proportioned. In complexion they were fair, and they wore their hair long and flowing down over their shoulders like women. They had horses of a size which suited them, about as big as greyhounds. They never ate meat or fish. They lived on various milk dishes, made up into junkets flavoured with saffron. They never gave their word, for they hated lies more than anything they could think of. Whenever they came back from the upper world, they would speak contemptuously of our own ambitions, infidelities and inconstancies. They had no wish for public worship, and what they revered and admired, or so it seemed, was the plain unvarnished truth. The boy used frequently to return to our upper world. Sometimes he came by the tunnel through which he had gone down, sometimes by another route. At first he was accompanied, but later on he came by himself. He made himself known only to his mother. He told her all about the country, the sort of people who lived there and his own relationship with them. His mother asked him to bring her back a present of gold, a substance which was extremely common in that country. He stole a golden ball, which he used when he was playing with the king's son. He hurried away from the game and carried the ball as fast as he could to his mother, using the customary route. He reached the door of his father's house, rushed in and tripped over the threshold. The little folk were in hot pursuit. As he fell over in the very room where his mother was sitting, the ball slipped from his hand. Two little men who were at his heels snatched the ball and ran off with it, showing him every mark of scorn, contempt and derision. The boy got to his feet, very red in the face with shame at what he had done. As he recovered his wits he realized that what his mother had asked him to do was very foolish. He set out back along the road which he usually followed, down the path to the river, but when he came to where the underground passage had been there was no entry to be found. For nearly a year he searched the overhanging banks of the river, but he could never find the tunnel again.

The passing of time helps us to forget our problems more surely than arguing rationally about them can ever hope to do, and our day-to-day preoccupations blunt the edge of our worries. As the months pass by we think less and less of our troubles. Once the boy had settled down among his friends and learned to find solace in his mother's company, he became himself once more and took up his studies again. In the process of time he became a priest. The years passed and he became an old man; but whenever David II, Bishop of St David's,[202] questioned him about what had happened, he would burst into tears as he told the story. He still remembered the language of the little folk and he could repeat quite a number of words which, as young people do, he had learnt very quickly.

The Bishop told me that these words were very like Greek. When they wanted water they said 'ydor ydorum', which means in Latin 'aquam offer'. In their language 'ydor' was the word for water, like Greek 'ὕδωρ' and just as 'ὑδρίαι' means water-vessels. In Welsh the word for water is 'dwfr'. When they wanted salt they said 'halgein ydorum', which means 'salem affer'. Salt is 'ἅλς' in Greek and 'halen' in Welsh. The Britons stayed a long time in Greece after the fall of Troy and then took their name from their leader Brutus, so that the early Welsh language is similar to Greek in many of its details.[203] It seems remarkable to me that I do not find so many languages agree as much over any other word as they do in this: 'ἅλς' in Greek, 'halen' in Welsh, 'halgein' in Irish, where *g* is inserted, and 'sal' in Latin, where, as Priscian tells us, *s* replaces the aspirate in

202. David FitzGerald was Gerald's uncle.
203. Cp. Geoffrey of Monmouth, *The History of the Kings of Britain*, I.3-11.

some words.[204] Just as '$\ddot{\alpha}\lambda\varsigma$' in Greek corresponds to 'sal' in Latin, so '$\dot{\epsilon}\mu\iota$' is 'semi' and '$\dot{\epsilon}\pi\tau\alpha$' is 'septem'. In French the word becomes 'sel', the vowel *a* changing to *e* as it develops from Latin. In English a *t* is added to make 'salt' and in German the word is 'sout'. In short you have seven languages, or even eight, which agree completely over this word.

If, careful reader, you should ask me if I think that this story of the little folk is really true, I can only answer with Augustine that 'miracles sent by Heaven are there to be wondered at, not argued about or discussed'.[205] If I reject it, I place a limit on God's power, and that I will never do. If I say that I believe it, I have the audacity to move beyond the bounds of credibility, and that I will not do either. I call to mind what Jerome said when asked a similar question: 'You will find many things quite incredible and beyond the bounds of possibility which are true for all that. Nature never exceeds the limits set by God who created it.'[206] As Augustine implied, I would put this story, and others of a similar nature, should the circumstance arise, among those which cannot be rejected out of hand and yet which I cannot accept with any real conviction.

Chapter 9
How we crossed the River Loughor and the two Gwendraeth streams; and what happened at Kidwelly.

Next we made our way through the open countryside towards the River Loughor. Not long after the death of Henry I, Hywel ap Maredudd from Brecknockshire fought a pitched battle here against the local English, killing quite a few of their regular troops.[207] We crossed the Loughor and the two Gwendraeth streams, and so came to Kidwelly Castle. It was in this region,

204. Reference to Priscian, *De arte grammatica*, XIII.5.25.
205. Saint Augustine. This is clearly a memory of *De civitate Dei*, XXI.4–8, but no sentence there quite fits.
206. I cannot trace the quotation.
207. This was 1 January 1136. Gerald stresses that the colonists were English. Some 500 were killed.

after the death of Henry I, King of the English, and at a moment when her husband, Gruffydd ap Rhys, Prince of South Wales, had gone to North Wales for reinforcements, that the Princess Gwenllian rode forward at the head of an army, like some second Penthesilea, Queen of the Amazons.[208] She was beaten in battle by Maurice of London, who ruled over the district at that time, and by Geoffrey, the Bishop's constable.[209] She was so sure of victory that she had brought her two sons with her. One of them, called Morgan, was killed, and the other, called Maelgwn, was captured. Gwenllian herself had her head cut off, and so did many of her followers.[210]

During the reign of Henry I, King of the English, Wales enjoyed a period of peace. Maurice of London, whom I have mentioned already, possessed in that area a forest, which was well stocked with game and especially with deer.[211] He did everything in his power to protect these animals. As always happens, his wife was only too well aware of her husband's foibles. She decided to play a trick on him. Adjacent to his forest and running down to the sea, he owned broad pasture-lands, where he grazed a great flock of sheep. His wife persuaded all his shepherds and household servants to be her accomplices and to help her in her trick. Maurice was a simple sort of man, but very jealous of his possessions. His wife took advantage of his credulity. One day she said to him: 'It seems very odd to me

208. Penthesilea, Queen of the Amazons, was killed by Achilles at the siege of Troy, as narrated in the sequel to the *Iliad* by Quintus of Smyrna called *Posthomerica* or *Where Homer Ends*.

209. This was Geoffrey, the constable of Roger, Bishop of Salisbury, who had probably not yet transferred Cydweli Castle to Maurice of London. Cp. p. 99, n. 108.

210. In 1136 Gruffydd ap Rhys ap Tewdwr went north to seek reinforce-ments from the sons of Gruffydd ap Cynan ab Iago, Prince of Gwynedd. Gwenllian, the wife of Gruffydd ap Rhys, was a natural daughter of Gruffydd ap Cynan. While her husband was away, Gwenllian fought a pitched battle against Maurice of London just north of Cydweli. She was beaten and killed. Her son Morgan was killed with her, and her son Maelgwn was captured. According to Sir Richard Colt Hoare, the battlefield is called Maes Gwenllian still.

211. Cp. p. 126, n. 185.

that you who own all these animals cannot control them better. Your deer do exactly as they wish. Instead of taking their orders from you, they seem to be telling you what to do! They run completely wild and there is just no limit to their depredations. They have now begun savaging our sheep. Our flocks were once so great that no one could count them. They are still large enough, but they are certainly reduced in number.' To prove her story she had two stags cut open and then padded their intestines with wool. Maurice was completely taken in by his wife's story and set his hounds to attack the deer.

Chapter 10
How we crossed the River Tywi in a boat. Carmarthen and the monastery of Whitland.

We crossed the River Tywi in a boat and travelled on to Carmarthen, leaving Llanstephan and Laugharne on the rocks by the seashore on our left. These were the two castles which Rhys ap Gruffydd took by assault after the death of Henry II, King of the English, the garrisons being forced to capitulate. Rhys then ravaged the provinces of Pembroke and Rhos with fire and sword, completely devastating the whole neighbourhood and besieged Carmarthen, but failed to take it.[212] Carmarthen means the town of Merlin, because, according to the *Historia Regum Britanniae*, Merlin was discovered there as the offspring of an incubus.[213]

This ancient town is enclosed by brick walls, parts of which still stand.[214] It is situated on the noble River Tywi, and

212. Immediately after the death of Henry II in July 1189, Prince Rhys ap Gruffydd attacked and captured the two castles of Laugharne and Llanstephan, ravaged Pembroke and Rhos, and besieged Carmarthen. Gerald had been sent home from Normandy by Richard I to promote peace in Wales. According to him he had some success (*De rebus*, I.21).

213. *The History of the Kings of Britain*, VI.17–18. Gerald says simply 'iuxta Britannicam historiam'.

214. Carmarthen is the site of a hill-fort of the Demetae known by the latinized Celtic name of Maridunum. Under the Romans it was an important centre where many roads met. In Gerald's day part of the Roman walls was still standing. The name clearly comes from 'caer' + 'maridunum'.

surrounded by woods and meadowlands. To the east lies Cantref Mawr, that is the Great Cantref, a safe refuge for the inhabitants of South Wales, because of its impenetrable forests. There, too, is Dinevor Castle, built on the top of a high hill which overlooks the River Tywi and which is held to be the royal seat of the princes of South Wales. In ancient times there were three royal castles in Wales: Dinevor in South Wales, Aberffraw in North Wales, on the island of Anglesey, and Pengwern in Powys, now known as Shrewsbury.[215] Pengwern means the head of the alder-grove. My pen quivers in my hand as I think of the terrible vengeance exacted in our own times by the King's troops on the subject people of the commote of Caeo in Cantref Mawr,[216] and I call to mind the lines:

> Fair dealing or stratagem, which seek you in your foe?[217]

And again:

> If justice fails, use any means you can or will.[218]

Near Dinevor, on the other side of the River Tywi, in Cantref Bychan, that is the Little Cantref, there is a spring which, like the fitful tide, ebbs and flows twice each twenty-four hours.[219]

Not far to the north of Carmarthen lies Pencader, which means the head of the chair. When, in our own days, Rhys ap Gruffydd was forced to surrender, more by a trick than by force of arms, and was carried off to England,[220] Henry II, King of the English,

215. This is very like Triad 85 in *Trioedd Ynys Prydein*, ed. Rachel Bromwich, Cardiff, 1961, p. 85:

> Arthur's Three Principal Courts:
> Caerleon-on-Usk in Wales,
> and Celliwig in Cornwall,
> and Penrhyn Rhionydd in the North.

216. This seems to be another reference to the death in battle of Gwenllian, wife of Gruffydd ap Rhys, at the hands of Maurice of London, in 1136, and the persecution which followed. Cp. p. 137.

217. Virgil, *Aeneid*, II.390.

218. Horace, *Epistolae*, I.1.66 (word order changed).

219. Cp. *The Topography of Ireland*, II.7.

220. This was in 1163. It follows on from the story on p. 122 of how Henry II crossed Nant Pencarn. In *The Conquest of Ireland*, II.31, Gerald says that

sent a knight from Brittany, in whose prudence and fidelity he could trust, with Guaidan, the Dean of Cantref Mawr, to conduct him, with orders to examine the site of Dinevor Castle and to report back on how strongly the terrain was fortified. This priest was told to lead the knight to the castle by the easiest route and to make his journey as pleasant as possible. Instead he made a point of taking him along the most difficult and inaccessible trackways. Whenever they passed through lush woodlands, to the great astonishment of all present, he plucked a handful of grass and ate it, thus giving the impression that in time of need the local inhabitants lived on roots and grasses. The knight went back to the King and reported everything worth mentioning that he had seen and heard. The district was quite uninhabitable, he said, inaccessible and virtually without roads, providing sustenance only for a bestial race of people, who were content to live there like animals. Thereupon the King made Rhys swear an oath of fealty and hand over hostages. Then he sent him back to his own affairs.

When we were travelling from Carmarthen to the Cistercian monastery called Whitland,[221] the Archbishop was told by messengers of how a young Welshman, who was coming to meet him in all devotion, had been murdered on the way by his enemies. He turned aside from the road, ordered the bloody corpse to be wrapped in his almoner's cloak, and with pious supplication commended the soul of the murdered youth to heaven. The next day twelve archers from the near-by castle of St Clears, who had killed the young man, were signed with the Cross in Whitland as a punishment for their crime.

We crossed three more rivers, the Taff, the Cleddau near Llawhaden and another branch of the Cleddau near Haverfordwest, and then came to Haverfordwest itself. Placed as it is between these two streams, this province has taken the name of Deugleddyf, for it is enclosed and its boundaries are marked

---

Rhys ap Gruffydd submitted on the advice of his uncle Owain Gwynedd. Rhys did homage at Woodstock and was soon back in Wales.

221. Whitland Abbey, or Blanchland, Alba Landa, and for Gerald Alba Domus, on the banks of the River Gronw, had been moved from Little Trefgarn, near Haverfordwest, c. 1151.

by the two rivers as if by two swords. The Welsh word 'cleddau' means sword in Latin.

Chapter II
Haverfordwest and Rhos.

In Haverfordwest first the Archbishop himself gave a sermon, and then the word of God was preached with some eloquence by the Archdeacon of St David's, the man whose name appears on the title-page of this book, in short by me. A great crowd of people assembled, some of them soldiers, others civilians. Many found it odd and some, indeed, thought it little short of miraculous, that when I, the Archdeacon, preached the word of God, speaking first in Latin and then in French, those who could not understand a word of either language were just as much moved to tears as the others, rushing forward in equal numbers to receive the sign of the Cross.[222]

When she heard that the Archbishop had come, an old woman of those parts, who had been blind for three years, sent her son to the place where the sermons were to be delivered, with orders that he should bring back something belonging to the Archbishop, if only a thread pulled from his vestments. The crowd was so great that the young man could not come near to the Archbishop. When everyone had gone home, he carried back to his mother the piece of turf on which the Archbishop had stood when he gave the sign of the Cross. She received this gift with great joy. She knelt down facing the east, prayed to God and pressed the turf to her mouth and eyes. So great were her faith and her devotion, and so strong was the miraculous power of the Archbishop, that she immediately regained the blessing of her sight, which she had lost completely.

The folk who lived in the neighbourhood came from Flanders, for they had been sent there by Henry I, King of the English, to colonize the district.[223] They are a brave and robust people, but

222. There is a much fuller account of the preaching at Haverfordwest in *De rebus*, II.18.

223. The Flemings seem to have come at various times, in 1105, 1107 and 1111.

very hostile to the Welsh and in a perpetual state of conflict with them. They are highly skilled in the wool trade, ready to work hard and to face danger by land or sea in the pursuit of gain, and, as time and opportunity offer, prompt to turn their hand to the sword or the ploughshare. They would be strong and contented, if only Wales could find the place which it deserves in the heart of its rulers, or at least if those put in charge locally would stop behaving so vindictively and submitting the Welsh to such shameful ill-treatment.

I must tell you about something which happened in the castle of Haverfordwest in our own time. A notorious freebooter was being held in chains in one of the towers there. Three boys, the son of the Earl of Clare, sent to Haverfordwest for his education, and two others, one of them the son of the castellan and the other his grandson, the child of his daughter, were in the habit of visiting the prisoner frequently.[224] They went to him to get arrows, for he was highly skilled in fitting iron heads to them and he would give them to the boys for their bows. One day, when the gaoler was absent, they asked permission for the robber to be brought out into the fresh air from his prison-chamber. He immediately slammed the door to and locked himself and the boys in. He had no sooner done this than the boys inside began to shout, and so did the occupants of the castle who were locked out. Thereupon he picked up an axe and with great ferocity threatened to kill the children. In the end he was promised his life and given every surety, with an indemnity as well.

A not dissimilar circumstance happened in one of the regions of France, in a place called Châteauroux.[225] The overlord of that district held prisoner in his castle a man whose eyes he had put out. From long familiarity with them this prisoner had committed to memory all the passage-ways of the castle and even the steps

224. Could this have been William de Clare, Earl of Gloucester, and the boy his son Robert, the victims of Ifor Bach's exploit in Cardiff Castle in 1158 cp. pp. 122-3)? It is clearly impossible to be precise.

225. Châteauroux in Berry is 'Castellum Radulphi' for Gerald. In 1187 and 1188 there was much fighting in that area between Henry II and Louis VII. Gerald has occasion to mention the place frequently in *De princ.*, III.1-2, III.10, etc.

which led up to the towers. One day, in a fit of anger and longing for vengeance, he seized the child of the castellan, his only son and heir, and dragged him up to the topmost crenellation of one of the towers. As he went up he locked all the doors behind him, and there he stood outlined against the sky, threatening to throw the boy over. A great shout arose and everyone screamed in anguish. The boy's father came running, and no one's distress was greater than his. He made every offer he could think of, in an attempt to obtain the release of his son. The prisoner replied that he would not give the boy up until the father had first cut his own testicles off, which deprivation he had himself suffered. The castellan went on with his appeals, but all in vain. In the end he pretended to agree, and had himself hit a mighty blow in the lower part of the body, to give the impression that he had mutilated himself. All those present groaned lugubriously. The blind man asked the castellan where he felt most pain, and he replied, falsely, that it was in his loins. Thereupon the blind man stepped forward to throw the boy over. The father was struck a second blow, and this time he said that the worst pain was in his heart. The blind man did not believe him, and he dragged the boy forward to the very edge of the parapet. The third time, to save his son, the father really did cut off his own testicles. He shouted out that it was his teeth which hurt most. 'This time I believe you,' said the blind man, 'and I know what I am talking about. Now I am avenged of the wrongs done to me, in part at least, and I go happily to meet my death. You will never beget another son, and you shall certainly have no joy in this one.' As he said this, he hurled himself over the battlements and plunged into the abyss, taking the boy with him. When he hit the ground his legs and arms were broken in many places, and the two of them died together. To save his son's soul the knight built a monastery on the spot. It is still there today. They call it the Scene of Sorrows.

It seems a remarkable thing to me that, although Richard FitzTancard had so many healthy brothers and was himself the youngest of the family, the others all predeceased him and it was upon him that the entire inheritance devolved, so that it is he who is now castellan of Haverfordwest.[226] In exactly the same way the overlordship of South Wales fell to Rhys ap Gruffydd, who also had so many healthy, handsome brothers, and yet they all died before him.[227]

When this Richard was a young lad, a holy man called Saint Caradog lived as a hermit at St Ismael's in the province of Rhos.[228] From time to time his father, and even more often his mother, used to send him to this Caradog with gifts of food, and in the end the holy father became so indebted to him that he would bless him and promise him the portion of his brothers and the entire inheritance of his father. One day it happened that Richard was caught in a downpour of rain and sought shelter in Caradog's cell. He had brought his hounds with him, for he was on a hunting expedition. No matter how much he shouted at them, or coaxed them, or even tried to entice them in with food, these dogs refused absolutely to come in out of the rain. Then the hermit smiled a gentle smile, made a slight gesture with his hand, and immediately they all trooped in.

In the normal course of nature the time came for Caradog to depart this life and he ended his days happily enough.[229] It was his dying wish that his body should be bequeathed to the church of St David's, but Tancard, Richard's father, had the presumption to lay hands on it. Tancard immediately fell ill, which caused him to change his mind quickly enough. This happened a second and a third time, just as in the case of Pharaoh, who,

226. Richard Tancard, castellan of Haverfordwest, died c. 1130. Of his sons only one, Richard FitzTancard, survived him, becoming lord of Haverfordwest in his turn.

227. Anarawd died in 1143, Cadell in 1175 and Maredudd in 1155.

228. This is Caradog Fynach, who settled in Rhos c. 1105. Gerald says 'apud Sanctum Hysmaelem in Rosensi provincia', but this cannot be St Ishmael's at the mouth of Milford Haven. Sir John Lloyd suggests Haroldston East, near Haverfordwest, which is dedicated to Saint Ismael (*A History of Wales*, II, 592). In the *Epistola ad capitulum Herefordense de libris a se scriptis*, Gerald claims to have written a *Vita Sancti Karadoci*. It was Gerald who proposed the canonization of Caradog to Pope Innocent III (*De invect.*, III.6–7).

229. Caradog died on 13 April 1124. He was buried in the cathedral at St David's.

when the plagues came, promised to let the Children of Israel go, but, when there was respite, hardened his heart.[230] At the third illness Tancard gave in and let the body go. As it was being carried across Newgale Sands on its way to St David's, the clouds opened and there was a heavy fall of rain, so that the whole countryside ran with water. When those who were in charge of the holy cortege emerged from shelter, they found the bier, which was covered with a silken pall, completely dry and not even damped by the rain. The corpse was carried on to St David's, and there with due solemnity it was buried in the left aisle of the church of Saint Andrew and Saint David, beside the altar of Saint Stephen the protomartyr. Even today it is the cause of many miracles, and so it will continue to be in the future.

A strange habit of these Flemings is that they boil the right shoulder-blades of rams, but not roast them, strip off all the meat and, by examining them, foretell the future and reveal the secret of events long past. Using these shoulder-blades, they have the extraordinary power of being able to divine what is happening far away at this very moment. By looking carefully at the little indents and protuberances, they prophesy with complete confidence periods of peace and outbreaks of war, murders and conflagrations, the infidelities of married people and the welfare of the reigning king, especially his life and death.[231]

In our own times it happened that a man of some position in these parts called William Mangunel,[232] who knew more about

230. Exodus, 8.15.

231. According to Sir Richard Colt Hoare, in his day the young women of Rhos still consulted a ram's shoulder-blade to discover whom they were to marry. Thomas Jones, op. cit. in n. 200, p. 133, records the use of hanging bones in Cardiganshire to determine the sex of unborn children and refers to the 'Slinneineachd' in Scotland. In *The Parson's Tale*, §.37, in *The Canterbury Tales*, the parson condemns 'thilke horrible swering of adjuracioun and conjuracioun . . . in a shulder-boon of a sheep'. The Chinese Archaeological Exhibition 'The Genius of China', held at the Royal Academy, London, from September 1973 to January 1974, included as items 88 and 89: 'Two ox scapulae treated for oracle-taking, excavated in 1971 at Anyang, Honan' (Catalogue, p. 75).

232. William Mangunel = Guillelmus Mangunel. There are several men with similar names in Gerald's writings: Philippus Mangunellus, Gerald's

divination than most people, had a wife who was pregnant by his own grandson. William was fully aware of all the circumstances. He took a ram from his own flock and in person presented it to his wife, giving her to understand that it was an offering from a neighbour. She sent it down to the cook. That same day, when they sat down to dinner, William with due deliberation passed the ram's shoulder-blade, boiled according to the recipe and now carefully cleaned, to his wife for her to examine, for he knew very well that she, too, had powers of divination. For some little time she inspected the prophetic bone, fingering the cracks and all its secret markings: then with a smile she threw it on the table. William still continued to appear quite unconcerned. He pressed his wife to tell him what she was laughing at and what her prognostication was. In the end she gave in to his importunate request. 'Husband,' said she, 'the man from whose flock this ram was taken has a wife who has broken her marriage vows. At this very moment she is pregnant from commerce with his grandson.' William peered gloomily at her. 'You never said a truer word,' he answered, and as he spoke his features were downcast. 'Indubitably all the facts support you, and that is all the worse for me. It is I who have to face this public disgrace.' Now that her peccadillo was uncovered, his wife strove in vain to hide her confusion. Her emotions were only too evident on her face. Shame and remorse in swift succession filled her breast. She blushed bright pink and then went deadly pale. Finally, as women will, she began to cry.

On another occasion the shoulder-blade of a goat was brought to a certain person instead of that of a ram, for when they are cleaned they are very similar. He felt all the indents in it and all the marks. 'Unhappy herd,' he cried, 'which never multiplied! Unhappy he who owned it, for he never had more than three or four in his herd!'

Many people foretold from the shoulder-blades the devastation of their homeland which was to follow the death of Henry I,

___

cousin, *De rebus*, XVIII; Galterus Mangenellus, Philip de Barry's son-in-law, *Invect.*, VI.18; and even a Willelmus Mangunel, *De princ.*, II.5. Could this have been a relation?

and this a year and a half or more before it happened.[233] They sold everything they possessed, both portable property and land, abandoned their homes and so by their prescience escaped disaster.

The story is told in Flanders, the land from which these people come, that a certain person sent one of these bones to his neighbour for inspection. As he jumped over a ditch, the man who was carrying it let out a fart through his exertions, and wished the stench on the nostrils of him to whom he was taking it. The man who received the bone turned it over and said without more ado: 'Well, brother, what you have wished on my nose you can stuff up your own!'

In our own days, and this is well worthy of report, it happened that a man who was inspecting one of these bones not only gave notice of a theft, the manner of the theft, the name of the thief and all the attendant circumstances, just by looking at it, but even said that he could hear a bell ringing and a trumpet sounding, just as had happened when the crime was being committed, although this was some little time before. It really is quite remarkable that occult prognostications of this sort seem to be able to reproduce events with the same imagined verisimilitude to the eyes and also to the ears.

Chapter 12
Pembrokeshire.

The province of Pembroke comes next after Rhos, lying towards the south and by the sea: indeed, a branch of the sea divides the two. Its main town, also called Pembroke, is the capital of Dyved. It is built high up on an oblong plateau of rock, and it extends along the north and the south of an inlet of the sea which runs down from Milford Haven. Hence its name Pembroke, which means the head of the estuary.

233. Henry I died on 1 December 1135. The Welsh immediately rose in revolt and attacked the Norman, English and Flemish colonists. As we have seen, there were two other prodigies: a lake and a reservoir burst their banks in Elfael (cp. p. 79).

THE JOURNEY THROUGH WALES

Arnulf de Montgomery was the first to build a fortification here, from wooden stakes and turf, in the days of Henry I, King of the English.[234] It was not very strong and it offered little resistance. When he went back to England, Arnulf left the fortress and a small garrison in the charge of Gerald of Windsor, a stalwart, cunning man, who was his constable and lieu-tenant.[235] Without more ado the inhabitants of South Wales began to lay siege to the place.[236] They had just lost their prince, Rhys ap Tewdwr, a warlike leader, who had been betrayed by his own troops in Brecknockshire, and they were left with his son, Gruffydd, who was still a boy.[237] Under cover of darkness fifteen knights deserted the fortress in desperation, clambered into a boat and tried to escape over the water. The very next morning Gerald transferred their estates to fifteen of their own men-at-arms, dubbing them there and then as knights. The siege lasted a long time, and those inside were greatly reduced and near the end of their tether. When they had hardly any provisions left, Gerald, who, as I have said, was a cunning man, created the impression that they were still well supplied and were expecting reinforcements at any moment: for he took four hogs, which was about all that they had, cut them into sections and hurled them over the palisade at the besiegers. The following day he thought of an even more ingenious stratagem. He signed a letter with his own seal and had it placed just outside the lodging of Wilfred, Bishop of St David's, who chanced to be in the neighbourhood.[238] There it would be picked up almost immediately, and the finder would imagine that it had been dropped accidentally by one of

234. Arnulf de Montgomery, younger son of Roger de Montgomery, Earl of Shrewsbury, built his first fortress at Pembroke c. 1091, in the reign of William Rufus.

235. Gerald of Windsor, castellan of Pembroke, the founder of the line of the Geraldines, was the grandfather of Gerald of Wales.

236. This was the uprising of 1096. The Welsh leaders of the attack on Pembroke were Uchtryd ab Edwin and Hywel ap Gronw.

237. Rhys ap Tewdwr, Prince of South Wales, was killed near Brecon in April 1093.

238. This was at Lamphey, two miles away. Wilfred seems to have been Bishop of St David's from c. 1083 onwards.

Gerald's messengers. The purport of the letter was that the constable would have no need of reinforcements from Arnulf for a good four months. When this despatch was read to the Welsh, they immediately abandoned the siege and went off home.

The next thing Gerald did was to marry Nest the sister of Gruffydd, Prince of South Wales, with the object of giving himself and his troops a firmer foothold in the country.[239] In the process of time she bore him a large number of children, both boys and girls. With the help of this family the sea-coast of South Wales was held secure by the English, and Ireland, too, was stormed, as is narrated in my *Vaticinal History*.[240]

In our own times it happened in this same castle of Pembroke that a man discovered some baby weasels inside a sheepskin in his house. Without hurting them, he carefully removed them, still inside the sheepskin, and put them somewhere else. When the mother came back, she looked for them everywhere, but could not find them. Her grief was very great. She went over to a jug of milk, which had been set aside for the man's son and heir, stood up on her hind legs, spat the venom which she had inside her body into the milk and so infected it with deadly poison. In this way she planned to seek vengeance for the loss of her own offspring by killing the man's son. The man had watched her doing all this, and he put the sheepskin back in its place. The weasel returned, in her motherly care torn between hope and despair, and found it there once more,

> Her grief proving pointless and there but to deceive.[241]

Her relief was only too plain, both from the squeaks which she emitted and the way she behaved. She rushed back to the jug and knocked it over, so that all the milk was spilt. In her gratitude for the return of her own babies, she was determined that her host's son should suffer no harm.

239. Gerald of Windsor married Nest, daughter of Rhys ap Tewdwr, c. 1100. She was the maternal grandmother of Gerald of Wales.

240. As explained on p. 68, n. 22, Gerald usually called *The Conquest of Ireland* by this name, *The Vaticinal History*.

241. I cannot trace this quotation.

In another place a female weasel brought her young out of the
bushes where they lived into the open, so that they could enjoy
the sunshine and the fresh air. Thereupon an evil kite carried
one of them off. The weasel led her remaining babies back into
their leafy home. In her grief as a mother she thought of a very
subtle revenge. She came out once more and lay down on a heap
of earth, pretending to die there in full sight of the predator.
Appetite comes with eating, and the greedy kite seized her and
carried her up into the air. The weasel then took her revenge.
She bit the kite with her poisonous teeth and it fell to the ground
dead.

Only about three miles from Pembroke Castle is the fortified
mansion known as Manorbier, that is the house of one Pyrrus.
The same man also owned Caldy Island, called by the Welsh
Ynys Byr, which means the Island of Pyrrus. There the house
stands, visible from afar because of its turrets and crenellations,
on the top of a hill which is quite near the sea and which on
the western side reaches as far as the harbour. To the north and
north-west, just beneath the walls, there is an excellent fish-
pond, well constructed and remarkable for its deep waters. On
the same side there is a most attractive orchard, shut in between
the fish-pond and a grove of trees, with a great crag of rock and
hazel-nut trees which grow to a great height. At the east end of
the fortified promontory, between the castle, if I may call it
such, and the church, a stream of water which never fails winds
its way along a valley, which is strewn with sand by the strong
sea-winds. It runs down from a large lake, and there is a water-
mill on its bank. To the west it is washed by a winding inlet of
the Severn Sea which forms a bay quite near to the castle and yet
looks out towards the Irish Sea. If only the rocky headland to
the south bent round northwards a little farther, it would make
a harbour most convenient for shipping. Boats on their way to
Ireland from almost any part of Britain scud by before the east
wind, and from this vantage-point you can see them brave the
ever-changing violence of the winds and the blind fury of the
waters. This is a region rich in wheat, with fish from the sea and
plenty of wine for sale. What is more important than all the rest

is that, from its nearness to Ireland, heaven's breath smells so wooingly there.

Of all the different parts of Wales, Dyved, with its seven cantrefs, is at once the most beautiful and the most productive. Of all Dyved, the province of Pembroke is the most attractive; and in all Pembroke the spot which I have just described is most assuredly without its equal. It follows that in all the broad lands of Wales Manorbier is the most pleasant place by far. You will not be surprised to hear me lavish such praise upon it, when I tell you that this is where my own family came from, this is where I myself was born. I can only ask you to forgive me.

In these parts of Pembroke, in our own times, unclean spirits have been in close communication with human beings. They are not visible, but their presence is felt all the same. First in the home of Stephen Wiriet,[242] then, at a later date, in the house of William Not,[243] they have been in the habit of manifesting themselves, throwing refuse all over the place, more keen perhaps to be a nuisance than to do any real harm. In William's house they were a cause of annoyance to both host and guests alike, ripping up their clothes of linen, and their woollen ones, too, and even cutting holes in them. No matter what precautions were taken, there seemed to be no way of protecting these garments, not even if the doors were kept bolted and barred. In Stephen's home things were even more odd, for the spirit there was in the habit of arguing with humans. When they protested, and this they would often do in sport, he would upbraid them in public for every nasty little act which they had committed from the day of their birth onwards, things which they did not like to hear discussed and which they would have preferred to keep secret.

If you ask me the cause and the explanation of an event of this sort, I do not know what to answer, except that it has often been

242. Stephen Wiriet is otherwise unknown. According to Sir Richard Colt Hoare, the Wiriet family was still living at Orielton, near Pembroke, in the early seventeenth century.

243. William Not is otherwise unknown. According to Sir Richard Colt Hoare, in his day the name still existed in Pembrokeshire.

the presage, as they call it, of a sudden change from poverty to wealth, or more often still from wealth to poverty and utter desolation, as, indeed, it was in both these cases. It seems most remarkable to me that places cannot be cleansed of visitations of this sort by the sprinkling of holy water, which is in general use and could be applied liberally, or by the performing of some other religious ceremony. On the contrary, when priests go in, however devoutly and protected by the crucifix and holy water, they are among the first to suffer the ignominy of having filth thrown over them. From this it appears that the sacraments and things pertaining to them protect us from actual harm but not from trifling insults, from attack but not from our own imaginings.

It is worth recording that in Poitou in our own time there was a woman possessed of a devil, which devil used to speak through her mouth, arguing and disputing most cleverly and astutely with intelligent and well-informed people.[244] He would upbraid these men with things which they had done in secret and did not wish to hear. If one of the Gospels or the relics of the saints were placed on the possessed woman's mouth, the devil would take refuge lower down her throat; and if they were then moved there, he would crawl down into her stomach. It was quite clear what parts of her body he was hiding in from the swellings and convulsive movements there; and when the relics were placed on her lower parts he would immediately climb up again. When they brought the holy sacrament and administered it to this possessed woman, the devil answered: 'You silly fools, what you are doing is of no use at all. You are giving her food for the soul, not for the body. My power is over her body, not over her soul.' When those whose inner secrets he had revealed came back from making confession and doing penance, he stopped reproaching them. 'What I have known, I have known,' he would say. To others he would issue this threat: 'I am silent now; and what I know, I know not.' From this it appears that after confession and penance these devils either forget the sins of mortal men, or else they no longer reveal them to their disgrace and shame. As

244. This story is told again in *Gemma*, I.17.

Augustine says: 'If man conceals, then God reveals; if man reveals, then God conceals.'[245]

It is a matter of concern for many people that lightning so often strikes our churches and other places of worship, damaging crosses and crucifixes before the very eyes of Him who sees all things and yet does nothing to stop it. I have been able to think of no better answer than that given by Ovid:

We envy what is best, storm-winds blow through the sky,
And Jove his thunder-bolts will aim at what stands high.[246]

In his own day, and with Philip I, King of the French, listening to him, Peter Abelard is said to have made a memorable reply to a certain Jew, who was urging the same sort of objection to the Christian religion. 'It cannot be denied', said he, 'that, as it rushes down from on high, lightning often strikes the loftier things on earth and those sublime in nature like itself. It is contrived in all malice by the devils in hell. Its immediate cause is a collision between the clouds, and it rushes downwards through the air in a zigzag direction. Nothing can prevent it from reaching its target. It sometimes strikes human beings, and it can do great harm to the faithful and the objects of their cult. No one ever saw lightning hit a public lavatory, or even heard of such a thing: by the same token it never falls on any of your Jewish synagogues.'[247]

In our own times there was an interminable dispute between a group of Cistercian monks in France and a certain knight, concerning the boundaries which divided their fields and the precise limits of their lands. One night a violent storm completely destroyed the crops in the fields belonging to the monks, while those of the knight remained untouched. The knight had some

245. I cannot trace this quotation.
246. Ovid, *Remedia Amoris*, 369–70.
247. I cannot trace the source of this anecdote. The great expert on lightning and other such natural phenomena was Gregory of Tours rather than Abelard. See my translation of *The History of the Franks*, Penguin Classics, pp. 50–52. Mrs Betty Radice tells me that Abelard's argument starts from Saint Jerome, *Epistulae*, LIV.13 (ed. L. Hilberg, *Corpus Scriptorum Ecclesiasticorum Latinorum*, Vol. LIV, 1910, pp. 479–81).

unkind things to say about the monks, for, according to him, God
in His wisdom had made it clear that the fields in question really
belonged to him. The abbot replied wittily enough that the
opposite was true. When the devils came riding they were
naturally enough friendly towards the knight, but they did all
they could to show their hostility towards the monks.

At about the same time, in this province of Pembroke which I
have been describing to you, a third manifestation occurred, in
the home of Elidyr of Stackpole.[248] It took the form of a young
man with red hair called Simon. This was a full incarnation, for
he could be seen and touched. He removed the household keys
from the man in charge of them, and with complete self-
assurance took on the function of steward. He administered the
household with such foresight and attention to detail, or so it
seemed, that in his hands everything prospered and nothing was
ever lacking. Elidyr and his wife had only to think of something
which they would like for their table or their day-to-day use,
mentioning it perhaps to each other, but certainly not to Simon,
and he would immediately procure it, without having been asked
to do so. 'You wanted this,' he would say, 'and I have got it for
you.' He knew all about their family finances, and the money
they were trying to save, and he would sometimes grumble at
them. Whenever they planned to avoid some particular expense,
or to practise some economy, he would say: 'Why on earth are
you afraid to spend this money? Your days are numbered. The
money you are making such an effort to hoard will never be of
any use to you. It will simply go to others.' He liked to see the
farm-labourers and household servants eat and drink well.
These things had been acquired by the sweat of their brow, he
would say, and it was only fair that they should enjoy them.
Whatever he made up his mind to do, whether it pleased his
master and mistress or not, for, as I have told you, he knew all
their secrets, he would carry out immediately, brooking no
opposition. He never went to church, and no Christian word
was ever heard on his lips. He never slept in the house, but
reported for work each morning with amazing punctuality. Then

248. Elidyr of Stackpole = Eliodorus de Stakepole. I cannot trace him
elsewhere. There is an Eustachius de Stakepole in *De iure*, VII.

by chance he was seen one night by some member of the family conversing with his fellow-demons by the water-mill and the pool. The next morning he was interviewed by his master and mistress. He was dismissed on the spot and he handed over the keys which he had held for forty days or more. When he left they questioned him closely and asked him who he really was. He said that he had been born to some rustic beldam in the same parish, fathered on her by an incubus who had appeared in the shape of her husband. He gave the husband's name and that of the man's father-in-law, who was dead. Then he revealed who his mother was. She was still alive. They looked into the matter with some care. The mother said that it was all true.

A somewhat similar case occurred in Denmark in our own lifetime. A priest appeared from nowhere and attached himself to the archbishop. He was discreet and hard-working, he had a great store of literary and historical knowledge, and he possessed a phenomenal memory. He did all he could to please the archbishop, and in a very short time the two became close friends. One day, when he was talking to the archbishop about happenings long past and events long forgotten, all of which were naturally of the greatest interest to that prelate, he mentioned the incarnation of our Lord. 'Before Jesus Christ was born in the flesh,' he said, 'devils had great power over human beings; but when He came, this power was greatly diminished. They were dispersed, some here, some there, for they fled headlong from His presence. Some hurled themselves into the sea. Others hid in hollow trees and in the cracks in rocks. I remember that I myself jumped down a well.' As he said this, he blushed for shame. Then he got up and left the room. The archbishop was greatly astonished, and so were all those with him. One after another they asked what he could possibly have meant and put forward their own suggestions. They waited a while, for they expected him to return at any moment. Then the archbishop sent one of his men to fetch him. His name was called and he was looked for everywhere, but he was never seen again. Not long afterwards two priests came back home, having been sent to Rome on a mission. The archbishop told them the story, and they asked him if he could remember the precise day and even the hour when it had happened. They listened carefully and then said that they had met the man on that very same day and at that moment in one of the passes through the Alps. He told them that he was on his way to the Roman curia on some business or other of his master's which had just cropped up. He made it clear that when he said his master he meant the archbishop. It was obvious enough that they had been tricked by a devil in human guise.

I must not forget to tell you about the falcons of this region. They are remarkable for their good breeding, and they lord it over the river birds and those in the open fields. When Henry II, King of the English, spent some time in this neighbourhood making preparations for his journey to Ireland, he occasionally went hawking.[249] By chance [250] he saw a noble falcon perched on a rock. He approached it sideways and then loosed at it a huge and carefully bred Norwegian hawk which he had on his left wrist. At first the falcon seemed slower in its flight. Then it lost its temper and in its turn became the aggressor. It soared to a great height, swooped fiercely down and gave the hawk a mighty blow in the chest with its sharp talons, striking it dead at the King's feet. As a result from this year onwards Henry II always sent to this region at nesting-time for some of the falcons which breed on the sea-cliffs. Nowhere in the whole of his kingdom could he find more noble or more agile birds. That is enough about falcons. Now I must return to our journey.

Chapter 13
Our journey through Camrose and Newgale.

From Haverfordwest we set out on our journey to St David's, which is about twelve miles away. First we passed through Camrose where, in the days of King Stephen, the relations and dependants of that distinguished young man, Gerald the son of

249. Henry II arrived in Pembroke on 21 September 1171 on his way to Ireland. He was delayed there by contrary winds for nearly a month.
250. This passage, from 'By chance . . . more agile birds', is repeated from *The Conquest of Ireland*, I.29.

William,[251] avenged his father's death on the men of Rhos with more ferocity than was necessary. Next we crossed Newgale Sands. At the time when Henry II, King of the English, was wintering in Ireland, a curious phenomenon occurred here.[252] It was seen, too, in many of the other western seaports. The wind blew[253] with such unprecedented violence that the shores of South Wales were completely denuded of sand, and the subsoil, which had been buried deep for so many centuries, was once more revealed. Tree-trunks became visible, standing in the sea, with their tops lopped off, and with the cuts made by the axes as clear as if they had been felled only yesterday. The soil was pitch-black, and the wood of the tree-trunks shone like ebony. By this strange convulsion of nature, the element through which ships were wont to move so freely became impassable to them, and the sea-shore took on the appearance of a forest grove, cut down at the time of the Flood, or perhaps a little later, but certainly very long ago, and then by slow degrees engulfed and swallowed up by the waves, which encroach relentlessly upon the land and never cease to wash it away. The tempest raged so fiercely that conger-eels and many other sea-fish were driven up on the high rocks and into the bushes by the force of the wind, and there men came to gather them.

In St David's we were given good accommodation by Peter, the Bishop of that diocese, a most friendly and hospitable man.[254] He had accompanied us on the whole of our journey.

Here ends the First Book.

251. I cannot trace elsewhere Gerald the son of William.
252. This was the winter of 1171–2.
253. This passage, from 'The wind blew ... to wash it away', is repeated from *The Conquest of Ireland*, I.36.
254. This is Peter de Leia, one-time Prior of the Cluniac house of Much Wenlock, who had been preferred to Gerald of Wales and consecrated Bishop of St David's on 7 November 1176. It is strange that Gerald, who elsewhere has no good word to say for him, here qualifies him as 'viro ... personali et liberali'. He had been with them ever since the journey began, that is presumably since they crossed into Wales about three weeks earlier, and it is curious that he has been mentioned only once before. Cp. p. 75.

BOOK II

Here begins the Second Book.

St David's is still the capital of Wales, but once it was also the metropolitan city of an archbishop. Nowadays it lives largely upon its past reputation and does not retain any real power. Once it was our venerable and unchallenged mother-church.[255]

255. Gerald clings to the fiction that St David's was 'once . . . the metropolitan city of an archbishop', 'urbs olim metropolitana'. His almost lifelong dream was that he himself might become Bishop of St David's without having to acknowledge subjection to Canterbury, and that he could then persuade the Pope to appoint him as Archbishop and give him the pallium. He seems genuinely to have believed that in doing so he would be restoring to St David's a dignity which it had held in the past. In this he was following the example set by Bernard, Bishop of St David's 1115–47.

Ironically enough, this involved him in considerable reliance upon *The History of the Kings of Britain*, for the author of which he professed nothing but scorn (cp. p. 117). Geoffrey had imagined three metropolitan sees in Britain: London, York and Caerleon (op. cit., IV.19). Dyfrig was made Archbishop of Caerleon (VIII.13). When Dyfrig resigned to become a hermit, David, Arthur's uncle, replaced him (IX.15). David died in his own abbey, in St David's (XI.3). Merlin had prophesied that 'Menevia shall be dressed in the pall of the City of the Legions' (VII.3). Gerald quotes this prophecy verbatim: 'Menevia pallio Urbis Legionis induetur' (p. 115). He then transmutes it into a fact: 'It was David who had the archbishopric moved to St David's' (p. 160). What then had happened to the pallium? According to Gerald, Samson was the twenty-fourth Archbishop of St David's after David. He fled to Brittany to avoid the yellow plague (pp. 161–2). He became Bishop of Dol. He took the pallium with him and wore it in Dol. Subsequent Bishops of Dol continued to wear it, 'usque ad nostra haec fere tempora', until they were eventually stopped by their metropolitan, the Bishop of Tours (p. 162). To return this non-existent pallium to St David's would simply be to restore its imagined archiepiscopal dignity to that bishopric. All this skates perilously over the fact that the Saint Samson who fled to Dol was Saint David's contemporary and had held no position in St David's; and that in Gerald's list of the 'archbishops' of St

I have therefore not forborne to weep at its obsequies, to follow its most mournful hearse and to lament with tearful sighs its ashes which remain half-buried. In short I propose to tell you in as few words as possible how the archbishop's pallium came to St David's, from where and at what time it was brought, how it was taken away again, how many prelates wore it and how many have been deprived of that honour, giving their names in both cases and bringing the story down to our own time.

Chapter 1
The see of St David's.

The histories of Britain tell us how in Caerleon-on-Usk, also known as the City of the Legions, at that great court which I have already described, Saint Dyfrig, who was then Archbishop, handed his high functions over to David, who was said to be the uncle of King Arthur. Dyfrig was already an old man, and he wanted to devote his last few years to the contemplative life.[256] It was David who had the archbishopric moved to St David's. As I have already explained in Book I, Caerleon was much more suited to be a metropolitan city.[257] St David's is in a remote corner of the country, looking out towards the Irish Sea. The

---

David's, Samson comes twenty-fourth after Saint David and so must have lived much later.

Gerald has already called St David's 'the metropolitan see of the country' (p. 77). He repeats the fiction in *De Invect.*, II.1. In *De Invect.*, II.10, he quotes a letter from the chapter of St David's to Pope Honorius II asking for the re-institution of the 'archiepiscopatus Menevensis' and the return of its 'dignitas metropolitana'.

For a masterly note entitled 'The Alleged Archbishopric of St David's', see Sir John Lloyd, *A History of Wales*, Vol. II, p. 486.

256. Dyfrig, latinized to Dubricius, a sixth-century Welsh churchman of credit and renown, ended his days on Bardsey Island. In life he had no connection with Llandaff, but his remains were translated there in May 1120. He is mentioned three times in *The Journey through Wales* (*Itin.*, I.5, II.1 and II.4). It was Geoffrey of Monmouth who elected him to the imaginary archbishopric of Caerleon (*Historia Regum Britanniae*, VIII.13, IX.1, IX.4, IX.12–15), and Gerald follows Geoffrey, as always when it suits him.

257. See pp. 114–15.

soil is rocky and barren. It has no woods, no rivers and no pasture-lands. It is exposed to the winds and to extremely inclement weather. It lies between two hostile peoples who are constantly fighting over it, the Flemings and the Welsh. However, these saintly men deliberately chose to establish the archbishopric there, for they wanted to live as far removed as possible from worldly upsets, preferring an eremitical existence to a pastoral one, so that they might enjoy a spiritual life which no one could take away from them. David was extremely devout and lived a most saintly life. My *Life of Saint David* gives abundant evidence of this.[258] Of all the miraculous events which you can read there, three in particular seem noteworthy to me: the story of his origin and conception;[259] the fact that thirty years before he was born it was known that he would become Archbishop;[260] and, most remarkable of all, the way in which, in full view of an astonished congregation, the ground on which he was standing rose up in the air one day when he was preaching at Llanddewi Brefi.[261]

From the time of David onwards,[262] twenty-five Archbishops occupied the see of St David's down the years. I give you their names.[263] First came David himself, then Eliud also called

258. *De vita S. Davidis archiepiscopi Menevensis.*
259. *V.S.D.*, I.
260. *V.S.D.*, II.
261. *V.S.D.*, VIII. According to the story 118 Welsh churchmen met at the Synod of Brefi in Cardiganshire to preach to a vast crowd against Pelagianism. None could make himself heard until Saint David arrived, whereupon the ground on which he stood rose to form a small hill and he was able to address the multitude.
262. Saint David seems to have lived from c. 520 to c. 588. He founded the monastery named after him and became its first Abbot. He is given the title of bishop, but he was certainly not an archbishop in the accepted sense.
263. I print them as they appear in MS D of Version III, except that I have omitted the *p* of Sampson. In Versions I and II they are: David, Kenauc, Eliud, Keneri, Morwal, Haernueu, Elwid, Gurneu, Llendivord, Gorwiust, Gugaun, Cledauc, Amman, Eluoed, Ethelemun, Elauc, Maiscoit, Sadernueu, Nortwal, Aser, Artwail, Idwalauri, Sampson. In short, Versions I and II have as extra names Keneri and Idwalauri, but they lack Catulus, Sulhaithuai, Novis and the second Sadurnueu, thus finishing up with twenty-three.

Theliau,[264] Keneu, Morwal, Haernueu, Elwaid, Gurnueu, Leudiwit, Gorwiust, Gogaun, Cledauc, Aman, Eludged, Elduven, Elave, Mailswid, Sadurnueu, Catalus, Sulhaithuai, Novis,[265] another Sadurnueu, Doithwal, Asser,[266] Archuail and Samson.[267]

The pallium was taken away in Samson's time.[268] The circumstances of its removal were as follows. During his period as Archbishop, an epidemic spread throughout Wales and killed a great number of people. They called it the yellow plague, but the doctors' name for it was the icteric disease. As a man of religion, Archbishop Samson had no fear of death, but he was persuaded to go on board a boat. The wind blew from the north-west, and it carried him and those with him safely to Brittany. By chance the see of Dol was vacant at the time, and Samson was immediately elected as Bishop. He had taken the pallium with him, and as a result succeeding bishops of Dol continued to wear it almost down to our own times. One of the archbishops of Tours put an end to the practice. That was how it came about, through indolence or poverty, or more probably as the result of the coming of the English to our island and the never-ending wars with the Saxons, that we Welshmen lost for all time the honour which we had once enjoyed.

Until the final subjugation of Wales by Henry I, King of the English, the Welsh bishops continued to be consecrated by the Bishop of St David's, and in the same way the Bishop himself was consecrated by his suffragans, without profession or submission to be made to any other church.

264. 'Eliud also called Theliau' is Saint Teilo, the patron of many a Llandeilo in South Wales.

265. 'Novis' is Nobis.

266. Asser, a relation of Nobis, later joined the court of King Alfred and died c. 910 as Bishop of Sherborne. He is the author of the *De rebus gestis Ælfredi*.

267. Samson is copied 'Sampson' in all three versions.

268. The earliest Latin *Vita* of Saint Samson of Dol seems to date back to the seventh century. He was associated with Childebert I, King of the Franks, who succeeded to his father Clovis in 511 and died in 558. Gerald places him last in his list of 'archbishops' and so nearly four centuries too late. Cp. p. 159, n. 255, for a fuller discussion.

From the time of Samson down to that of Henry I, nineteen
Bishops occupied the see. Their names were as follows:[269]
Kuielm, Retherth, Eluin, Lunuerc, Nergu, Sulidir, Eneuris and
Morgeneu, who was the first Bishop of St David's to eat meat.
He was murdered by pirates in his own city.[270] On the very
night when he was killed, he showed himself in a vision to a
certain bishop in Ireland, pointed to his wounds and said:
'Because I ate flesh, I am become flesh.' Then followed Nathan,
Iewan, who was Bishop for one night only, Arwistel, Morgenen-
nith, Eruin, Tramerin, Joseth, Bleidhud, Sulghein,[271]
Abraham[272] and Wilfred.[273]

From the subjugation of Wales down to the present day only
three men have held the bishopric: Bernard in the time of
Henry I,[274] David II in the time of King Stephen,[275] and Peter,
the Cluniac monk, in the time of Henry II.[276] At the express
command of the Kings concerned, all three were consecrated
in Canterbury.[277] So also was the fourth, Geoffrey, prior and
canon of Llanthony, who succeeded them and was promoted to
the bishopric in the time of King John. It was Hubert, Arch-

269. I print them as they appear in MS D of Version III. In Versions I and
II they are: Ruelm, Retherch, Elgiun, Morbiu, Lunuerd, Nergu, Sulhidir,
Eneuris, Morgeneu, Nathan, Johannes, Augustus, Morgenueth, Blethuth,
Eruin, Tramerin, Joseph, Blethuth, Sulgen, Abraham, Wilfridus. By the
addition of Morbiu and the repetition of Blethuth this makes twenty-one.

270. Morgeneu was killed by Danish pirates in 999.

271. Sulghein or Sulien was Bishop of St David's from c. 1072 until he
resigned and was succeeded by Abraham in 1078. Abraham was killed by
Norse pirates in 1080 and Sulghein became Bishop again from then until
1085, when he resigned a second time. He died in 1091.

272. Abraham was Bishop from 1078 until 1080.

273. Wilfred or Wilfre was Bishop from 1085 until his death in 1115.

274. Bernard was consecrated on 19 September 1115 and he died in
1147.

275. David II, Gerald's uncle, was consecrated on 19 December 1148
and he died on 8 May 1176.

276. Peter de Leia was consecrated on 7 November 1176 and he died on
16 July 1198.

277. Bernard was consecrated at Westminster by Archbishop Ralph.
David II was consecrated at Canterbury by Archbishop Theobald. Peter de
Leia was consecrated at Canterbury by Gilbert Foliot, Bishop of London.

bishop of Canterbury, who had him elected and who consecrated him.[278]

From what we read, no Archbishop of Canterbury, except Baldwin, the present one, has ever entered Wales, either before the subjugation or after it. With praiseworthy devotion to the service of the Cross, from whence cometh our salvation, Baldwin has undertaken the task of travelling through our rough, remote and inaccessible countryside. In an attempt to encourage people to take the Cross, he has planned to celebrate Mass in every one of the Welsh cathedrals.[279]

Until recent times the see of St David's was in no way subject to Canterbury. Bede makes this clear, as we can read in his *Ecclesiastical History*.[280] After the conversion of King Ethelfrid and the English people, Augustine, Archbishop of the English and legate of the apostolic see, summoned all the Welsh bishops to confer with him at a place where the lands of the Welsh and the West Saxons met. With typical Roman arrogance Augustine remained seated when the seven bishops arrived, making no effort to stand up to greet them. When they saw how proud he was, they immediately set off home again, determined to treat both him and his ordinances with the utmost contempt. On their way to the meeting they had visited a saintly anchorite of their own nation and asked him to advise them from his own long experience. On their way home they announced to everyone they met that they would never acknowledge Augustine as their Archbishop. 'If he will not stand up to meet us now,' they kept repeating, 'he will have an even poorer opinion of us if we swear allegiance to him.'

That there were then seven Welsh bishops whereas there are now only four can easily be accounted for. There were probably

278. Geoffrey was consecrated at Westminster on 7 December 1203 by Archbishop Hubert Walter. He died in 1214.

279. That is in Llandaff, St David's, Bangor and St Asaph.

280. Bede, *Historia Ecclesiastica*, II.2: '... nor would they recognize Augustine as their archbishop'. The story of the meeting of Saint Augustine and the seven Welsh bishops in 602 or 603 at the place which Bede calls Augustine's Oak is given in that same chapter. According to Sir John Lloyd (op. cit., I, p. 174), Augustine's Oak is probably Aust in Gloucestershire.

more cathedrals in Wales in those days than there are now; or maybe Wales itself was bigger, stretching right down to the Severn.

Of all the bishops thus deprived of their rank as metropolitans, only one, Bernard, the first Anglo-Norman Bishop of St David's, made any public move to claim back the rights of his own church. He sent a number of carefully prepared and extremely expensive appeals to the Roman curia. He would have been successful in his suit, but witnesses who appeared before Pope Eugenius III at Meaux in France swore, rightly or wrongly, that he had made profession and submission to the see of Canterbury.[281] It was with some confidence that he had undertaken to do battle with such formidable adversaries on this issue, for he could rely upon three sets of circumstances which were favourable to his cause: he had the ear and the close personal interest of King Henry I, he was living in a time of peace, and as a result this was a time of plenty. He was so sure of himself and so convinced that right was on his side that, when he travelled through Wales, he occasionally had an archbishop's cross carried before him.

However commendable he may have been in other respects, Bernard was remarkable for his insufferable pomposity and ambition. From the moment when he left the court and was sent to this outpost by the King, his sole desire was to return to the more easy circumstances of an English bishopric. Almost all those sent to Wales from England suffer from this same malady. He alienated much of the land held by his church without either advantage to himself or profit to anyone else. He disposed of other church lands in the most improvident and foolish fashion, so that, when ten carucates[282] were demanded in lieu of military service, without watching what he was doing he would give twenty or thirty. Where he had himself, injudiciously, it is true,

281. Bernard argued the case with Popes Innocent II (1130–43), Lucius II (1144–5) and Eugenius III (1145–53). He appeared before Eugenius III at Meaux in 1147, but Archbishop Theobald of Canterbury, who was there to oppose him, made it clear that Bernard had submitted to Canterbury at his consecration in 1115. Gerald refers repeatedly to this contest in his writings.

282. A carucate was as much land as could be tilled by one plough pulled by eight oxen in one year.

and without much enthusiasm, instituted holy and canonical obsequies in honour of Saint David, he would perform only one of them, or at the most two or three.[283]

I will tell you briefly how I think things stand today concerning these two sees of Canterbury and St David's which I have been discussing. Canterbury enjoys royal favour, immense wealth, the services of a great number of suffragan bishops, who are, moreover, well endowed, and the presence of many learned men who are highly skilled in literature and the law. All these advantages are completely lacking in St David's, and no just consideration is ever given to its plight. It will be extremely difficult for it ever to recover its former position, except perhaps by some fundamental upheaval and revolution in human affairs, such as has been known to happen sometimes in a king's dominions.

St David's cathedral was founded in honour of Saint Andrew the Apostle. The place where it stands is called the Valley of Roses.[284] A better name for it would be the Valley of Marble, for it is in no sense rosy or remarkable for roses, whereas there are plenty of rocks all over the place. The churchyard is bounded on the north side by the River Alun, a muddy and unproductive stream. It runs under the Llech Lafar Stone,[285] a slab of marble polished by the feet of those innumerable people who have walked across it. I have written about the size, texture and name of this stone in my *Vaticinal History*.[286] What follows is my description of how Henry II, King of the English, crossed over this stone on his return from Ireland, as he went into the cathedral of Saint Andrew and Saint David to pray.[287]

283. Gerald is very critical of Bishop Bernard. He was often absent on the King's business, but he instituted a number of necessary reforms and rebuilt part of his cathedral.

284. Gerald writes 'Vallis Rosina'.

285. The Llech Lafar Stone = 'lapide Lechlavar' means the Talking Stone.

286. By *The Vaticinal History* Gerald means, as always, *The Conquest of Ireland*.

287. The long passage 'The King . . . twelve miles away', except for three sentences, 'A wit . . . at all', is repeated from *The Conquest of Ireland*, I.38.

The King had left the following garrisons behind in Ireland: in Dublin, Hugh de Lacy,[288] to whom he had given Meath in fee, with twenty knights to support him; with him, FitzStephen[289] and Maurice FitzGerald,[290] together with twenty more knights; in Waterford, Humphrey de Bohun, Robert FitzBernard and Hugh de Grainville, with forty knights; and in Wexford, William FitzAldelm and Philip de Braose,[291] with twenty knights. At first light on the day after Easter Sunday he embarked in the outer harbour at Wexford. The wind blew from the north-west and after an uneventful crossing he landed in St David's port about noon.[292] Dressed as a pilgrim, on foot and leaning on a staff, he went to pray in Saint David's cathedral. As he came to the white gate, he met a procession of the church canons, who received him with due honour and reverence.

As the procession advanced, the clergy walking one by one and with proper ceremony, a Welsh woman threw herself at the King's feet and made a complaint about the Bishop of St David's.[293] This was explained to the King by an interpreter. Nothing could be done there and then about her petition, so she gestured violently with her hands and, with everyone listening, had the impudence to shout in a loud voice: 'Revenge us today, Llech Lafar! Revenge the whole Welsh people on this man!' She was held back and then driven away by those who understood the Welsh language. As she went she shouted even more loudly and violently. She repeated the well-known fiction and prophecy of Merlin, so often heard, that a king of England, who had just conquered Ireland, would be wounded in that country by a man with a red hand, and then, on his return to St David's would die as he walked over Llech Lafar. This was the name of the stone which served as a bridge over the River Alun, the stream which marks

288. Hugh de Lacy, like most of the other knights listed in this paragraph, is mentioned repeatedly in *The Conquest of Ireland*. He was assassinated in 1186.

289. Robert FitzStephen was the son of the Princess Nest by Stephen, constable of Cardigan, and thus an uncle of Gerald of Wales.

290. Maurice FitzGerald was the son of the Princess Nest by her husband Gerald of Windsor and thus both a half-brother of Robert FitzStephen and another uncle of Gerald of Wales.

291. Philip de Braose was the uncle of William de Braose (cp. p. 81, n. 53).

292. This was Easter Monday, 17 April 1172, and Henry II landed at Porth Stinian.

293. This was Gerald's uncle.

the boundary of the cemetery on the north side of the cathedral. The stone was made of very beautiful marble, polished over the whole of its length by the feet of all those who had walked across it. It was ten feet long, six feet wide and one foot deep. In Welsh the name Llech Lafar means the Talking Stone. There is an age-old legend about this stone that once, when a corpse was being carried across it, it burst into speech and in the effort split down the middle, the crack still being visible today. Because of this heathen superstition, attributed to the stone in bygone days, they have given up carrying corpses across it.

It so happened that the King knew all about the prophecy. When he reached the stone he stopped and eyed it closely. Then, without further hesitation, he walked boldly over it. As soon as he was across he turned round, glared at the stone and with no small indignation made this trenchant remark about the soothsayer: 'Merlin is a liar. Who will trust him now?' A wit, who was there among the crowd, heard the King's remark, and pretended to take umbrage at the insult offered to the prophet. 'You are not the king who is to conquer Ireland,' he said. 'Merlin was not talking about you at all.' Henry went into the cathedral, which had been founded in honour of Saint Andrew and Saint David. He prayed there with great feeling and heard Mass. This was said by a chaplain who, by divine providence, was the only priest present among such a crowd who had not yet broken his fast. The King had a meal and then rode off to Haverfordwest Castle, which is about twelve miles away.

Two stories worth mentioning, or so I think, are first that, in our own lifetime, when David II was Bishop, the River Alun ran with wine, and secondly that the Pistildewi, that is Saint David's Spout, a spring which flows through a narrow channel into the churchyard from the east, several times ran with milk.[294]

The jackdaws in the cathedral have become so accustomed to kindly treatment from the local priests that you will find them tame and used to human beings. They never fly away from anyone dressed in black.

In clear weather the mountains of Ireland can be seen from St David's. The Irish Sea can be crossed in one short day.

294. Saint David prayed for running water for his cathedral and the Pistildewi began to flow (V.S.D., V). There is no mention there of its running with milk.

William Rufus, the son of King William the Bastard and the second of the Norman Kings in England, penetrated far into Wales in his own day.[295] He looked around him, and from these rocky headlands could just make out Ireland. He is supposed to have said: 'I will collect a fleet together from my own kingdom and with it make a bridge, so that I can conquer that country.' This was reported to Murchard, Prince of Leinster in Ireland.[296] He thought for a while and then asked: 'When the King made this mighty threat, did he add "If God so wills"?' He was told that Rufus had not mentioned God at all when he spoke. Murchard found this very reassuring. He replied: 'Since this man puts all his trust in human agencies and none in the power of God Almighty, I have no reason to fear his coming.'

Chapter 2
Our journey through Cemais and our stay in St Dogmael's monastery.

Early the next morning the Archbishop celebrated Mass at the high altar in Saint David's cathedral: then he hurried off through Cemais to meet Prince Rhys in Cardigan.[297] He left the Archdeacon of St David's, that is myself, behind there, with orders that I should preach to the people.

I want to tell you about two events which happened in the cantref of Cemais, one fairly recently and the other some time ago. In our own days a young man who lived in this neighbourhood, and who was lying ill in bed, was persecuted by a plague of toads. It seemed as if the entire local population of toads had made an agreement to go to visit him. Vast numbers were killed by his friends and by those looking after him, but they

295. This was in 1097.

296. This is Murtough MacMurrough, nephew of Dermot MacMurrough, King of Leinster.

297. Rhys ap Gruffydd, Prince of South Wales, had been there to meet Archbishop Baldwin and Gerald in Radnor. Now he was waiting for them in Cardigan as they entered the region under his direct control, and he stayed with them until they crossed the River Dovey and so left his dominions.

grew again like the heads of the Hydra. Toads came flocking from all directions, more and more of them, until no one could count them. In the end the young man's friends and the other people who were trying to help were quite worn out. They chose a tall tree, cut off all its branches and removed all its leaves. Then they hoisted him up to the top in a bag. He was still not safe from his venomous assailants. The toads crawled up the tree looking for him. They killed him and ate him right up, leaving nothing but his skeleton. His name was Seisyll Esgairhir, which means Longshanks. I read somewhere that, by the judgement of God, which is never unjust, even if it is sometimes hard to understand, another man was persecuted in the same way by a large species of rodents, called rats.

In the same cantref,[298] in the time of King Henry I, a rich man who lived on the northern slopes of the Prescelly Mountains dreamed three nights in succession that, if he put his hand in a stone which stuck out above the gushing water of a near-by spring called the Fountain of Saint Bernacus, he would find there a gold torque. On the third day he did what he had been told to do in his dreams. He was bitten in the finger by a viper and died from the wound. It is true that many treasures have been discovered as the result of dreams, and in all sorts of circumstances. It seems to me that dreams are like rumours: you must use your common sense, and then accept some but refuse to believe others.

I must tell you about an extraordinary event which occurred in our own time in Llanhyver Castle, which is the chief stronghold in Cemais.[299] After besieging it with a force of armed men, Rhys ap Gruffydd captured Llanhyver Castle from his own son-in-law, a young nobleman called William FitzMartin. He did this at the instigation of his son Gruffydd, a cunning, artful man.

298. This passage 'In the same cantref . . . to believe others' is copied from *The Conquest of Ireland*, I.42, but it is worded differently.

299. Llanhyver is Nanhyver or Nevern. Rhys ap Gruffydd captured the castle from William FitzMartin in 1191. William FitzMartin, son of Martin of Tours, the first Norman ruler of Cemais, married Angharad, daughter of Lord Rhys.

It was in direct contravention of a whole series of oaths which he had sworn in person on the most precious relics to the effect that William should be left in all peace and security in his castle. Rhys then handed the castle over to Gruffydd. In so doing he broke another oath which he had sworn, mentioning Gruffydd by name and promising that he would never permit him to hold Llanhyver Castle.

Ill-gotten gains bring nothing but remorse.[300]

'Vengeance is mine; I will repay, saith the Lord,' through the mouth of His prophet.[301] God ordained that soon afterwards the castle should be taken away from Gruffydd, who was the real author and contriver of this plot, and handed over to his brother Maelgwn, the man he hated most in all the world. About two years later Rhys was planning to disinherit his own daughter, his grandsons and his two granddaughters. Instead he was made prisoner in a battle with his sons and locked up in this very same castle.[302] God took vengeance on him in the most apposite way, for, as he well deserved, he was disgraced and discountenanced in the very place where he had perpetrated a base and shameful crime.

At the time when he suffered this misfortune, and this is well worth bearing in mind, he had stolen the torque of Saint Cynog of Brecknockshire and had hidden it in Dinevor. For this act alone he deserved to be captured and locked up, as an example of the judgement of God.

We spent the night in St Dogmael's monastery, where we were lodged very comfortably. The next day we were in Cardigan or Aberteivi, which means the spot where the River Teifi meets the sea, and there we were entertained by Prince Rhys. A crowd assembled on the Cemais side of the river, not far from the bridge, with Prince Rhys and his two sons, Maelgwn and Gruffydd, in the middle, and the word of God was preached with great effect, first by the Archbishop and then by me, the Arch-

300. Ovid, *Amores*, I.10.48.
301. Romans, 10.19.
302. This was in 1194.

deacon of St David's. We persuaded a great number of people to take the Cross. One of those who did so was the only son and the sole comfort of his mother, a woman far advanced in years. As she gazed at him, she was inspired by God to say: 'Jesus Christ, our most dear Lord, I give You heartfelt thanks for having judged me worthy to bear a son whom You have deigned to accept into Your service.' There was present another woman, one of the matrons of Cardigan, whose reaction was quite different. She seized her husband firmly by the cloak and the belt, and, with everyone watching, brazenly prevented him from going up to the Archbishop and taking the Cross. Three nights afterwards she heard an awesome voice say in a dream: 'You have taken my servant away from me. Therefore the thing you hold most dear shall be taken away from you.' She related this vision to her husband and they were both struck with horror and amazement. However, they went to sleep again, and this time the woman most unfortunately overlaid her little boy, whom she loved very much but whom she had most unwisely allowed to get into bed with her. The husband told the local bishop about his wife's dream and of how she had been punished. He then took the Cross. His wife made no further objection. In fact she sewed the sign on his shoulder with her own hands.

In a green field just by the bridge-head where the sermons had been given those who had been present marked out a site for a chapel in commemoration of what had happened there. In their devotion they planned that the altar should be on the exact spot where Archbishop Baldwin had stood when he preached. Later on crowds of sick people thronged to this spot from all parts of the country and many miracles were performed there, but I have no time to tell you about them.[303]

303. According to Sir Richard Colt Hoare, in his day the spot was still called Park y Cappell or Chapel Field.

Chapter 3
The River Teifi, Cardiganshire and Newcastle Emlyn.[304]

Near by flows a noble river called the Teifi. It is better stocked
with the finest salmon than any other stream in Wales. Near
Cilgerran,[305] at a spot called Cenarth Mawr, on the topmost
point of a rock which Saint Llawddog hollowed out with his own
hands, there is a flourishing fishing-station. The waters of the
Teifi run ceaselessly over this rock, falling with a mighty roar
into the abyss below. Now it is from these depths that the salmon
ascend into the concave rock above, which is a remarkable leap,
about as far as the height of the tallest spear. This may seem hard
to believe, but it is the nature of the fish to perform such feats.
This particular species has developed the habit of leaping into
the air. Indeed, it is from the Latin word 'saltus' that it takes its
name as 'salmon'.[306] I have already described its habits in my
Topography of Ireland.[307]

This is how the salmon contrives to leap. When fish of this species
swimming, as is natural, against the course of the water – for fish
swim upstream, just as birds fly into the wind – come to some apparently insurmountable obstacle, they twist their tails round towards
their mouths. Sometimes, in order to give more power to their leap, they
go so far as to put their tails right in their mouths. Then with a great
snap, like the sudden straightening of a bough which has long been
held bent, they jerk themselves out of this circular position and so
leap from the lower pool to the one above, to the great astonishment
of anyone who happens to be watching.

The church dedicated to Saint Llawddog, his mill, the bridge
with its fishing-station and a most attractive garden all stand
together on a small plot of ground.

304. Emlyn was a cantref of Dyfed.
305. There was a Norman castle at Cilgerran, built in 1109 by Gilbert
Strongbow, Earl of Striguil.
306. The word salmon comes from 'salmonem', C.L., which is clearly
cognate with 'salire'.
307. This graphic description is repeated from *The Topography of Ireland*,
II.42.

The Teifi has another remarkable peculiarity. Of all the rivers in Wales, and of those in England south of the Humber, it is the only one where you can find beavers. In Scotland, or so they tell me, there is again only one stream where beavers live, and even there they are rare. I thought that[308] it would be useful to include a paragraph or two at this point about the habits of these animals: the way in which they convey their building materials from the woods to the water; with what artistry they construct their dams in the middle of rivers from the materials which they have collected; how they protect their dwellings in Western countries and in the East against those who hunt them; and a word about their tails, which are fish-like, so to speak, rather than what one would expect in a land animal. Beavers build their castle-like lodges in the middle of rivers. They have an extraordinary method of conveying and carting timber from the woods to the water, for they use other beavers as waggons. The beavers of one team [309] gnaw

down the branches, and then another group has the instinct to turn over on their backs and to hold this wood tightly against their bellies with their four feet. Each of these last grips a branch in its teeth which sticks out on either side. A third group holds tightly on to this cross-branch with its teeth and pulls the animal in question along backwards together with its load. Anyone who witnesses this manoeuvre cannot fail to be impressed. Badgers use a not dissimilar device when they are cleaning out their sets, which they arrange to their satisfaction by digging into the soil and scraping at it with their paws. It is remarkable that in both species of animal there are to be found slaves which are prepared to accept a debasement of their natural habits and to suffer at the same time a certain wear and tear of the skin on their backs.

There in some deep and tranquil bend of the river the beavers piece together with such skill the logs of wood which form their lodge that no drop of water can easily enter and no storm however

308. The long passage 'I thought that ... taken for fish' is repeated in *The Description of Wales*, I.5.

309. The passage 'The beavers of one team ... on their backs' is repeated from *The Topography of Ireland*, I.25–6.

violent do harm to it or loosen it. They have no reason to fear any attack, except that of us human beings, and even we must bring our weapons shod with iron. When they are building a lodge, they bind the logs together with willow-wands. The number of storeys placed one above the other varies according to the rise in the water-level which they foresee. They plan their construction so that it just protrudes from the water, with connecting doorways inside to lead from one storey to another. Whenever they have decided that it is necessary, they can keep a lookout from the top and watch the rising waters when the river is in spate. As the years pass and the willow-wands keep on growing, the lodge is constantly in leaf and becomes, in fact, a grove of willow-trees, looking like a natural bush from the out-side, however artificially constructed it may be within.

The beaver can remain in the water as long as it chooses; and when under the water it can hold its breath,[310] as do toads and hairy seals, which last creatures mark the ebb and flow of the tide by the alternate smoothness and roughness of their fur. These three species of animals live indifferently under the water or in the air. Beavers have short legs, a broad body and no tail to speak of,[311] or at the best very short ones, and they are made rather in the shape of moles or badgers. It is worth noting that the beaver has only four teeth, two at the top of the mouth and two below. These teeth are very broad and sharp, and the animal uses them to cut with, as if they were an adze. Near their lodges they build underground hiding-places in the river-bank, carefully protected retreats which they dig into the dry earth. When the hunter comes to prise the beaver out and strives his hardest to poke sharpened poles down into its den, the creature hears the attack and knows that danger threatens. It retreats as fast as it can to the protection of its dam; but first, while still in the river-bank, it stirs up the water all round the entrance to its hole, scraping at the earth with its feet to form a muddy mixture, thus making the clear transparent river all thick and foul. In

310. It is true, apparently, that beavers have watertight valves in their nose and ears.

311. This is an odd statement = caudis nullis vel quasi mutilatis.

this way by its own stratagem it finds an answer to the wiles of its enemy, who is standing on the bank above, holding his three-pronged spear and waiting for the beaver to spring out.

In Eastern countries, when the beaver finds that it cannot evade the dogs which are following it by its scent, it saves itself by self-mutilation. By some natural instinct it knows which part of its body the hunter really wants. The creature castrates itself before the hunter's eyes and throws its testicles down. It is because of this act of self-castration that it is called 'castor' in Latin.[312] If a beaver which has already lost its testicles is hard pressed a second time by the hounds, it rushes to the top of a hillock, cocks up one of its hind-legs and shows the hunter that the organs which he is really after have already been cut off. In his oration *Pro Scauro*[313] Cicero says of beavers: 'They ransom themselves by cutting off that part of their bodies for which they are most commonly pursued.' Juvenal says the same:

> This beast
> Himself a eunuch makes, but saves his life at least,
> Without his testicles.[314]

So does Saint Bernard:

> The beaver saves his life by offering at full speed
> Those vital organs which the lustful hunters need.[315]

In order to save its skin, which is much sought after in the West, and in the East that medicinal part of its body which is so greatly prized there, the beaver thus does what it can to escape from the traps laid by the hunter, giving evidence of remarkable instinct and cunning, but even so not saving itself completely. Beavers have

312. The word 'castor' comes via Greek from the Hebrew for musk, because of the castoreum produced in the creature's abdominal glands. Needless to say, it has nothing to do with 'castrare', C.L. On the other hand 'castor' also means 'aries castratus'.

313. Apart from a few fragments, Cicero's *Pro Scauro* is lost. This quotation is taken from Isidore of Seville, *Etymologiae*, XII.2.21.

314. Juvenal, *Satires*, 12.34–6, also borrowed via Isidore.

315. Gerald adds this third quotation to the two provided by Isidore. I cannot trace it.

broad short tails,[316] thick, like the palm of the hand, which they use as a rudder when they are swimming. All the rest of their body is hairy, but this part is smooth and slippery, and, like the seal's tail, completely without hair. They are very common in Germany and the Arctic regions: and there, in times of fasting, the great leaders of the Church eat these tails instead of fish, accepting them for their flavour and their colouring, for in this, they say, they could be taken for fish. It would seem that what is true of the whole remains true of the whole, whereas what is true of the part is true of that part only; but in normal circumstances the part cannot be generically different from the whole.

From the castle which I have just mentioned [317] we made our way towards Lampeter,[318] leaving Crug Mawr,[319] that is the Big Hill, on our left soon after riding out of Cardigan. It was on this spot that, a short time after the death of Henry I, King of the English, Gruffydd, son of Rhys ap Tewdwr, gained a great victory over the English in pitched battle.[320] They were left without a leader, for, as I told you earlier on, Richard of Clare had just been murdered near Abergavenny,[321] and as a result Gruffydd was able to beat them at the very first encounter. There is a tumulus at the top of this hill.[322] The local inhabitants say that it adjusts itself to the size of anyone who goes there. They also maintain that if as evening falls you leave your arms there in good condition you will find them broken to pieces the next morning.

316. The passage 'Beavers have broad short tails ... from the whole' is repeated from *The Topography of Ireland*, I.26.

317. Cardigan Castle, p. 171.

318. Lampeter, *Pons Stephani* for Gerald, is still Llanbedr Steffan in Welsh.

319. Cp. Nennius, *Historia Brittonum*, 74, where Crug Mawr is the last of the 'mirabilia Britanniae'.

320. This was the Battle of Crug Mawr, 1136, in which Gruffydd ap Rhys defeated Stephen, constable of Cardigan Castle, Robert FitzMartin and Gerald's two uncles, William and Maurice FitzGerald.

321. Cp. p. 108, n. 142.

322. Cp. Nennius, *Historia Brittonum*, 74: 'Sepulchrum ... in cacumine montis qui cognominatur Crucmare'.

Chapter 4
Our journey through Lampeter, the Abbey of Strata Florida, Llanddewi Brefi and the church of Saint Padarn the Great.

A sermon was preached the next morning in Lampeter, first by the Archbishop, then by me, Archdeacon of St David's, and finally by two Abbots of the Cistercian order, John of Whitland [323] and Seisyll of Strata Florida. [324] These last two accompanied us faithfully as far as these parts and then came on to North Wales. Many persons were induced to take the Cross. We reached Strata Florida that night and stayed there for a while. From there we journeyed on, leaving on our right the lofty mountains of Moruge, called Elenydd in Welsh. [325] Here we were met near the side of a wood by Cynwrig ap Rhys, [326] who was accompanied by a band of lightly armed young men. Cynwrig was tall and handsome, with fair curly hair. He was dressed according to the custom of his race and country, for he wore only a thin cloak and beneath that a shirt. His feet and legs were bare, and he seemed to care nothing for the thorns and thistles.

323. This abbey, Alba Domus for Gerald, translated from Ty Gwyn, more properly Whitland or Alba Landa, was moved from Little Trefgarn and re-founded on the River Gronw c. 1151. It was the first Cistercian house in Wales.

324. Strata Florida, or Ystrad Fflur, originally a colony of Whitland, was a Cistercian house founded on the little River Fflur in 1164. It was later moved two miles away to the banks of the River Teifi. Seisyll, obviously a Welshman, preached again in Anglesey (*Itin.*, II.7).

325. Gerald's 'montani de Moruge . . . quae Kambrice dicuntur Elennith' are the hills of Plinlimmon. Cp. p. 225, n. 496.

326. Cynwrig ap Rhys ap Gruffydd was the third son of the Lord Rhys. He died in 1237. I translated 'natura munitus' as 'he had a natural dignity' before I read Sir John Lloyd's ironic half-sentence: '. . . the tall and handsome Cynwrig, singled out as a young man by Giraldus Cambrensis for special admiration, played no part in the political strife of his day and carried his goodly presence to the grave without having in any way disturbed the tenor of his long life of dignified inaction' (*A History of Wales*, Vol. II, pp. 577–8).

He had a natural dignity, which owed nothing to affectation: he was, as it were, a man adorned by nature, not by art. In the presence of their father, Prince Rhys, we preached a sermon to his three sons, Gruffydd, Maelgwn and Cynwrig. These brothers vied with each other about taking the Cross. In the end Maelgwn promised faithfully that he would accompany the Archbishop to the King's court, and that once there he would abide by their advice, always supposing that they wanted him to do so.[327]

We next passed through Llanddewi Brefi, that is David's church at Brefi, situated on the top of the hill which rose up under Saint David's feet when he was preaching there.[328] This was at the great synod of all the bishops, abbots and priests of Wales, who assembled on this spot in the presence of the people to rebut the Pelagian heresy, which long before had been put an end to in Britain by Saint Germanus, Bishop of Auxerre, but which had then started up again in those parts like some recurrent plague or epidemic.[329] With loud acclamation and with the unanimous agreement of all present, David was elected as Archbishop, especially in view of the miracle which had just occurred, although he was reluctant and tried to refuse the honour.[330] What is more, as I have already told you, Saint Dyfrig, in his archiepiscopal court at Caerleon, had only recently resigned this honour to him, naming him personally and appointing him as his successor. As a result the metropolitan see was moved from Caerleon to St David's.[331]

That night we stayed at Llanbadarn Fawr, that is the church

327. Sir John Lloyd is equally ironic about Gruffydd: 'It was, perhaps, an instance of his adroit manoeuvring that, while professing great anxiety to join the crusade . . ., he contrived that the impetuous Maelgwn should actually go with the archbishop' (op. cit., p. 577, n. 20). Of course, Maelgwn never went. He died in 1230 and was buried at Strata Florida.

328. Cp. p. 161, nn. 261 and 262.

329. Cp. Geoffrey of Monmouth, *The History of the Kings of Britain*, VI.13, and Bede, *Ecclesiastical History*, I.10 and 17.

330. Cp. p. 159, n. 255, and p. 161, n. 262.

331. Cp. p. 115, n. 156, and p. 159, n. 255. Cp. also Geoffrey of Monmouth, op. cit., IX.15 and VII.3.

of Saint Padarn the Great.[332] The following morning we attracted many people to the service of Christ.

It is a remarkable fact that this church, like so many others in Ireland and Wales, has a layman as what is called its abbot. There has come about a lamentable use and custom by which the most powerful people in a parish have been appointed by the clergy as stewards in the first place, or rather as patrons and defenders of the churches. In the process of time their greed has grown greater and they have usurped full power, in their impudence appropriating all church lands and assuming secular possession, leaving to the clergy nothing but their altars, with their tenths and oblations. Even these last they have made over to their own sons and other relations who are actually in the church. These so-called defenders of the churches, who are really bent on destroying what they should protect, have taken the name of abbots, presuming to attribute to themselves not only a title but also lands to which they have no right. We found the church of Llanbadarn Fawr reduced to this sorry state. An old man called Ednywain ap Gweithfoed, who had grown grey in iniquity, was usurping the office of abbot, while his sons officiated at the altar. In the reign of King Henry I, when the English were still in control of Wales, Saint Peter's monastery in Gloucester administered this church in peace and tranquillity. After Henry's death the English were driven out and the monks expelled.[333] As I have explained, laymen took forcible possession of the church and brought in their own clergy.

It happened in the reign of King Stephen, who succeeded to Henry I, that a certain knight from Brittany, who had travelled in many lands, to visit the homes of different peoples and to study their way of life, came by chance to Llanbadarn. One feast-day, when the clergy and the parishioners were awaiting the coming of their abbot, so that Mass could be celebrated, this knight was there to witness the abbot's arrival, in the midst of a crowd of other people. What he actually saw was a band of about twenty young men, all armed and equipped according to the local custom. He asked which was the abbot. They pointed

332. Saint Paternus or Saint Padarn was a contemporary of Saint David.
333. This was in 1135.

out to him a man with a long spear in his hand, who was walking in front of the others. The knight gazed at him with amazement. 'Has the abbot no other vestments?' he asked. 'Has he no other staff to use, instead of the spear which he is carrying?' 'No,' they said. 'Upon my soul!' answered the knight. 'What I have seen today really is a novelty! I have never heard of anything so odd!' Without more ado he gave up travelling, put an end to his studies and went straight back home.

This wicked people, this depraved generation, maintains that a certain bishop of this church,[334] for it was once a cathedral, was murdered by their predecessors. It is mainly by this argument that they justify their seizure of church property and of church authority in Llanbadarn Fawr. Nobody has ever complained about their conduct. I have therefore come to the conclusion that, for the moment at least, it is better to say no more about this sorry state of affairs, for fear of infuriating this wicked people.[335]

Chapter 5
How we crossed the River Dovey in boats and so came to the territory of the sons of Cynan.[336]

We made our way to the River Dovey, which divides North Wales from South Wales. Here the Bishop of St David's [337] and Rhys ap Gruffydd both left us to go home.[338] With a kind

334. Gerald again harks back to the time before the division of the country into dioceses, when the head of a monastic institution was often called a bishop.

335. Perhaps Gerald implies that he had expected Archbishop Baldwin to put an end to the scandal in Llanbadarn Fawr, but that, as the Archbishop had taken no action, he himself could do nothing.

336. 'The territory of the sons of Cynan', 'terra filiorum Canani', is that part of North Wales which was ruled over by Gruffydd and Maredudd, the two sons of Cynan ab Owain Gwynedd (d. 1173). In 1188 Gruffydd held Meirionydd and Ardudwy, and Maredudd held Eifionydd. After the death of Rhodri ab Owain Gwynedd in 1195 they greatly enlarged their territories.

337. Peter de Leia.

338. When they crossed the River Dovey, they left behind the diocese of St David's and the territory ruled over by Lord Rhys.

solicitude much to be praised in so distinguished a person, Rhys had accompanied us from Cardigan Castle and right across Cardiganshire as far as the river. We crossed the Dovey in boats and so left the diocese of St David's. Now we were in Merioneth,[339] the territory of the sons of Cynan, the first province of Gwynedd to those coming from that direction and part of the diocese of Bangor. We spent the night in Towyn.

Early the next morning Gruffydd ap Cynan came to meet us, humbly and devoutly begging the Archbishop's pardon for having been so slow to do so. That same day we were rowed across the two branches of the River Mawddach. Maelgwn ap Rhys found a ford near the sea. It was he who had promised to accompany the Archbishop to the King's court.[340] That night we slept at Llanfair, that is Saint Mary's church, in the commote of Ardudwy.

This territory of Cynan, and especially Merioneth, is the rudest and roughest of all the Welsh districts. The mountains are very high, with narrow ridges and a great number of very sharp peaks all jumbled together in confusion. If the shepherds who shout to each other and exchange comments from these lofty summits should ever decide to meet, it would take them almost the whole day to climb down and up again.

They use very long spears in this area. Just as the bow is the chief weapon in South Wales, so here in Gwynedd they prefer the spear. A cuirass of chain-mail offers no resistance to one of these lances when it is thrown a short distance as a javelin.

The next morning Maredudd, the younger son of Cynan, came to meet us with a number of his people just as we were crossing a bridge. Quite a few of them were inspired to take the Cross. A very fine young man in Maredudd's suite, one of his close associates, was about to have the Cross sewn on his cloak. The young prince burst into tears when he saw how worn and

339. Merioneth, in Welsh Meirionnydd, takes its name from Meirion, grandson of the Brythonic chieftain Cunedda, who conquered North Wales at the beginning of the fifth century. Cp. Rachel Bromwich, *Trioedd Ynys Prydein*, Triad 81.C.18: '... and the Offspring of Cunedda Wledig ...'
340. Cp. p. 179.

threadbare the garment was, and he threw his own cloak round the man's shoulders.

Chapter 6
How we crossed the Traeth Mawr and the Traeth Bychan. Nefyn, Caernarfon and Bangor.

We crossed the Traeth Mawr and the Traeth Bychan. These are two arms of the sea, one large and one small. Two stone castles have been built there recently. The one called Deudraeth belongs to the sons of Cynan and is situated in the Eifionydd area, facing the northern mountains.[341] The second, which is called Carn Madryn, belongs to the sons of Owain:[342] it is on the Lleyn peninsula, on the other side of the river, and it faces the sea.[343] 'Traeth' in the Welsh language means a tract of sand where the tide comes in, but which is left bare when the sea ebbs. Before this we had crossed over two fine rivers, the Dysynni, which is between the Mawddach and the Traeth Mawr, and the Artro, which is between the Traeth Mawr and the Traeth Bychan.[344] That night, which was the Eve of Palm Sunday, we slept at Nefyn.[345] There I myself, Archdeacon of St David's, discovered the works of Merlin Silvester, which I had long been looking for, or so I would like you to think.[346]

Beyond Lleyn there is a small island occupied by some extremely devout monks, called the Coelibes or Colidei.[347]

341. Sir Richard Colt Hoare could not identify Deudraeth.

342. Owain Gwynedd died in 1170.

343. Carn Madryn Sir Richard Colt Hoare found easily: '. . . it stands on a lofty insulated hill, rising immediately above the well-wooded grounds of Mr Parry at Madryn Ucha'.

344. This is the sentence added many years later in Version III in which Gerald wrongly puts the River Dysynni between the River Mawddach and the Traeth Mawr, and the River Artro between the Traeth Mawr and the Traeth Bychan.

345. 9 April 1188.

346. In Version III Gerald wrote 'dicitur invenisse'; in Versions I and II he had written 'invenit'. I do not understand the purpose of the change.

347. 'Coelibes' = presumably celibates. 'Colidei' or 'Culdei' = cultores Dei, cp. Du Cange, *Glossarium*, Vol. II, p. 427.

Either because of its pure air, which comes across the sea from Ireland, or through some miracle occasioned by the merits of the holy men who live there, the island has this peculiarity, that no one dies there except in extreme old age, for disease is almost unheard of. In fact, no one dies there at all, unless he is very old indeed. In Welsh the place is called Ynys Enlli, and in the Saxon tongue Bardsey Island. The bodies of a vast number of holy men are buried there, or so they say, among them that of Daniel, Bishop of Bangor.[348]

The next morning the Archbishop gave a sermon and many people took the Cross. On the way to Bangor we passed through Caernarfon, that is Arfon Castle. It is called Arfon, the region facing Mon, because it is opposite the island of Mona. Our road led us to a valley, where the going was hard, with many steep climbs up and down.[349] We dismounted from our horses and proceeded on foot, in intention at least rehearsing what we thought we would experience when we went on our pilgrimage to Jerusalem. We walked the whole length of the valley, and we were very tired by the time we reached the farther end. The Archbishop sat himself down on an oak-tree, which had been completely uprooted and overturned by the force of the winds, for he needed to rest and recover his breath. As he reclined there, he joked with his attendants, which was a wonderful thing for so venerable a person to do. 'Which of you, now, in all my company, can soothe my tired ears by whistling a tune?' he asked, although he knew very well how difficult this would be, seeing how exhausted they all were. He maintained that he himself could do so, if he really wanted to. At this moment a bird in a near-by coppice began to sing very sweetly. Some said that it was a green woodpecker, called 'pic' in French, which was making a hole in an oak-tree with its strong beak and tapping away as hard as it could. Others maintained that it was an oriole, remarkable for its gold and yellow colouring, which sometimes

348. This is Saint Deiniol, who flourished in the mid sixth century. Dubricius, in Welsh Dyfrig, was also buried on Bardsey Island.

349. According to Sir Richard Colt Hoare this is the valley called Nant y Garth.

whistles sweetly instead of singing.[350] It is called an oriole because it is as bright as gold. Someone remarked that the nightingale was never seen in those parts. The Archbishop smiled and replied jokingly: 'If it never comes to Wales the nightingale is a very sensible bird. We are not quite so wise, for not only have we come here but we have traversed the whole country.'

We spent that night at Bangor, the metropolitan see of Gwynedd, where we were well entertained by the local bishop.[351] The next morning Mass was celebrated by the Archbishop before the high altar. On the right of the altar stood Gwion, Bishop of Bangor. He was hard pressed by the Archbishop and a number of other people, importuned, in fact, rather than persuaded, and in the end there was nothing for it but that he himself should take the Cross. This caused great concern to his flock assembled in the church, for both men and women present wept and wailed very loudly.

Chapter 7
The island of Anglesey or Mona.

After this we crossed by boat over a small arm of the sea to the island of Mona or Anglesey, which is about two miles distant. There Rhodri, the younger son of Owain, came to meet us reverently, with all the inhabitants of the island and quite a few from the adjacent mainland.[352] Confession was heard in a place near the seashore where the surrounding rocks form a sort of circular theatre.[353] The Archbishop gave a sermon, and so did

350. Thomas Jones suggests a yellow-hammer.

351. Gwion, a Welshman, was consecrated as Bishop of Bangor at Amesbury on 22 May 1177 by Archbishop Richard. He was present at the coronation of King Richard I on 3 September 1189.

352. This was Rhodri ab Owain Gwynedd, who was constantly harassed by Gruffydd and Maredudd ap Cynan.

353. According to Sir Richard Colt Hoare this was at Cerrig y Borth in the parish of Llandysilio, the spot where Rhodri and his men sat is called Maen Rodi, and the place where Baldwin stood is known as Carreg Iago from Carreg yr Archjagon.

Alexander, the local Archdeacon, who acted as our interpreter,[354] and Seisyll, the Abbot of Strata Florida.[355] Many of the common people were persuaded to take the Cross. A band of youths who formed part of Rhodri's household sat on a rock facing us. The Archbishop addressed them personally, and the other preachers did the same, exhorting them again and again, as if trying to extract blood from a stone, but not one of them could be persuaded. It came to pass within three days, as if by divine vengeance, that these very same young men, with many others, set off in pursuit of a local band of robbers. The thieves beat them and put them to flight, some being killed there and then, and others mortally wounded. The Cross which they had previously scorned they now of their own free will marked on their own bodies. Only a short time before Rhodri had taken the daughter of Prince Rhys as his mistress, this being incest, for she was his close blood-relation and a cousin three times removed.[356] He paid no attention at all to the sensible advice given to him by the Archbishop. He had taken this woman to gain the support of Rhys against his own brothers' sons, whom he had disinherited.[357] Soon afterwards he was dispossessed of all his lands by these same nephews.[358] Despite his illicit act, he met with disappointment instead of the support on which he had counted.

The island of Anglesey contains three hundred and sixty-three vills, and this is considered to be the equal of three cantrefs. The word cantref is the same in Welsh and Irish: it means about as much land as goes to make up a hundred vills.

Three islands lie off the shores of Britain,[359] in different

354. See p. 114, n. 154.

355. See p. 178, n. 324.

356. This seems really to have been a marriage. A little later in 1193 Rhodri married the daughter of Reginald, King of Man.

357. That is Gruffydd and Maredudd ap Cynan.

358. In 1195 the young Llywelyn ab Iorwerth Drwyndwn, with the help of Gruffydd and Maredudd ap Cynan, beat Dafydd ab Owain Gwynedd at the Battle of Aberconwy, and Rhodri, brother of Dafydd, was deposed. Rhodri died the same year.

359. Cp. Rachel Bromwich, *Trioedd Ynys Prydein*, p. 229.

directions but all of about the same size: the Isle of Wight to the
south, Anglesey to the west and the Isle of Man to the north-
west. The first two are near the coast, being divided from it by
narrow straits of sea-water. The third, the Isle of Man, is much
farther away, lying midway between Ulster in Ireland and
Galloway in Scotland.

The island of Anglesey is an arid stony land, rough and un-
attractive in appearance. It is rather like the cantref of Pebidiog,
round St David's, to look at, but in its natural productivity it is
quite different. This island produces far more grain than any
other part of Wales. In the Welsh language it has always been
called 'Môn mam Cymru', which means 'Mona the Mother of
Wales'. When crops have failed in all other regions, this island,
from the richness of its soil and its abundant produce, has been
able to supply all Wales.

You will find much on Anglesey which is worthy of your
attention. I have thought it a good idea to choose a few of these
features and to insert a description of them here. There is, for
example, a stone almost in the shape of a human thigh-bone
which has this extraordinary property, so often proved true by
the local inhabitants, that, however far away it is carried, it
returns of its own accord the following night. Hugh, Earl of
Shrewsbury, who, in the reign of King Henry I, forcibly
occupied the whole island and the adjacent mainland,[360] heard
of the properties of this stone. To test it, he had it attached by
iron chains to another much larger stone and then thrown far
out to sea. Early the next morning, to everyone's astonishment,
they found it back again in its usual place, to which it always
returned. As a result the Earl issued a public edict that no one
from this time onwards should be so presumptuous as to move it
from its place. In another attempt to test the stone, a countryman
had it tied to his own thigh. His leg became gangrenous, but the
stone returned to its place. It is also said that if a couple come to
have intercourse on this spot, or near by, which they do fre-

360. This was Hugh de Montgomery, Earl of Shrewsbury, who, with Hugh
the Fat of Avranches, Earl of Chester, invaded and ravaged Anglesey in
1098.

quently, great drops of sweat drip from the stone. The same thing happens if a man and a woman simply fondle each other there. If they do have intercourse, no child is ever born as a result of what they have done. A little cottage which once stood there is now completely derelict and, as you can see for yourself, the stone is completely surrounded by a wall of rock.

On the same island there stands a stony hill, not very big and not very high. If you stand on one side and shout, no one on the other side can hear you. It is called ironically the Listener's Rock. There is a similar hill in the north of Great Britain, in Northumberland, so called by the English because it is north of the Humber. If a loud horn or trumpet is sounded there on one side, it cannot be heard on the other.

On Anglesey there is also a church dedicated to the holy Saint Tyfrydog. Hugh, Earl of Shrewsbury,[361] who had conquered Anglesey and parts of Wales, shut his dogs up there one night. The next morning he found them all raving mad, and he himself died within a month.[362] Some pirates from the Orkneys made their way into one of the island ports in their long ships. When he heard of their approach, the Earl, who was on a mettlesome horse, dashed wildly into the sea to attack them. Magnus, who was in command of the expedition, stood on the prow of the leading ship and shot an arrow at the Earl, who was completely clad in iron from the top of his head to the soles of his feet, all except for his eyes. The arrow struck his right eye and penetrated his brain, so that he fell mortally wounded into the sea. From where he stood Magnus glared down at the dying man. In his pride and insolence he is said to have shouted: 'Leit loupe,' which is Danish for 'let him leap.' From that moment onwards the English lost their control of Anglesey.[363]

In our own times Henry II, King of the English, led an army

361. Gerald writes 'comes Hugo Cestrensis' in mistake for 'Slopes-buriensis'. This whole paragraph concerns Hugh de Montgomery, Earl of Shrewsbury, not Hugh d'Avranches.

362. This event occurred in 1098 in the church of Llandyfrydog.

363. The invader was Magnus Barefoot, King of Norway, who was raiding Man and Anglesey. Apparently the pirates sailed away immediately after killing Hugh de Montgomery.

into Gwynedd. He was defeated in battle in a narrow wooded pass near Coleshill, that is the hill of coal.[364] He thereupon sent a fleet to Anglesey, and began ravaging and plundering this church of Saint Tyfrydog and other holy places throughout the island. He was punished by God, for the local inhabitants attacked the invaders, few as they were against many and un-armed against those wearing armour. Many of Henry's troops were killed, and many were captured and thrown into chains, for the islanders won a bloody victory.[365] As I have made clear in my *Topography of Ireland*, both the Irish and the Welsh are more prone to anger and revenge in this life than other nations, and similarly their Saints in the next world seem much more vindictive.[366]

Two great noblemen were sent to the island by the King. They were my own uncles: Henry, son of King Henry I and uncle of King Henry II, the child of Nest, the nobly born daughter of Rhys ap Tewdwr, Prince of Dyved in South Wales;[367] and Robert FitzStephen, Henry's brother, but by a different father.[368] Robert was a man who, in our own time, led where others followed, for it was he who soon afterwards invaded Ireland. I have recorded his deeds in my *Vaticinal History*. Henry behaved far too rashly and, with no support from his troops, fell in the

364. This was the Battle of Coed Eulo, fought in 1157. Owain Gwynedd took up his position at Basingwerk. His two sons Dafydd and Cynan pre-pared an ambush in the great forest which stretched from Coleshill to Hawarden. Henry II rode straight into this: Eustace FitzJohn and Robert de Courcy were slain, the King was in grave danger, and Henry of Essex was disgraced, for he dropped the royal standard and ran away. He was accused of treason, beaten in a judicial duel by Robert de Montfort in 1163 and forced to become a monk in Reading Abbey.

365. Henry II had sent a fleet to meet him at Rhuddlan or Degannwy. Instead the ships entered the harbour of Moelfre and the knights began ravaging Anglesey, especially the churches of Llanbedr Goch, Llanfair Mathafarn Eithof and Llandyfrydog. Henry FitzHenry was killed and Robert FitzStephen was wounded.

366. Cp. *The Topography of Ireland*, II.55.

367. Henry FitzHenry was the son of the Princess Nest, Gerald's grand-mother, by King Henry I.

368. Robert FitzStephen was the son of Nest by Stephen, constable of Cardigan. He is mentioned repeatedly in *The Conquest of Ireland*.

THE JOURNEY THROUGH WALES

first line of battle, pierced by a number of spears, to the great grief of his soldiers. Robert was badly wounded and escaped with great difficulty to his ships, abandoning all hope of defence.

Close to Anglesey and almost adjoining it, there is a small island inhabited by hermits, who live in the service of God by the labour of their hands.[369] They are remarkable in that, should they have ever quarrelled with each other for reasons of human frailty, a species of small mice, which abound on the island, consume most of their food and drink, and befoul the rest. As soon as their argument is over, the plague of mice disappears immediately. It is not to be wondered at if God's servants occasionally disagree. Jacob and Esau struggled with each other in Rebecca's womb;[370] and Paul and Barnabas had their differences.[371] The disciples of Jesus disputed as to which of them was the greatest.[372] These are the temptations which assail us frail human beings. Virtue is often made the more perfect by our very weakness, and by tribulation our faith becomes the more constant. In Welsh this island is called Ynys Lannog, which means Priests' Island, because so many of the Saints have been buried there. No women are ever allowed on the island.

On Anglesey we saw a dog which was without a tail. It had not been born that way, but had lost its tail by some accident. All the puppies which descended from it, whether through a bitch or a male dog making no difference, had the same defect from birth. It is a remarkable fact that a fault in the parent should be handed down naturally to all its descendants. In England I once saw a knight called Erchembald, who came from Devonshire. While he was still in his mother's womb, his father refused to recognize him as his own son. For reasons of jealousy, he accused his wife of adultery because he was suspicious of her. At the boy's birth nature settled the argument. As the result of a

369. Priestholm, or Ynys Lannog, took its Welsh name from the mythical Glannog. Gerald spells it Enislannach and gives it a false etymology from 'llan'.

370. Genesis, 25.22.   371. Acts, 15.39.
372. Mark, 10.43.

blow from a lance which he had received in battle, the father had a scar just below his nose in the middle of his upper lip. By some miracle of nature, when the child was born, he, too, had a scar in the same place. I myself saw Erchembald's son, whose name was Stephen, and there is no doubt that he had the same mark. A chance accident had become a natural defect. In the case of Earl Alberic, the son of Alberic, Earl de Vere, I can again bear witness of a natural miracle. When his mother, the daughter of Henry of Essex, was already pregnant, the father did all he could to obtain a divorce from her, because of her father's disgrace.[373] When the child was born, he had a defect in one of his eyes, exactly similar to that which the father had received in an accident. It is possible that physical peculiarities of this sort may be produced in a child because the mother remembers something which she has seen, concentrating on it and thinking of nothing else. I have read of a queen who had a painting of a Negro in her bedroom. She spent much of her time staring at it, with the result that when she had a baby it was black. Quintilian says that this was because of the picture.[374] The same thing happened to the speckled sheep which Laban chose from his flock to give to his nephew Jacob: through the variation in the rods which Jacob set up they brought forth ringstraked lambs.[375] Sometimes a child is marked by something which has greatly affected the father's imagination, for it does not have to be the mother. There is a well known case of a man who, on his way home, saw someone who, by a nervous tic, kept fidgeting himself in front and behind. The man went to bed with his wife and they had intercourse. The tic which he had seen affected him so much that he could not stop thinking about it. The two had a son and,

373. Alberic de Vere III, whom Queen Matilda made 1st Earl of Oxford in 1142, married as his third wife Lucy, daughter of Henry of Essex. When Henry was disgraced in 1157 (cp. p. 189, n. 364), Alberic wanted to rid himself of Lucy, according to Gerald, and alleged that the son whom she was bearing was illegitimate. He died many years later in 1194 and his eldest son, here unborn, became Alberic de Vere IV, 2nd Earl of Oxford.

374. Gerald wrote 'regina ... quam et Quintilianus per picturam excusavit': but I cannot trace the quotation.

375. Genesis, 30.25–42.

from the moment of his birth, he was afflicted with the same nervous convulsion.

Chapter 8
How we crossed the River Conway in a boat.
Dinas Emrys.

When we returned to Bangor from Anglesey we were shown the tombs of Owain Gwynedd and his brother Cadwaladr, who were buried in a double vault in the cathedral by the high altar. Because he had committed public incest with his first cousin, Owain had been excommunicated by the blessed martyr Thomas and remained so until his death. The Bishop of Bangor was therefore ordered to watch for an opportunity of removing his body from the cathedral and to do this as quickly as possible.[376]

We then continued our journey along the coast, with the sea on one side and a steep cliff on the other, until we came to the River Conway, the waters of which are fresh. Not far from the source of the Conway, where the mountains of Snowdonia begin and stretch away to the north, stands Dinas Emrys, meaning the hilltop of Ambrosius, where Merlin made his prophecies, while Vortigern sat beside the pool.[377] There were two Merlins. The one called Ambrosius, who thus had two names, prophesied when Vortigern was King. He was the son of an incubus and he was discovered in Carmarthen, which means Merlin's town, for it takes its name from the fact that he was found there.[378] The second Merlin came from Scotland. He is called Celidonius, because he prophesied in the Calidonian Forest. He is also called Silvester, because once when he was fighting he looked up into the air and saw a terrible monster. He went mad as a result and

376. Owain Gwynedd died on 23 November 1170. He had married as his second wife Cristin, daughter of Gronw ab Owain ab Edwin and thus his first cousin. He refused to give her up and as a result he was excommunicated by Archbishop Thomas. The Bishop of Bangor was Gwion. Cadwaladr died in 1172.

377. Cp. Geoffrey of Monmouth, *The History of the Kings of Britain*, VI.19, and for the prophecies the whole of Bk VII.

378. ibid., VI. 17–18, and Nennius, *Historia Brittonum*, 40–42.

fled to the forest where he passed the remainder of his life as a wild man of the woods.[379] This second Merlin lived in the time of Arthur. He is said to have made more prophecies than his namesake.

I shall pass over in silence what was done by Owain's sons in our own days, when he himself was dead or dying.[380] In their desperate attempts to gain the inheritance, they showed a complete disregard of brotherly ties. I have decided not to omit another event which happened in our own time and which I really must include. Owain ap Gruffydd,[381] Prince of North Wales, had many sons, but only one of them was legitimate.[382] This was Iorwerth Drwyndwn, which is the Welsh for flatnosed. He in his turn had a legitimate son called Llywelyn.[383] At the time of our journey through Wales this Llywelyn, who was then only about twelve years old, began to attack his two uncles, Dafydd and Rhodri, the sons of Owain by his first cousin Cristin. Although they shared between them as their inheritance the whole of Gwynedd except the land of Cynan, and although Dafydd was strongly supported by the English in that he had married the sister of King Henry II, by whom he had a son,[384] in a few years Llywelyn drove them out of almost the whole of Gwynedd. They had their own wealth to draw on

379. Cp. p. 138 and p. 248. Merlin, the son of the incubus, disappears from Geoffrey of Monmouth's story after the miraculous conception of Arthur.

380. Cp. p. 186, n. 358.

381. His full name was Owain Gwynedd ap Gruffydd ap Cynan.

382. By his second wife, Cristin, Owain had Dafydd and Rhodri, and these Gerald counts as illegitimate. Four sons by various women predeceased him: Rhun, Llywelyn, Cadwallon and Cynwrig (cp. p. 186, n. 358). Hywel was the son of an Irish woman called Pyfog. Cynan's mother is not known. This leaves the two legitimate sons, not one, of his wife Gwladus, daughter of Llywarch ap Trahaearn: Iorwerth Drwyndwn mentioned here, and Maelgwn.

383. Iorwerth Drwyndwn married Marared, daughter of Madog ap Maredudd. Their only son was to become Llywelyn Fawr. He was born early in 1173 and so was fifteen in 1188. Llywelyn Fawr married King John's illegitimate daughter Joan c. 1205.

384. Dafydd married Emma of Anjou, half-sister of Henry II, in 1174. Their son was Owain ap Dafydd.

and the support of other rich men, but they were born in incest. Llywelyn was completely destitute of lands and money, but he was legitimate and he could therefore trust in the vengeance of God. He left them nothing but what, in his own magnanimity and on the advice of his good counsellors, he chose to give them, . for he pitied them still and felt some family responsibility for them. This shows how much those who commit adultery and incest are displeasing in the eyes of God.

Chapter 9
The mountains of Snowdonia.

I must not fail to tell you about the mountains which are called Eryri [385] by the Welsh and by the English Snowdon, that is the Snow Mountains. [386] They rise gradually from the land of the sons of Cynan and extend northwards near Degannwy. When looked at from Anglesey, they seem to rear their lofty summits right up to the clouds. They are thought to be so enormous and to extend so far that, as the old saying goes: 'Just as Anglesey can supply all the inhabitants of Wales with corn, so, if all the herds were gathered together, Snowdon could afford sufficient pasture.' To these grazing-grounds Virgil's words can well apply:

> And what they crop by day the shorter night renews,
> Thus feeding all the flocks thanks to its cooling dews. [387]

At the very top of these mountains two lakes are to be found, each of them remarkable in its own way. One has a floating island, which moves about and is often driven to the opposite side by the force of the winds. Shepherds are amazed to see the flocks which are feeding there carried off to distant parts of the lake. It is possible that a section of the bank was broken off

385. Eryri = the haunt of the eagles.
386. Gerald writes 'Snaudune, id est nivium montes' = Snowdonia, not merely the summit, which in Welsh was 'Y Wyddfa Fawr' = Great Burial-place, where Rhita the Giant was buried.
387. Virgil, *Georgics*, 11.201-2 ('carpunt' for 'carpent', 'reponit' for 'reponet').

in times long past and that, bound together in a natural way by the roots of the willows and other shrubs which grow there, it has since become larger by alluvial deposits. It is continually driven from one bank to another by the violent winds, which in so elevated a position never cease to blow, and it can never anchor itself firmly to the shore again. The second lake has a remarkable and almost unique property. It abounds in three different kinds of fish, eels, trout and perch, and all of them have only one eye, the right one being there but not the left. If the careful reader asks me the cause of such a remarkable pheno-menon, I can only answer that I do not know. It is worth noticing that in Scotland, too, in two different places, one to the east and one to the west, the fish called mullet are found in the sea with only one eye. They lack the left eye but have the right one.

There is a remarkable eagle which lives in the mountains of Snowdonia. Every fifth feast-day [388] it perches on a particular stone, hoping to satiate its hunger with the bodies of dead men, for on that day it thinks that war will break out. The stone on which it takes its stand has a hole pierced nearly through it, for it is there that the eagle cleans and sharpens its beak. An eagle is said to know the place where it can find its prey, but not the time. A raven knows the time, but not the place.

Chapter 10
How we travelled through Degannwy, Rhuddlan and the cathedral town of Llanelwy or St Asaph. The quicksand and Coleshill.

We crossed the River Conway, or rather an arm of the sea below Degannwy, leaving on our right the Cistercian monastery of Conway, which is on the western bank of the river. [389] We then

388. Gerald wrote 'qualibet quinta feria'.
389. In 1186 the monks of Strata Florida founded a daughter-house at Rhedynog Felen, not far from Carnarfon. This soon moved to Conway. The words 'leaving . . . river' were added in Version II (c. 1197) and cannot be taken as evidence that the monks had already moved in 1188.

followed the road to Rhuddlan, a fine castle on the River Clwyd, which belongs to Dafydd, Owain Gwynedd's eldest son by his cousin.[390] We were suitably entertained that night by Dafydd himself, who pressed us to stay.

Not far from Rhuddlan, in the province of Tegeingl,[391] there is a spring which not only ebbs and flows like the sea every twenty-four hours but frequently rises and falls at other times, both day and night. Trogus Pompeius says that there is a town belonging to the Garamantes with a spring which alternately runs hot and cold in the night and the day.[392]

In the morning many folk were persuaded to dedicate themselves to Christ's service. From Rhuddlan we travelled the short distance to the small cathedral town of St Asaph or Llanelwy. Mass was celebrated there by the Archbishop. We set out again almost immediately. We passed through a district where there is a rich vein of silver and successful mining-works, and where, by delving deep,

> They penetrate the very bowels of the earth.[393]

We spent the night in the small priory at Basingwerk.[394]

The next morning, not without considerable apprehension, we rode across an extensive quicksand. On our right we passed the forest of Coleshill, the hill of coal. It was there in our own time that Henry II, King of the English, was badly mauled when he made his first assault on Wales. In his youthful ardour and rash enthusiasm he was unwise enough to push on through this densely wooded pass, to the great detriment of his men, quite a few of whom were killed.[395] Henry II invaded Wales three times: first North Wales, here, on this spot; secondly South

390. Cp. p. 193, n. 382.

391. Tegeingl < the tribal name Deceangli.

392. In effect this story is in Saint Augustine, *De civitate Dei*, XXI.5 and again XXI.7. Cp. p. 129, n. 191.

393. Ovid, *Metamorphoses*, I.138.

394. In 1131 Ranulf II, Earl of Chester, established the Abbey of Basingwerk as a house of the order of Savigny. It was transferred to the Cistercians in 1147.

395. Cp. p. 189, n. 364. This was in 1157.

Wales, along the coastal road through Glamorgan and Gower, penetrating as far as Carmarthen and Pencader, which means Cathedral Head, and returning towards Radnor via Elenydd and Maelienydd; [396] and thirdly Powys, near Oswestry. [397] He was unsuccessful in all three of these expeditions, simply because he placed no confidence in the local leaders, who were experienced and familiar with the conditions, preferring to take advice from men who lived far away from the Marches and knew nothing of the habits and customs of the inhabitants.

In every military expedition, just as the craftsman is to be trusted in his own trade, so advice should be sought from those who are resident in the country, who by experience have become familiar with local circumstances and who know the customs and habits of the inhabitants. It is, moreover, to the great advantage of such men that the power of a hostile people, whose implacable enmity and hatred they have incurred by long continuous warfare, should now be weakened or destroyed.

That is what I wrote in my *Vaticinal History*. [398]

In this wood at Coleshill a young Welshman was killed as he tried to make his way through the King's battle-lines. A greyhound which he had with him watched over his master's body for nearly eight days without food. With a fidelity remarkable in a brute beast it defended his corpse from the attacks of other dogs, wolves and birds of prey. [399] What son to his father, what Nisus to Euryalus, [400] what Polynices to Tydeus, [401] what Orestes to Pylades [402] would have shown such affectionate regard? In appreciation of what had happened and as a mark of

396. Cp. pp. 121–2. This was in 1163.

397. This was in 1165. Cp. p. 201, n. 417.

398. This passage is repeated from *The Conquest of Ireland*, II.38. It is repeated a second time in *The Description of Wales*, II.8.

399. This was in 1157. Cp. p. 189, n. 364.

400. Nisus and Euryalus, the two friends who accompanied Aeneas to Italy, perished in the night attack on the Rutilian camp. Cp. Virgil, *Aeneid*, IX.176–502.

401. Statius, *Thebaid*, VII.9 and VIII.664.

402. Orestes, son of Agamemnon and Clytemnestra, was the close friend of Pylades, son of Strophius and Anaxibia, e.g. Ovid, *Remedia Amoris*, 589.

favour to the dog, which had almost died of starvation, the English, who nevertheless hated the Welsh, had the corpse buried with all due ceremony, although it was almost putrid by this time.

Chapter 11
How we crossed the River Dee. Chester.

Below Chester we crossed a ford over the River Dee, which the Welsh call Dwfr Dwy, and so came to Chester itself on the Day of Absolution, the third day before Easter.[403] Just as the River Wye separates Wales from England in the south, near Striguil Castle,[404] so the River Dee divides the two countries in the north at Chester Castle. The local inhabitants maintain that the Dee moves its fords every month and that, as it inclines more towards England or Wales in this change of channel, so they can prognosticate which nation will beat the other or be unsuccessful in war in any particular year. The river has its source in Lake Bala.[405] It is rich in salmon, yet this fish is never found in the lake. You will find it true that the Dee is never swollen by rain but that it often rises when the winds blow.

Chester boasts of being the burial-place of the Holy Roman Emperor Henry V. After having imprisoned Pope Paschal, his earthly and spiritual father, he made penitence for what he had done and went into voluntary exile, ending his days as a saintly hermit in this country, or so they say.[406] In the same way they maintain that King Harold is buried there.[407] He was the last

403. 14 April 1188.
404. Striguil Castle is in Chepstow.
405. The Welsh name is Llyn Tegid. It is also called Pimblemere. Gerald was one of the first to record this name and he wrote Pemmelsmere.
406. Henry V, Holy Roman Emperor, 1081–1125, married Matilda, daughter of Henry I of England, in 1114. He had considerable trouble with Pope Paschal II. He died in Utrecht on 23 May 1125 and was buried in Spier. Walter Map, *De nugis curialium*, has the story that his death was false and that he really went into exile to do penance for his sins. Gerald had heard that he came to Chester. He repeated this in *De Invect.*, VI.25.
407. According to William of Poitiers, William the Conqueror refused to

of the Saxon kings in England and, as a punishment for his perjury, he was defeated by the Normans in pitched battle at Hastings. He was wounded in many places, losing his left eye through an arrow which penetrated it, but, although beaten, he escaped to these parts. It is believed that he led the life of an anchorite, passing his days in constant attendance in one of the local churches, and so came contentedly to the end of life's journey. The real identity of these two persons, which had hitherto been kept secret, was revealed only when they each made their last confession.

In Chester I saw cheese made from deer's milk, something which I had never heard of before. The Countess of Chester, the Earl's mother, kept tame deer.[408] From their milk she made three small cheeses, shaped them in a mould and presented them to the Archbishop.

In this same neighbourhood, in our own days, there was born a deer-cow.

A stag served a cow. From this union there was born a deer-cow. All its forequarters as far back as the groin were bovine; but its rump, tail, legs and hoofs were like those of a deer, and it had a deer's colouring and shaggy hair. It stayed with the herds, for it was more of a domestic animal than a wild one.[409]

Again in our time a bitch near here had a litter by a monkey and produced puppies which were ape-like in front but more like a dog behind. When the warden of the soldiers' quarters saw them, he was amazed at these prodigies of nature. Their deformed and hybrid bodies revolted this country bumpkin. He killed the

---

give Harold's mutilated body to his mother Gytha, Earl Godwine's widow, but ordered William Malet to go and bury it on the sea-shore. Cp. my *The Bayeux Tapestry and the Norman Invasion*, 1973, p. 54. Inevitably there were rumours that Harold had escaped and was living on in obscurity either in Waltham Abbey or in Chester.

408. The Earl was the young Ranulf III, born 1170. He was to marry Constance of Brittany in 1189, but for the moment his widowed mother was acting as his hostess.

409. The passage 'A stag . . . a wild one' is repeated from *The Topography of Ireland*, II.22.

whole lot of them out of hand with a stick. His master was very annoyed when he learned what had happened, and the man was punished. Still in our own lifetime there was to be seen in Chester a deformed woman, who was born without hands. Nature in some sense compensated her for the defect. Her feet were so loosely articulated, her toe-joints being long and easily moved this way and that, that she could sew just as finely as other women. Whatever they do with their hands with scissors and thread, she could do with her feet, despite her deformity, to the great astonishment of all who saw her.

Chapter 12
How we journeyed through Whitchurch, Oswestry, Powys and Shrewsbury.

We observed the feast of Easter with due solemnity in Chester and, as the result of the Archbishop's sermons, many people took the Cross. Then we set out for Whitchurch and Oswestry. As we entered their territory, we were met by the princes of Powys, Gruffydd ap Madog, Elise and others, with a number of their local supporters.[410] Quite a few were persuaded to take the Cross, but most of them had already done so, thanks to the efforts of Reiner, the local Bishop.[411] In the presence of the Archbishop, Gruffydd, the local prince, publicly renounced his cousin Angharad, Owen Gwynedd's daughter, whom, according to the vicious habit of the country, he had long considered as his wife.[412] We spent the night at Oswestry, that is the Tree of Saint Oswald.[413] We were entertained most splendidly and sumptu-

410. Gruffydd Maelor ap Madog ap Maredudd died in 1191. Elise ap Madog was his younger brother.

411. Reiner, Bishop of St Asaph, apparently lived on until 1224.

412. Gruffydd Maelor had married Angharad, daughter of Owain Gwynedd, who was his first cousin.

413. For Gerald this is 'apud Oswaldestroe, id est Oswaldi arborem', and in Welsh Croes Oswallt. It was supposed to be named from the stake on which Penda of Mercia fixed the head of Saint Oswald, King of Northumbria, after the Battle of Maserfield in 642.

ously in the English fashion by William FitzAlan, a hospitable young nobleman, who had himself pressed us to stay.[414]

It had happened in these parts some time before, when Bishop Reiner was preaching the Cross, that a certain rather forceful young man was being pressed very firmly to accept it himself, as many of his friends had already done. 'I will take no notice of what you say,' he answered, 'until, with this spear which I hold in my hand, I have first avenged my master's death.' He was referring to Owain ap Madog, a man of some distinction, who had only recently been maliciously and treacherously murdered by Owain Cyfeiliog, his own first cousin.[415] While he was thus venting his anger and desire for revenge, he brandished his spear with great violence. As he did so, this strong spear broke in pieces and fell to the ground from his two hands. He was left holding nothing but the butt. He was alarmed and terrified by this omen, which he accepted as a sign that he must indeed take the Cross, and this he did without further argument.

In this third district of Wales, which is called Powys, there are some excellent stud-farms. A superb race of blood-stock is now bred there, tracing its descent from the Spanish horses which Robert de Belesme, Earl of Shrewsbury, had gone to some pains to have imported long ago.[416] The horses which are sent out from Powys are greatly prized: they are extremely handsome and nature reproduces in them the same majestic proportions and incomparable speed.

It was here that Henry II, King of the English, entered Powys, at the head of an expedition which was noble and expensive enough, although it achieved nothing.[417] He murdered out of

414. William FitzAlan of Oswestry and Clun died in 1210.

415. Owain Fychan ap Madog ap Maredudd, a younger brother of Gruffydd and Elise, had been murdered at Gwern y Figyn in 1187, not by Owain Cyfeiliog, but by this last's two sons Gwenwynwyn and Cadwallon.

416. Robert de Belesme became Earl of Shrewsbury in 1098. He was dispossessed and sent into exile by Henry I in 1102.

417. This was the campaign of 1165. Although it was August it rained heavily and Henry II's large army was bogged down in the forests and wild uplands. In rage he mutilated twenty-two of his hostages, blinding Cadwallon

hand the hostages whom he had taken, but then was forced to withdraw because of a sudden and unexpected fall of rain. The previous day the leaders of the English army had burnt down certain Welsh churches, with their villages and churchyards. As a result the sons of Owain Gwynedd, supported by a band of young soldiers who were with them, bitterly harangued their father, and his fellow-princes, too, swearing that they would never in future spare any English churches. Everyone present was on the point of agreeing to this, but Owain, who was well known among his peers for his great wisdom and moderation, quelled the tumult. 'I do not agree with you at all,' he said. 'On the contrary, we ought to be pleased with what has happened and rejoice. Unless we have God on our side, we are no match for the English. By what they have done they have alienated Him. He can avenge Himself and us, too, in the most striking way. Let us accordingly promise God devoutly that from this moment on we will pay greater reverence and honour than ever before to all churches and holy places.' On the night which followed these events, the English army, as I have told you already, learned what the wrath of God could bring.

From Oswestry we made our way towards Shrewsbury, round which flows the River Severn. There we stayed for a few days to rest and recover our breath. By the Archbishop's preaching and by the elegant sermons delivered by me, Gerald, Archdeacon of St David's, we persuaded many folk to take the Cross. We also excommunicated Owain Cyfeiliog, because he alone of all the Welsh princes had made no move to come with his people to meet the Archbishop.[418] This Owain was much more fluent in speech than the other Welsh princes and he was well known for the sensible way in which he managed his land. He had frequently opposed the plans of his own leaders and had espoused the cause

---

and Cynwrig, the two sons of Owain Gwynedd (cp. p. 193, n. 382), and Maredudd Ddall, the son of Prince Rhys.

418. Owain Cyfeiliog ap Gruffydd ap Maredudd was so called to distinguish him from Owain Gwynedd ap Gruffydd ap Cynan. Cyfeiliog was the commote in Powys in which the first Owain had been settled by his uncle Madog in 1149.

of Henry II, King of the English, so that he had become a close friend of that King. One day when he was sitting at table with the King in Shrewsbury, Henry passed to him one of his own loaves, to do him honour, as the custom is, and to show a mark of his affection. With the King's eyes on him, Owain immediately broke the loaf into portions, as if it were Communion bread. He spread the pieces out in a row, again as if he were at Holy Communion, picked them up one at a time and went on eating until they were all finished. Henry asked him what he thought he was doing. 'I am imitating you, my lord,' answered Owain. In this subtle and witty way, he was alluding to the well-known avariciousness of the King, who had the habit of keeping church benefices vacant for as long as possible so that he could enjoy the revenues.

At this point I want to stress to you with what equity, prudence and princely moderation three rulers have governed the three parts of Wales in our times: in Gwynedd Owain Gwynedd, son of Gruffydd ap Cynan; in South Wales Maredudd ap Gruffydd, Owain's nephew, who died young;[419] and in Powys this Owain Cyfeiliog. Two other princes were famous for their generosity: Cadwaladr ap Gruffydd in Gwynedd,[420] and Gruffydd ap Madog of Bromfield in Powys.[421] In South Wales Rhys ap Gruffydd deserved high praise for his liberality and independent spirit.[422] In Gwynedd Dafydd ab Owain[423] and in Glamorgan in South Wales Hywel, son of Iorwerth of Caerleon,[424] maintained their good faith and credit by observing a strict neutrality between the Welsh and the English.

419. Maredudd ap Gruffydd ap Rhys, who died in 1155 aged twenty-five, was the older brother of Prince Rhys.
420. Cadwaladr ap Gruffydd ap Cynan died in 1172.
421. Gruffydd Maelor ap Madog ap Maredudd died in 1191. Maelor is the Welsh for Bromfield.
422. Rhys ap Gruffydd ap Rhys, the Prince Rhys, died in 1197.
423. Dafydd ab Owain Gwynedd died in 1203 in exile in England.
424. For Hywel ab Iorwerth of Caerleon see p. 119.

Chapter 13
Our journey over Wenlock Edge, through Bromfield, Ludlow Castle and Leominster, and so back to Hereford.

From Shrewsbury we continued our journey along a rough and narrow road called Malplace,[425] which led to Wenlock Edge. The Archdeacon of Shrewsbury was called Peche[426] and the Dean was a Daiville or De Eyville.[427] It happened in our lifetime that a Jew who was travelling towards Shrewsbury in their company heard the Archdeacon refer casually to the fact that his jurisdiction began in Malplace[428] and stretched as far as Malpas,[429] near Chester. He thought for a moment about the surnames of the Archdeacon and the Dean, and then said wittily: 'It will be a miracle if I ever arrive home safely after travelling in a region where the Archdeacon is Sin, the Dean is called Devil and the archdeaconry stretches from Evil Street to Evil Pass!'

From Wenlock we pressed on via the little priory of Bromfield, the imposing castle of Ludlow and through Leominster, and so came at length to Hereford, leaving Maelienydd and Elfael on our right. We thus described a full circle and returned once more to the place from which we had begun this rather exhausting journey through Wales.

We worked very hard to make a success of our mission. About three thousand men were signed with the Cross, all of them highly skilled in the use of the spear and the arrow, most experienced in military affairs and only too keen to attack the enemies of our faith at the first opportunity. They were all sincerely and warmly committed to Christ's service. If only the Crusade itself had been prosecuted with an urgency and forethought on a par with the enthusiasm and devotion of these men whom we collected! By the judgement of God, which is sometimes hard to

425. Gerald writes 'Malam plateam'.
426. Richard Peche was Archdeacon of Shrewsbury c. 1180–c. 1190.
427. Gerald writes 'Diabolus'.
428. This is again 'Mala platea'.
429. 'Malum passum.'

understand but never unjust, it was delayed because of the
dilatory behaviour of the Holy Roman Emperor,[430] the dis-
sensions which arose between our own kings,[431] and the unexpected and premature death of the King of Sicily,[432] who had
been foremost among all the great rulers in supplying the Holy
Land with corn and provisions in its moment of maximum
distress. The consequences of his death were that a violent
quarrel ensued among our kings over their rights to the suzerainty,
the roads across Europe were left unprotected, the faithful
beyond the sea suffered severely from hunger and want, and they
were left surrounded by their enemies in their moment of need.

These things are allowed to happen, since adversity tempers
our understanding and we gain strength from our very weakness,
just as gold is refined by smelting. As Saint Gregory the Great
said: 'When we are opposed in our good intentions, this is a test
of our endurance, not a judgement against us. Who does not
agree that it was a good thing that Paul sailed to Italy, even
though he suffered so much in the shipwreck? Amidst the
violence of the waves, the ship of his heart stood firm.'[433]

Chapter 14
A description of Baldwin, Archbishop of Canterbury.

I have given you a brief account of Baldwin's mission, which was,
so to speak, a prelude to his going on the Crusade. You must not
think it out of order if I now describe his physical appearance
and personality. He was a swarthy man, with an honest, venerable face, only moderately tall, of good physique and inclined to
be thin rather than corpulent. He was modest and sober, and of
great abstinence and self-control, so that very little criticism was
ever levelled against him. He was a man of few words, slow to

430. Frederick I Barbarossa was drowned in Cilicia on 10 June 1190 and
the German contribution to the Third Crusade was small.
431. There was much hostility between Richard I of England and Philippe
Auguste of France.
432. William II, King of Sicily, died in 1189.
433. Saint Gregory the Great, *Epistolae*, IX.122.

anger, temperate in all his feelings and emotions, 'swift to hear, slow to speak, slow to wrath'.[434] He had studied humane letters[435] from his early youth and had always seen himself as one of our Lord's servants. By the purity of his personal life he was an inspiration to his people. Of his own free will he resigned the position of Archdeacon to which he had been promoted in the canonical hierarchy,[436] and, steadfastly scorning the pomps and vanities of this world, with saintly devotion he became a monk in the Cistercian order.[437] In his way of life he had always been more of a monk than anything else, and within a year he was elected as Abbot. A few more years passed, and he was promoted to be Bishop and then Archbishop.[438] He had been faithful in small things: now he was given far-reaching authority. However, as Cicero said, 'Nature has produced nothing which is wholly perfect.'[439] When he was raised to great power, he was unable to cast off the gentle and innate kindliness which he had always shown as a private individual. He sustained his people with his staff, instead of castigating them with his stick, acting more like a mother offering her breasts than a father wielding his rod, and he was publicly criticized for his laxness. His kindness of heart made him weak and ineffectual, and the Church lost all sense of discipline. He was clearly a better monk than abbot, a better abbot than bishop and a better bishop than archbishop. When Pope Urban wrote to him, he addressed him as follows: 'Urban, Bishop, servant of the servants of God, sends greetings to the most fervent monk, the warm Abbot, the luke-warm Bishop, the negligent Archbishop, etc.'[440]

The quarrel between the throne and the priesthood over the

434. James, I.19.
435. From here to the end of the chapter is repeated, with some changes, in V.S.R., XXIX.
436. This was in Exeter.
437. This was in the Abbey of Ford in Devonshire.
438. Baldwin was consecrated Bishop of Worcester on 10 August 1180. He was enthroned as Archbishop of Canterbury on 19 May 1185.
439. Cicero, De inventione, II.1 ('omni ex parte' for 'omnibus ex partibus').
440. This is quoted again in De iure, I (Rolls Series, Giraldi Cambrensis opera, Vol. III, p. 124), and in Spec., II.25. The Pope is Urban III.

Church in England seems never-ending, and tyranny in the island is becoming worse and worse. All the same, despite Baldwin's lack of leadership, it is clear that, in our own lifetime, Saint Thomas, his predecessor [but one] as Archbishop of Canterbury, won a glorious victory for the freedom of the Church by fighting on until he was martyred.[441] Then the malady returned and the disease gathered new strength. God's decisions are sometimes hard to understand, but they are never unjust.[442] All that the great martyr so successfully achieved when he put an end to the innumerable malpractices inflicted by the throne upon the Church of God, only after long altercations, it is true, and by paying for it with his life, all this He has allowed to be wasted through the slackness, not to say cowardice, of the man who first replaced him. Although it grieves me immensely to say it or to hear it said, this has proved an immense setback to His own Church. It all could have been made good again in the days of Saint Thomas' second successor, but not by behaving feebly when faced with unrepentant evil. This was no time for patient dissimulation. What was needed was firm handling and straight talking, if need be up to the point where blood would flow a second time. When the martyr's first successor lay on his death-bed,[443] only a short time before he died, he heard in the night as he slept this horrifying cry come down from heaven: 'You have torn my Church asunder! I in my turn will uproot you from the earth!' If only it had been from the land of the dying instead of from the land of the living, from the land which we leave empty behind us and not from the Promised Land, from the land of sweat and travail, not from the land of sweetness and light! God's decisions are indeed hard to understand, but they are never unjust. If only Saint Thomas had been succeeded, in the first place or the second, it makes no odds, by an archbishop who fought with all his might to defend what the holy martyr won in the face of such resistance, what he held on to so manfully,

441. Saint Thomas Becket, Archbishop of Canterbury, was murdered in his own cathedral on 29 December 1170.

442. This is a favourite statement of Gerald's: cp. pp. 74, 170.

443. Richard of Dover, the successor to Saint Thomas, died in 1184.

at the loss of his life, it is true, but with such benefit to all, leaving his earthly crown battered, but winning in heaven a crown untarnished and incorruptible, the English clergy, so miserably suppressed and unceasingly downtrodden, would still rejoice in the freedom which is its due. That freedom is now lost to the Church, probably for all time, certainly for as long as the present line of kings endures, unless more priestly blood is shed. We have thrown it away deliberately, but God in His wisdom has already planned, or so I believe, for it to flower again in the future: so that in the end this freedom by miracles may be reborn, through a new steadfastness on the part of some archbishop, the undying glory of the martyred Thomas and a fresh fervour of the faithful, torpid so long and lulled to sleep; and our strong faith, now grown so cold, may once again burn bright with all the fire of Christian charity, its dying embers blown to flame by renewed signs and prodigies, as if by bellows and the winnowing-fans.

This second successor to the martyr, having heard of the insults offered to our Saviour and the holy Cross, lately attacked by Saladin, took the Cross himself.[444] He obeyed Christ's call by accepting the task of preaching the Crusade with great vehemence both near and far. Then he set out on his journey, taking ship at Marseilles, crossing the deep sea and landing without mishap in the port of Tyre. He made his way to Acre, where he found our troops besieging and besieged. When he joined them, many of our soldiers, and, indeed, almost all of them, were in a state of desolation and despair, for they had been deserted by their leaders. They were worn out by waiting so long for supplies, sadly afflicted by hunger and want, and made ill by the inclement climate. He was about to end his own life there in the Holy Land: but he gave them such succour as he could, by gifts and presents, by his words and by the example of his own life, embracing them in Christian charity.[445]

444. Saladin beat the Templars and the Hospitallers at Tiberias in May 1187. In July he beat the united Christian army at Hittin. On 2 October 1187 he entered Jerusalem.
445. Archbishop Baldwin died at the siege of Acre on 19 November 1190.

May He who is alone 'the way, the truth, and the life',[446] the way without offence, the truth without shadow of doubt, the life without end, teach their 'hands to war' and their 'fingers to fight'; and direct their journeyings, their lives and every act into the way of truth, together with the whole body of God's elect, to the glory of His name and the palm of faith which He Himself planted. Amen.

Here ends Gerald's Journey.

446. John, 14.6.

THE DESCRIPTION OF WALES

FOR STEPHEN, ARCHBISHOP OF CANTERBURY, [447]
THE FIRST PREFACE TO THE DESCRIPTION OF
WALES.

Some time ago I set out in three books *The Topography of Ireland*, with its natural curiosities until then unknown, taking three years over the task. Next I completed *The Vaticinal History of the Conquest of Ireland*, in two books, which took me two years. Then I published the Archbishop's *Journey through Wales*, thus preventing his far from easy mission from ever being forgotten. I now propose, in this short treatise, to write a *Description of Wales*, my own country, and to describe the Welsh people, who are so very different from other nations. These new fruits of my labours I dedicate to you, Stephen,[448] Archbishop of Canterbury, so famous both for your piety and for your learning,[449] just as I did my *Journey*. It may seem an insignificant gift to one so distinguished, because, of course, you are used to receiving such fine presents.

Some, indeed, take exception to what I have done. In their concern for me, they see me as a painter who, rich in precious

447. This is the reading of Version II. Version I had 'Huberto', instead of 'Stephano'. MS T, the lost variant of Version I, the prefaces of which are copied out in *Symb. Elect.*, III, had only the heading 'In Kambriae descriptionem praefatio prima'.

448. Version I had 'Huberte'. MS T, the lost variant of Version I, had 'Hugo Lincolniensis episcope'.

449. So Version II and MS T. Version I had 'quem discretio pariter morumque venustas laudabilem reddunt' in MS V, and the same without 'pariter' in MS N. As the Rev. James F. Dimock says in the notes to his edition, p. 155: 'The alteration, from the *discretion* and *polished manners* in the address to Hubert, to the *religion* and *learning* in that to St Hugh and Stephen Langton, is worth remarking.'

colours, the master of his art, a second Zeuxis,[450] strives with great skill and industry to portray a humble cottage or some other subject by its very nature base and ignoble, when they were expecting me to paint a temple or a fine palace. They are surprised that, from all the great and striking subjects which the world can offer, I choose to extol in my writings and to adorn with all the flowers of my rhetoric those rugged countries, Ireland, Wales and Britain.

Others again rebuke me more harshly, saying that I should not squander on such insignificant themes the gifts which God has given me, or sit up late at night wasting my time praising princes, who have no interest in literature and are so tight-fisted, and who refuse to recommend or reward works of great literary merit. They add, moreover, that these talents which I have so lavishly received from God, as if from heaven above, should be used for sublime subjects and for God's greater glory. 'Every good gift and every perfect gift'[451] comes from God, as from a never-failing source, and it should be used in praise of Him from whose bounty nothing offered from a grateful heart can ever go unrewarded. Distinguished writers have composed and published admirable histories of other countries. I have been inspired to think that it may be a useful and praiseworthy service to those who come after me if I can set down in full some of the secrets of my own native land. By writing about such humdrum matters I can rescue from oblivion those deeds so nobly done which have not yet been fully recorded. What could my own crude and feeble efforts add to the Fall of Troy,[452] to Thebes[453] or Athens,[454] or to what happened on the coast of Latium?[455] Besides, just to do again what had been done already

450. Zeuxis, the Greek painter who fl. 424–400 BC, was famous for his portrayal of inanimate objects. Cp. Cicero, De inventione, II.1, which Gerald had just been reading, as n. 439 proves.

451. James, I.17.

452. This is no doubt from Virgil, Aeneid, Books II–III, rather than from Homer's Iliad.

453. This is no doubt from the Thebaid of Statius, which Gerald knew well.
454. This is no more than a general statement.
455. Virgil, Aeneid, Book VII.

would be to achieve nothing. That is why I have decided instead to write the history of my own country. It is a tale as yet untold, I have worked hard at it, and it will cause pleasure to my own relations and my countrymen. Later on perhaps I can slowly and painstakingly advance to greater things. From such small beginnings you can judge with what success I shall turn to some major work, when opportunity offers. I must, of course, apply myself unstintingly to that, but in the meantime I have other things to write. It is surely better that I should have practised my skills on these *œuvres de jeunesse*, rather than let my days slip gently by in idleness and sloth, the root-cause of all evil. I have enjoyed writing these minor works, preludes and preambles, if you will, to the great treasure-house of that Wisdom which transcends all Wisdom,[456] the quintessence of all knowledge, which shows us how to rule and to inspire mankind. All other arts must follow on behind, as if attendant on their Queen, and worship where she treads. Thus in my early days I have been laying foundations firm and strong on which to build this structure, reserving my later years, with God to lead me on and if my life is preserved, for the composition of a great masterpiece upon a theme both sacred and sublime. As the poet says:

Firm faith should be the theme of our maturer years.[457]

Thanks to it I have the right to linger on the way, but only for a season: for in the writing of that major work I am prepared to live my life and die.[458]

Before beginning my masterpiece, I must ask for a short respite, to give me time to lay before my public the little book on *How to Bring Up a Prince* which I have so often promised them,[459] this *Description of Wales* which I hold in my hand, and my *Topography of Britain*.[460]

456. Gregory of Nazianzus, *Orationes*, II.16. It is quoted again in *Symb. Elect.*, XXIV.

457. Lucan, *Pharsalia*, VIII.282.

458. What does he mean? The *Symbolum Electorum?* The *Gemma Ecclesiastica?*

459. *How to Bring Up a Prince* was not finished until 1216.

460. *The Topography of Britain* was never written. Gerald often refers to it

For the subject which I am now treating I have often had to consult Gildas. Of all the British writers he seems to me to be the only one worth copying. He puts on parchment the things which he himself saw and knew. He gives his own strong views on the decline and fall of his people, instead of just describing it. His history may not be all that polished, but at least it is true. It is Gildas, then, whom I, Gerald, propose to follow. I only wish I could emulate his life and ways; but at least I can imitate what he tried to do, with more understanding perhaps than literary skill, more in my soul than by my pen, more in my enthusiasm than by my style, more in my life than by my works.[461]

THE SECOND PREFACE. TO THE SAME.[462]

When, amid my various literary pursuits, I first applied the keen edge of my studious mind to the writing of history, I decided to begin by describing to the best of my ability my own country and the regions adjacent to it, so that I should not appear ungrateful to my native land. Once I had made this gesture, I planned, with God to lead me on and if my life were preserved, to proceed in orderly fashion to more advanced and maybe more useful matters. A number of famous men, whom I have met and who are known to me personally, show such contempt for literature that they are in the habit of immediately locking up in their cupboards the excellent works which I present to them, condemning them, as it were, to perpetual imprisonment. This present little book will shortly be placed in your hands. I therefore beg you, you who are so distinguished, not to allow these fruits of my industry, which have such need of publicity, to be shut up in the dark. Like my previous book, this one has been

---

as an eventual companion volume to *The Topography of Ireland* and *The Description of Wales*.

461. The *De excidio et conquestu Britanniae* of Gildas was written c. 550.

462. Version I has only 'Ad eundem'. MS T, the lost variant of Version I, the prefaces of which are copied out in *Symb. Elect.*, III, had 'In Kambriae descriptionem praefatio secunda'.

written for you. It is modest enough, but it may well prove acceptable to someone in the future. Will you please be generous enough to make sure that it is widely publicized, so that its merits may become known? I shall consider myself sufficiently rewarded for my trouble if you will withdraw a moment from your prayers and other pressing occupations and read it yourself. Failing that, perhaps you will ask someone to read it to you. Nowadays no one ever pays for books: and I do not seek or expect any other reward. Among men in high places there seems to be a conspiracy against authors. There would, of course, be nothing all that extraordinary if a man like you, who excels all others now alive by his virtues, by his abilities, both natural and acquired, his irreproachable morals and his munificence,[463] were able to distinguish himself by his generosity, a virtue which others have long since abandoned. If I wanted to sing your praises in one short pithy sentence, I would apply to you the lines which Martial wrote about Trajan when he was serving under Diocletian:

> You should be praised for this, that in bad times
> You have been good, despite your captain's crimes.[464]

When he wanted to praise that great man's character, Virgil wrote about Maecenas:

> You're powerful, famous, you have great friends in need,
> But no one saw you do an unkind deed.[465]

Men criticize me,[466] especially those who call themselves my friends, because I am so keen on literary pursuits that I pay too

463. All this rings a trifle false when one remembers that it was applied in turn to Hubert, Saint Hugh of Lincoln and Stephen Langton.

464. Martial, *Epigrams*, XII.6.11, adapted. Martial has the second line, but for the first 'Nunc licet, et fas est: sed tu sub principe duro ...'

465. According to the Rev. James F. Dimock, in the notes to his edition, p. 162, n. 4, this is taken from what is printed in Scaliger's *Catalecta Virgilii* (1617, p. 95) as 'C. Pedonis Albinovani in Maecenatis obitum elegeia', with 'clarus' here for 'carus'.

466. From 'Men criticize me ...' to the end of the Second Preface is copied with minor variations from *The Conquest of Ireland*, Introduction, except for the quotation from Horace.

little attention to the things of this world and my own personal affairs, with the result that I am slow to gain promotion. There is no respect paid any more to authors, they say, whether they are historians or poets. Now that our leaders are no longer literate, no one, they say, has any more time for humane letters. If you want to become famous today, you must try some other approach. All this I accept. I have no doubt about it at all, for it is obviously true. Our princes collect round them men of little principle and their courts are full of people on the make. Only ambitious men study any more for the Law or enter the Church. For all that,

Each man must follow his own bent.[467]

As far as I am concerned, ever since I was a boy, I have been inspired by a love of literature, and the art of writing has had a peculiar attraction for me. I have always had a great thirst for knowledge, and I have pursued my researches into the works of nature farther than most of my contemporaries. For the benefit of those who will come after, I have also rescued from oblivion some of the remarkable events of our own times. This cannot be achieved without great labour, but I have enjoyed doing it. The research-work necessary if one is to find out just what really happened is not at all easy. Even when one has discovered the truth in all its detail, there still remains the task of ordering one's facts, and this is difficult, too. To maintain a correct balance from beginning to end, and, indeed, throughout the whole course of one's narrative, and to exclude all irrelevant material, is not easy. Then there is the problem of the choice of words and expressions, and of how to perfect one's style, if one wants to write well. It is one thing to set out the course of events in proper sequence, but you still have the difficult problem of deciding what words to use and how best to express what you want to say. Writing is an exacting business. First you decide what to leave out, and then you have to polish up what you put in. What you finally commit to parchment must face the eagle eye of many readers, now and in the future, and at the same time

467. Virgil, *Bucolics*, II.65.

run the risk of meeting hostile criticism. The words one speaks
fly off on the wind and are heard no more: you can praise or
condemn, but it is soon forgotten. What you write down and then
give to the world in published form is never lost: it lasts for ever,
to the glory or ignominy of him who wrote it. As Seneca says:
'The critical reader mulls over what is said well and what is ill-
expressed, enjoying them both, for he is looking for faults. He
wants to find good things which he can praise, but he is only too
ready to laugh at anything ridiculous.'[468] To this the poet adds:

> He picks on what is bad, is prompt to sneer,
> And soon forgets the good he should revere.[469]

Among the pursuits which we should most admire, there are
other things to be said in favour of the studious life. 'History,'
says Seneca again, 'is the recording of past events, the testimony
of the ages, the light of truth, a living memory, a guide for
conduct and a reminder of what happened long ago.'[470] I find
this sort of work the more attractive in that it seems to me to be
more praiseworthy to write something worth quoting oneself
than simply to keep on quoting other people, and better to be
admired by others for one's own compositions than to be a sound
critic of what others have composed. It is good to praise others,
but it is better to be praised by them. I am strengthened and
encouraged by these pleasing thoughts: I would rather be like
Jerome than Croesus; to riches themselves I prefer the man who
scorns them. This, then, is my joy and my delight. My modest
way of life suits me better than any rich living could do; I prefer
my honest poverty to affluence which I do not want. What one
owns must always perish, but what I have will live. Possessions
pass away, but my skills live for ever. Fame I prefer to money, I
would rather have glory than wealth.

468. This is not Seneca but Sidonius Apollinaris, *Epistolae*, III.14, repeated
here with considerable variation.
469. Horace, *Epistolae*, II.2.262–3.
470. This is not Seneca but Cicero, *De oratore*, II.9.

HERE BEGIN THE CHAPTER-HEADINGS OF
GERALD THE WELSHMAN'S BOOK
The Description of Wales

Book 1

1. The first book deals with the length and breadth of Wales, its natural features and its rugged surface.
2. The whole of Wales is divided into three parts.
3. The genealogy of the Welsh Princes.
4. The number of cantrefs, royal palaces and cathedral sees in Wales.
5. The noble rivers which divide Wales and mark its boundaries, and the two mountain-ranges from which they take their source.
6. The fertility of Wales and its attractiveness.
7. The origin of the names Cambria and Wales.
8. The nature, manners and customs of the Welsh people. Their boldness, agility and courage.
9. Their frugality and parsimony.
10. Their hospitality and eating-habits.
11. How the Welsh cut their hair, take care of their teeth and shave off their beards.
12. Their natural acumen and shrewdness. Their musical instruments, florid rhetoric and originality when speaking in public.
13. Their choral music and part-singing.
14. Their witticisms and play on words.
15. Their boldness and confidence in speaking up for themselves.
16. Welsh soothsayers, who behave as if they are possessed.
17. Their respect for noble birth and ancient genealogy.

18. How they received the true religion long ago, their piety and their devotion to the Christian faith.

The chapter-headings of Book II

1. In Book II the inconstancy and instability of the Welsh are considered; and their failure to keep their word or carry out their promises.
2. They live on plunder and have no regard for the ties of peace and friendship.
3. Their weakness in battle: how shamefully and ignobly they run away.
4. Their desire to own land and the quarrels between brothers which ensue.
5. The greediness of the Welsh and the demands which they make on people.
6. The crime of incest, and the abuse by which church livings are both shared and handed down from father to son.
7. The sins of the Welsh, through which they lost first Troy and then Britain.
8. How the Welsh can be conquered.
9. How the Welsh should be governed once they have been conquered.
10. How the Welsh can best fight back and keep up their resistance.

BOOK I

Chapter I[471]
The length and breadth of Wales, its natural features and its rugged surface.

Cambria is called Wales nowadays, that having become its usual name, although it is a foreign word and not really correct.[472] It is two hundred miles long and about one hundred miles wide. It takes some eight days to travel the whole length, from the mouth of the River Gwygir in Anglesey to Portskewett in Gwent.[473] In breadth it stretches from Porth-mawr, that is the Great Port, near St David's, to Rhyd-helyg,[474] the Welsh for Willow Ford, called Walford in English, this being a journey which lasts four days. Because of its high mountains, deep valleys and extensive forests, not to mention its rivers and marches, it is not easy of access. The Britons who were left alive took refuge in these parts when the Saxons first occupied the island, and they have never been completely subdued since, either by the English or the Normans. Those who retreated to the southern corner of the island could not continue their resistance, for their territory has no natural protection. It is called Cornwall, after their leader Corineus.[475] There was a third group of Britons left un-

471. The chapters are numbered in the chapter-headings as given on pp. 218-19, but not at the beginning of each individual chapter.

472. There is much debate about the origin of the words 'Cymry' and in Latin 'Cambria'. Juvenal, *Satires*, VIII.249, has 'Cimbros', but they were Germanic. A tribal name 'Combroges' has been suggested. Wales < Wallia. Cp. *Desc.*, I.7, p. 254.

473. Gerald has 'Yoiger', variant 'Horger', and 'portum Eskewin'. Cp. Rachel Bromwich, *Trioedd Ynys Prydein*, p. 228, with 'Phorth Wygyr y Mon' and 'Porth Ys(g)ewin yg Gwent'.

474. Gerald has '*Ridhelic*', variants '*Rid helig*', '*Rithelic*'.

475. Cp. Geoffrey of Monmouth, *The History of the Kings of Britain*, I.12.

conquered, and these occupied Brittany, in southern Gaul.[476]
They were moved there by the tyrant Maximus, long before the
fall of Britain.[477] Their young soldiers supported Maximus in
many hard battles, and in gratitude the imperial authorities gave
them these lands which stick out from Gaul.

Chapter 2
Wales is divided into three parts.

From time immemorial Wales has been divided into three more
or less equal parts. When I say equal I mean in value rather than
in size. These are Gwynedd, or North Wales; South Wales,
called in Welsh Deheubarth,[478] which really means Right-Hand
Wales, a sub-section of which, containing seven cantrefs, has
been given the name of Demetia or Dyved; and Powys, which is
in the middle and stretches eastwards. The reason for this three-
fold division is as follows. Rhodri Mawr, or Roderick the Great,
who ruled over all Wales, had three sons, Merfyn, Anarawd and
Cadell.[479] Rhodri divided Wales between them. He gave North
Wales to Merfyn, Powys to Anarawd and South Wales to Cadell.
The people agreed to this last arrangement, and so did all three
brothers, for, although South Wales was by far the largest region,
it was much the least attractive, for it was ruled by a great number
of local chieftains, called 'uchelwr' in Welsh, who were in
constant rebellion and hard to control.[480] Cadell's brothers predeceased him and in the end he ruled over all Wales.[481] So did
his successors down to the time of Tewdwr.[482] Tewdwr's suc-

476. Gerald writes 'Armoricum australis Galliae sinum'.
477. This is the Maximianus of Geoffrey of Monmouth, *The History of
the Kings of Britain*, V.12–16.
478. For Deheubarth, cp. p. 94, n. 97.
479. Rhodri Mawr inherited Gwynedd from his father Merfyn Frych in
844. He died in 878. His three best known sons were Anarawd who died in
916, Cadell who died c. 909 and Merfyn who died in 904. There were three
others, Aidan, Meuruc and Morgant.
480. The word 'uchelwr' = high man.
481. Neither of these statements is true. Gerald may have believed them,
or he may have been trying to support the Prince Rhys.
482. Again, this is not true.

cessors in their turn were, like him, rulers of the whole of Wales:
Rhys ap Tewdwr, Gruffydd ap Rhys and Rhys ap Gruffydd,
who is the present prince.[483]

Chapter 3
The genealogy of the Welsh Princes.

This is the line of descent of the Princes of South Wales: Rhys
ap Gruffydd, Gruffydd ap Rhys, Rhys ap Tewdwr, Tewdwr ap
Cadell, Cadell ab Einon, Einon ab Owain, Owain ap Hywel Dda
or Hywel the Good, Hywel ap Cadell, Cadell ap Rhodri Mawr.
In short the Princes of South Wales descend from Cadell ap
Rhodri Mawr.[484]

The Princes of North Wales trace their descent from Merfyn
in the following way: Dafydd ab Owain, Owain ap Gruffydd,
Gruffydd ap Cynan, Cynan ab Iago, Iago ab Idwal, Idwal
ap Meurig, Meurig ab Anaudreg, Anaudreg ap Merfyn, Merfyn
ap Rhodri Mawr.[485]

483. The later princes of the line of Deheubarth certainly descended from
Cadell. Rhys ap Tewdwr died in 1093, his son Gruffydd ap Rhys ap Tewdwr
in 1137, and his grandson, Rhys ap Gruffydd ap Rhys, the Lord Rhys, who
plays such a big part in *The Journey through Wales*, in 1197.

484. This line of descent of the rulers of Deheubarth is correct. Hywel
Dda, the son of Cadell, died c. 950. Owain ap Hywel Dda died c. 988. Einon
ab Owain died in 984. The dates of the deaths of Cadell ab Einon and Tewdwr
ap Cadell are not known. Then the descent follows as in the previous footnote.

485. The line of descent of the rulers of Gwynedd, called here by Gerald
'Nortwallia', is wrong at the beginning. They start, not from Merfyn, but
from Anarawd ap Rhodri Mawr. Idwal Foel ab Anarawd died in 942.
Meurig ab Idwal Foel died in 986. Idwal ap Meurig died in 996. Iago ab
Idwal died in 1039. The date of the death of Cynan ab Iago is not known.
Gruffydd ap Cynan died in 1137. Then come Owain Gwynedd ap Gruffydd
who died in 1170, and Dafydd ab Owain Gwynedd who married Emma,
half-sister of Henry II, was dispossessed by Llywelyn Fawr in 1197 and
lived the rest of his life in England, dying in 1203. Apart from beginning
wrongly with Merfyn, Gerald has introduced Afandreg, whom he spells
wrongly Anaudrech, and who was a daughter of Merfyn, in the place of
Idwal Foel ab Anarawd. It is a tangled skein.

Anarawd had no children. As a result the Princes of Powys do not descend from Rhodri Mawr.[486]

You have to bear in mind that the Welsh bards, singers and jongleurs kept accurate copies of the genealogies of these princes in their old manuscripts, which were, of course, written in Welsh. They would also recite them from memory, going back from Rhodri Mawr to the time of the Blessed Virgin Mary,[487] and then farther still to Silvius, Ascanius and Aeneas.[488] They then continue the line back to Adam himself. I have deliberately shortened my family-trees and omitted all this, because I felt that genealogies so protracted and remote might seem ridiculous to many of my readers.

Chapter 4
The number of cantrefs, royal palaces and cathedral sees in Wales.

South Wales contains twenty-nine cantrefs, North Wales twelve and Powys six. Three of these last are now occupied by the English and the Normans, for the county called Shropshire was formerly part of Powys. The place where Shrewsbury Castle now stands used to be called Pengwern, which means the Head of the Alder Grove.

There used to be three royal palaces in Wales: Dinevor in South Wales, formerly at Caerleon-on-Usk, but now moved; Aberffraw in North Wales; and Pengwern in Powys.[489] Wales now contains fifty-four cantrefs in all. Cantref or cantred, a word made up from 'cant' meaning a hundred and 'tref' meaning a

486. Gerald is now in a muddle. Anarawd certainly had children, as set out in the previous footnote. Gerald means that the rulers of Powys do not descend from Merfyn, and that is correct. The line of Owain Cyfeiliog went back to Bleddyn who died in 1075 and before him to Cynfyn ap Gwerstan.

487. There has been much argument about this rather surprising statement, but it is there in all the manuscripts: 'ad beatam Virginem'.

488. Silvius, the son of Ascanius, himself the son of Aeneas.

489. Cp. Rachel Bromwich, *Trioedd Ynys Prydein*, Triad 85, with Caerleon-on-Usk, Celliwig and Penrhyn Rhionydd.

THE DESCRIPTION OF WALES

vill, is a term used in both Welsh and Irish for a stretch of land which contains a hundred vills.

There are four cathedral sees in Wales. St David's, in South Wales, is on the Irish Sea. Its patron saint is the Archbishop David. In former times this was the metropolitan see and contained twenty-four cantrefs.[490] Nowadays it has twenty-three only, for Erging, called Archenfield in English, which used to be in the diocese of St David's, is now in that of Llandaff. The see of St David's had twenty-five archbishops in succession. Since the removal of the pallium it has had twenty-four bishops. If you want to know their names, the order in which they came and how the pallium was removed, you must look in my *Journey through Wales*.[491]

The see of Llandaff is also in South Wales, on the Severn Sea and near Cardiff Castle. Bishop Teilo is its patron saint.[492] It contains five cantrefs and a quarter of another one, called Senghennydd.[493]

The see of Bangor is in North Wales, between Anglesey and the mountains of Snowdonia. Abbot Daniel is its patron saint.[494] It contains some nine cantrefs.

In North Wales, too, is the tiny cathedral of St Asaph.[495] Powys makes up this diocese. Bishop Asaph is its patron saint. It contains about six cantrefs.

Chapter 5
The noble rivers which divide Wales and mark its boundaries, and the mountain-ranges from which they take their source.

Wales is divided by a number of fine rivers which mark its boundaries. They take their source from two different mountain-ranges: Elenydd in South Wales, which the English call Moruge,

490. Cp. p. 159, n. 255. 491. *The Journey through Wales*, II.1.
492. Cp. p. 126, n. 184.
493. Senghennydd in Glamorgan is now Eglwysilan.
494. Cp. p. 184, n. 348. 495. Llanelwy in Welsh.

because of the marshlands on its summits;[496] and Eryri in North Wales,[497] called Snowdon in English, meaning the Snow Mountains. These last are so extensive and so rich in pasture-land that, if all the herds in Wales were driven together, Snowdon could feed them for a very long time. In Snowdonia there are two lakes, one of which has a floating island, while the other is filled with one-eyed fish. I have told you about these in *The Journey through Wales*:

It is worth noticing at this point that in Scotland, too, in different places, one to the east and one to the west, the fish called mullet are found in the sea with only one eye. They, too, lack the left eye but have the right one.[498]

The Severn, which is a noble river, rises in the Plinlimmon mountains. It flows round Shrewsbury Castle, then by Bridgnorth Castle, on through the city of Worcester and then through Gloucester, with its iron-works. A few miles below Gloucester it runs into the Severn Sea, which takes its name from it. For many years this river formed the boundary between Cambria and Loegria, or Wales and southern England. It took its Welsh name of Hafren from that of a girl, the daughter of Locrinus, who was drowned there by her stepmother.[499] The Latin aspirate has changed into *S*, just as happens when Greek words are borrowed by Latin, and so we now say Sabrina, or Severn. Other examples of this are 'sal' for 'hal', 'semi' for 'hemi', 'septem' for 'hepta'.[500]

The River Wye rises in these same Plinlimmon mountains. It flows by the castles of Hay and Clifford, through the city of Hereford, by Wilton Castle and Goodrich, through the Forest of

496. Elenydd is supposed to be derived from the River Elan. These hills are now called Plinlimmon, or Pumlumon in Welsh. No one knows where Gerald found the word 'Moruge', which is no doubt cognate with 'marais' MF < 'mariscus' VL. Cp. p. 178, n. 325.

497. Eryri = the haunt of the eagles.

498. This is repeated from *The Journey through Wales*, II.9.

499. Cp. Geoffrey of Monmouth, *The History of the Kings of Britain*, II.5, where the girl is called Habren.

500. Cp. pp. 135–6.

Dean, which is full of deer and where iron-ore is mined, and so comes to Striguil Castle,[501] below which it enters the sea. It forms the modern boundary between England and Wales.

The Usk takes its source, not from Plinlimmon, but from the mountains of Cantref Bychan. It flows by the most important castle in Brecknockshire, called Aberhonddu, which means the Honddu Falls,[502] for it is there that the Honddu joins the Usk. Any place where one river joins another is called 'aber' in Welsh. Then it passes Abergavenny Castle and Usk Castle, flows through Caerleon, the ancient City of the Legions, and enters the Severn Sea not far from Newport.

The River Rhymney rises in the Brecknockshire mountains. It flows by Rhymney Castle and through Rhymney Bridge, and then enters the sea. From the same range of mountains comes the Taff. It runs rapidly through the cathedral city of Llandaff, to which it gives its name, comes out at Cardiff Castle and so enters the sea.

The River Avon comes down from the mountains of Glamorgan, running between the two famous Cistercian monasteries of Margam and Neath. The River Neath rises in the Brecknockshire mountains, flows by Neath Castle and then enters the sea. Both of these rivers form the most dangerous quicksands.

The River Tawe also has its source in the mountains of Brecknockshire. It flows by Abertawe Castle, called Swansea in English. The Loughor runs into the sea at Loughor Castle and the Gwendraeth at Kidwelly. The Tywi, another fine river, comes down from Plinlimmon, separates Cantref Mawr from Cantref Bychan, flows by Llandovery Castle, Dynevor Castle and Carmarthen Castle, and enters the sea at Llanstephan Castle. Dynevor is where the royal palace of South Wales used to be: it is well protected by its site and surrounded by woods. Carmarthen is where Merlin was discovered, hence its name.[503]

501. Striguil Castle is in Chepstow.
502. Gerald writes 'Aberhotheni' and 'Hotheni'. Aberhonddu is Brecon.
503. Cp. Geoffrey of Monmouth, *The History of the Kings of Britain*, VI.17. Carmarthen < 'caer' + 'maridunum'.

The River Taff rises in the Prescelly Mountains, not far from Whitland Abbey. It flows by St Clears Castle and runs into the sea near Abercorran or Laugharne.

From the same mountains come the two Cleddau streams. Between them is the region called Deugleddyf, which is named after them. One runs by Llawhaden Castle and the other through Haverfordwest, and so they join the sea. Deugleddyf means Two Swords in Welsh.

Another fine river which rises in Plinlimmon is the Teifi. This flows down from the upper part of Cantref Mawr and Cardiganshire, not far from the pasturelands of the rich monastery of Strata Florida. Lower down it divides Cardiganshire from Dyved and runs into the Irish Sea. This is the only river in Wales which has beavers. If you want to read about their remarkable habits, you must look in *The Journey through Wales*. There are more fine salmon there than in any of the other Welsh rivers. It is possible that *The Description of Wales* may fall into the hands of many readers who do not possess *The Journey through Wales*. I have therefore decided to repeat here the account of the many curious habits of the beaver which you could find in my other book.

I thought[504] that it would be useful to include a paragraph or two at this point about the habits of these animals: the way in which they convey their building materials from the woods to the water; with what artistry they construct their dams in the middle of rivers from the materials which they have collected; how they protect their dwellings in Western countries and in the East against those who hunt them; and a word about their tails, which are fish-like, so to speak, rather than what one would expect in a land animal. Beavers build their castle-like lodges in the middle of rivers. They have an extraordinary method of conveying and carting timber from the woods to the water, for they use other beavers as waggons. The beavers of one team gnaw down the branches, and then another group has the instinct to turn over on their backs and to hold this wood tightly against their bellies with their four feet. Each of these last grips a branch in its teeth which sticks out on either side. A third group

504. The next five paragraphs, 'I thought that ... taken for fish', are repeated from *The Journey through Wales*, II.3.

holds tightly on to this cross-branch with their teeth and pulls the animal in question along backwards together with its load. Anyone who witnesses this manoeuvre cannot fail to be impressed. Badgers use a not dissimilar device when they are cleaning out their sets, which they arrange to their satisfaction by digging into the soil and scraping at it with their paws. It is remarkable that in both species of animals there are to be found slaves which are prepared to accept a debasement of their natural habits and to suffer at the same time a certain wear and tear of the skin on their backs.

There in some deep and tranquil bend of the river the beavers piece together with such skill the logs of wood which form their lodge that no drop of water can easily enter and no storm however violent do harm to it or loosen it. They have no reason to fear any attack, except that of us human beings, and even we must bring our weapons shod with iron. When they are building a lodge, they bind the logs together with willow-wands. The number of storeys placed one above the other varies according to the rise in the water-level which they foresee. They plan their construction so that it just protrudes from the water, with connecting doorways inside to lead from one storey to another. Whenever they have decided that it is necessary, they can keep a lookout from the top and watch the rising waters when the river is in spate. As the years pass and the willow-wands keep on growing, the dam is constantly in leaf and becomes, in fact, a grove of willow-trees, looking like a natural bush from the outside however artificially constructed it may be within.

The beaver can remain in the water as long as it chooses; and when under the water it can hold its breath,[505] as do toads and hairy seals which last creatures mark the ebb and flow of the tide by the alternate smoothness and roughness of their fur. These three species of animals live indifferently under the water or in the air. They have short legs, a broad body and no tail to speak of,[506] or at the best very short ones, being made rather in the shape of moles or badgers. It is worth noting that the beaver has only four teeth, two at the top of the mouth and two below. These teeth are very broad and sharp, and the animal uses them to cut with, as if they were an adze. Near their lodges they build underground hiding-places in the river-bank, carefully pro- tected retreats which they dig into the dry earth. When the hunter comes to prise the beaver out and strives his hardest to poke sharpened poles down into its den, the creature hears the attack and knows that

505. Cp. p. 175, n. 310.   506. Cp. p. 175, n. 311.

danger threatens. It retreats as quickly as it can to the protection of its dam; but first, while still in the river-bank, it stirs up the water all round the entrance to its hole, scraping at the earth with its feet to form a muddy mixture, thus making the clear transparent river all thick and foul. In this way, by its own stratagem it finds an answer to the wiles of its enemy, who is standing on the bank above, holding his three-pronged spear and waiting for the beaver to spring out.

In Eastern countries, when the beaver finds that it cannot evade the dogs which are following it by its scent, it saves itself by self-mutilation. By some natural instinct it knows which part of its body the hunter really wants. The creature castrates itself before the hunter's eyes and throws its testicles down. It is because of this act of self-castration that it is called 'castor' in Latin.[507] If a beaver which has already lost its testicles is hard pressed a second time by the hounds, it rushes to the top of a hillock, cocks up one of its hind-legs and shows the hunter that the organs which he is really after have already been cut off. In his oration *Pro Scauro*[508] Cicero says of beavers: 'They ransom themselves by cutting off that part of their bodies for which they are most commonly pursued.' Juvenal says the same:

> This beast
> Himself a eunuch makes, but saves his life at least,
> Without his testicles.[509]

So does Saint Bernard:

> The beaver saves his life by offering at full speed
> Those vital organs which the lustful hunters need.[510]

In order to save its skin, which is much sought after in the West, and in the East that medicinal part of its body which is so greatly prized there, the beaver thus does what it can to escape from the traps laid by the hunter, giving evidence of remarkable instinct and cunning, but even so not saving itself completely. Beavers have broad short tails, thick, like the palm of the hand, which they use as a rudder when they are swimming. All the rest of their body is hairy, but this part is smooth and slippery, and, like the seal's tail, completely without hair. They are very common in Germany and the Arctic regions; and there, in times of fasting, the great leaders of the Church eat these tails instead of fish, accepting them for their flavour and their colouring, for in this, they say, they could be taken for fish.

507. Cp. p. 176, n. 312.   508. Cp. p. 176, n. 313.
509. Cp. p. 176, n. 314.   510. Cp. p. 176, n. 315.

The Ystwyth rises in the same mountains of Plinlimmon. It flows through the upper parts of Penweddig in Cardiganshire and then enters the sea below Aberystwyth Castle.

The Dovey,[511] which is a fine river, has its source in the snow-clad mountains of Snowdonia. For a considerable part of its course it divides South Wales from North Wales. From the same mountains comes the great River Mawddach, which flows through Traeth Mawr and Traeth Bychan, two tracts of sea-sand, one large, one small. In the same way the Dysynni and the Artro run through Merioneth and the land of Cynan. The Conway flows down from the northern bastion of Snowdon and joins the sea below Degannwy Castle. The Clwyd has its source on the flanks of the same mountain. It flows by Rhuddlan Castle and so comes to the sea. The Dyfrdwy, called the Dee by the English, springs from Lake Bala, runs through Chester, leaves Coleshill Wood and Basingwerk far away on its right, passes near a rich vein of silver, and where it joins the sea forms a dangerous quicksand. It marks the northern border between Wales and England, just as the Wye is now the southern border.

Chapter 6
The fertility of Wales and its attractiveness.

The southern part of Wales, Cardiganshire and more especially Dyved, is particularly attractive because of its flat fields and long sea-coast. Gwynedd in the north is better defended by nature. The people who live there are more robust and the soil is richer and more fertile. If all the herds in Wales were driven together, the mountains of Snowdonia could supply them with pasture. In the same way Anglesey is so productive that it could supply the whole of Wales with corn over a long period. That is why Anglesey is called in Welsh 'Môn mam Cymru', which means the Mother of Wales.

Merionethshire and the Land of Cynan is wilder and less accessible than the other regions. The men of that part of Wales

511. For Gerald the Dovey is 'Devi fluvius'. In modern Welsh it is the Dewi.

are very skilful with their long spears. Those of the south, especially Gwent, use the bow to great effect.

It is thought that the Welsh language is richer, more carefully pronounced and preferable in all respects in North Wales, for that area has far fewer foreigners. Others maintain that the speech of Cardiganshire in South Wales is better articulated and more to be admired, since it is in the middle and the heartland of Wales. In both Cornwall and Brittany they speak almost the same language as in Wales. It comes from the same root and is intelligible to the Welsh in many instances, and almost in all. It is rougher and less clearly pronounced, but probably closer to the original British speech, or so I think myself. In the same way, in the southern parts of England, and especially in Devon, the speech is nowadays purer than elsewhere. It may well be that it retains more features of the original language and the old ways of speaking English, whereas the northern regions have been greatly corrupted by the Danish and Norwegian invasions. You have some proof of this and, indeed, you can be quite sure about it, for you will find that, when Bede, Rhabanus Maurus, King Alfred and many other such people wrote in English, they used this particular dialect.[512]

Chapter 7
The origin of the names Cambria and Wales.

Cambria took its name from the leader Camber,[513] who was the son of Brutus. Brutus was a descendant of Aeneas, his father being Silvius and his grandfather Ascanius. It was Brutus who led the last of the Trojans to this western island, after they had been held captive in Greece. He ruled them peacefully for many years, and, when he died, he gave his name to the country and the

512. Bede, of course, was a Northumbrian, Alfred was born in Wantage and Rhabanus Maurus of Fulda became Bishop of Mainz. A ll in all, this does not make much sense.

513. All this paragraph except the last two sentences is taken bodily from Geoffrey of Monmouth, *The History of the Kings of Britain*, II.1.

people. He divided the kingdom of Britain between his three sons. To Locrinus, his eldest son, he gave the middle part, from the Humber to the Severn, and this was called Loegria after him. To his youngest son, Albanactus, he gave the land north of the Humber, which thus took the name of Albania. To Camber, his second son, he bequeathed the territory west of the Severn, now known as Cambria. Just as the correct name of the country is Cambria, so the people should be called Cymry or Cambrenses. Some say that their language is called Cymric, the 'lingua Kambrica', from 'cam Graecus', which means Crooked Greek because of the similarity of the two tongues, caused by their long stay in Greece.[514] This is arguable and quite possible, but I do not think that it is the correct derivation.[515]

The name Wales does not come from that of a leader called Walo, or from a queen called Gwendolen, as we are wrongly told in Geoffrey of Monmouth's fabulous *History*,[516] for you will find neither of these among the Welsh who ever lived. It is derived from one of the barbarous words brought in by the Saxons when they seized the kingdom of Britain. In their language the Saxons apply the adjective 'vealh' to anything foreign, and, since the Welsh were certainly a people foreign to them, that is what the Saxons called them. To this day our country continues to be called Wales and our people Welsh, but these are barbarous terms.

That is enough about the size of the country, its rugged surface, the family trees of its princes, where its rivers spring

514. This is another memory of Geoffrey of Monmouth, *The History of the Kings of Britain*, I.16. Writing of his mythical Brutus he says: 'Brutus then called the island Britain from his own name, and his companions he called Britons. His intention was that his memory should be perpetuated by the derivation of the name. A little later the language of the people, which had up to then been known as Trojan or Crooked Greek, was called British, for the same reason' (Penguin Classics, p. 72). Geoffrey's words are: '... loquela gentis quae prius troiana sive curvum grecum nuncupabatur ...' Gerald wrote: 'Eorum autem qui Kembraec, linguam Kambricam, a Kam Graeco, hoc est, distorto Graeco ... dictam asserunt ...'

515. Nor do I. Cp. p. 220, n. 472.

516. This is the Gwendolen of Geoffrey of Monmouth, *The History of the Kings of Britain*, II.3-6.

from and the etymology of its two names. I shall now begin to tell you about the character and peculiarities of the people.

Chapter 8
The nature, manners and customs of the Welsh. Their boldness, agility and courage.

The Welsh people are light and agile. They are fierce rather than strong, and totally dedicated to the practice of arms. Not only the leaders but the entire nation are trained in war. Sound the trumpet for battle and the peasant will rush from his plough to pick up his weapons as quickly as the courtier from the court. One cannot say here, as elsewhere, that

> the farmer's toil is one long round.[517]

They plough the soil once in March and April for oats, a second time in summer, and then they turn it a third time while the grain is being threshed. In this way the whole population lives almost entirely on oats and the produce of their herds, milk, cheese and butter. They eat plenty of meat, but little bread. They pay no attention to commerce, shipping or industry, and their only preoccupation is military training. They are passionately devoted to their freedom and to the defence of their country: for these they fight, for these they suffer hardships, for these they will take up their weapons and willingly sacrifice their lives. They esteem it a disgrace to die in bed, but an honour to be killed in battle. They agree with the words of the poet:

> Turn peace away,
> For honour perishes with peace.[518]

No wonder they cherish their freedom, for these are the descendants of

> The sons of Aeneas who fought for liberty.[519]

517. Virgil, *Georgics*, II.401.
518. Cp. Lucan, *Pharsalia*, II.101, but it is not that.
519. Virgil, *Aeneid*, VIII.648 ('Eneadae' for 'Aeneadae').

It is a remarkable fact that on many occasions they have not hesitated to fight without any protection at all against men clad in iron, unarmed against those bearing weapons, on foot against mounted cavalry. They are so agile and fierce that they often win battles fought against such odds. In where they live and in their behaviour they are rather like the men described by the poet:

> These people who live in the north
> Are happy in their error. Bravely they rush forth
> To meet their foe. To them mankind's besetting dread
> Of death means nothing. Cowards live, but they instead
> Will be reborn tomorrow [520]

They use light weapons which do not impede their quick movements, small leather corselets, handfuls of arrows, long spears and round shields. They wear helmets and sometimes iron greaves. Their leaders ride into battle on swift mettlesome horses which are bred locally. Most of the common people prefer to fight on foot, in view of the marshy uneven terrain. The horsemen will often dismount, as circumstance and occasion demand, ready to flee or to attack. They go barefoot or else wear boots made from untanned leather roughly sewn together. By marching through the deep recesses of the woods and climbing mountain-peaks in times of peace, the young men train themselves to keep on the move both day and night. In peace they dream of war and prepare themselves for battle by practising with their spears and their arrows. At this point I must tell you what, in our own lifetime, Henry II, King of the English, wrote back in reply to Manuel Comnenus, Emperor of Constantinople, when that ruler asked for information about the geographical conditions, way of life and things worth seeing in the island of Britain. Manuel sent envoys to deliver his letter.[521] Among other things in Henry's reply the following sentence is worth quoting: 'In one part of the island there is a race of people called the Welsh who are so brave and untamed that, though unarmed themselves, they do not hesitate to do battle with fully armed

520. Lucan, *Pharsalia*, I.458–62.
521. Manuel Comnenus, born 1120, Emperor of Constantinople 1143–80.

opponents.'[522] They are so ready to shed their blood for their country that

> For fame they sacrifice their lives.[523]

This is all the more surprising because the wild animals in the island are not particularly fierce, whereas the Welsh show no sign of losing their ferocity. These wild animals are very numerous, especially stags and deer, because they are rarely hunted. In the northern parts of the island, in the Peak District,[524] stags have become so numerous in our own lifetime that they have been known to charge hunters with their hounds and trample them to death.

Chapter 9
Their frugality and parsimony.

The Welsh are given neither to gluttony nor to drunkenness. They spend little on food or clothes. Their sole interest in life consists of caring for their horses and keeping their weapons in good order, their sole preoccupation the defence of their fatherland and the seizing of booty. From morning to evening they eat nothing, devoting their whole energy to what business they have in hand and their whole day to their affairs, leaving everything else to chance. In the evening they eat a modest meal. If food is short or if they have none at all, they wait patiently for the next evening. Neither hunger nor cold can deter them. They spend the dark and stormy nights in observing the movements of their enemies.

522. Where does the quotation end? Gerald says simply 'inter cetera hoc'. The line from Virgil, the wild animals and the excursion to the Peak District all seem more typical of Gerald than of Henry II.

523. Virgil, *Aeneid*, V.230 ('velint' for 'volunt').

524. Gerald has 'in borealibus insulae finibus versus Pech'.

Chapter 10
Their hospitality and eating habits.

In Wales no one begs. Everyone's home is open to all, for the Welsh generosity and hospitality are the greatest of all virtues. They very much enjoy welcoming others to their homes. When you travel there is no question of your asking for accommodation or of their offering it: you just march into a house and hand over your weapons to the person in charge. They give you water so that you may wash your feet and that means that you are a guest. With these people the offering of water in which to wash one's feet is an invitation to stay. If you refuse the offer, it means that you have only dropped in for refreshment during the early part of the day and do not propose to stay the night.

In Wales young people go about in groups and families, under their chosen leader. They spend their time in exercise and in practising with their weapons, with the result that they are ready at a moment's notice to protect their homeland. They enter anyone's house without asking permission, as if it were their own.

Guests who arrive early in the day are entertained until nightfall by girls who play to them on the harp. In every house there are young women just waiting to play for you, and there is certainly no lack of harps. Here are two things worth remembering: the Irish are the most jealous people on earth, but the Welsh do not seem to know what jealousy is; and in every Welsh court or family the menfolk consider playing on the harp to be the greatest of all accomplishments. When night falls and no more guests are expected, the evening meal is prepared, varying according to what the house has to offer, and to the number and importance of the men who have come. You must not expect a variety of dishes from a Welsh kitchen, and there are no highly seasoned titbits to whet your appetite. In a Welsh house there are no tables, no tablecloths and no napkins. Everyone behaves quite naturally, with no attempt whatsoever at etiquette. You sit down in threes, not in pairs as elsewhere, and they put the food in front of you, all together, on a single large trencher containing enough for three, resting on rushes and green grass. Sometimes they serve the main dish on bread, rolled out large and thin, and baked fresh each day. In ancient books you will find these thin breads called 'lagana'.[525] That noble youth from whom the Welsh claim their descent [526] and whose mode of living they still in part maintain ate his food off thin bread in the same way:

'How sad!' Ascanius cried. 'We've scoffed the platters, too!'[527]

The whole family waits upon the guests, and the host and hostess stand there making sure that everything is being attended to. They themselves do not eat until everyone else has finished. If there is a shortage of anything, it will be they who go without. Finally the time comes to retire to rest. Alongside one of the walls is placed a communal bed, stuffed with rushes, and not all that many of them. For sole covering there is a stiff harsh sheet, made locally and called in Welsh a 'brychan'.[528] They all go to bed together. They keep on the same clothes which they have worn all day, a thin cloak and a tunic, which is all they have to keep the cold out. A fire is kept burning all night at their feet, just as it has done all day, and they get some warmth from the people sleeping next to them. When their underneath side begins to ache through the hardness of the bed and their upper-most side is frozen stiff with cold, they get up and sit by the fire, which soon warms them up and soothes away their aches and pains. Then they go back to bed again, turning over on their other side if they feel like it, so that a different part is frozen and another side bruised by the hard bed.

525. The word 'lagana' seems to be a Latin neuter plural here; cp. 'simila ... ad laganas faciendas', *The Account-book of Beaulieu Abbey*, ed. S. F. Hockey, 1975, p. 291.

526. Ascanius, the son of Aeneas. Cp. p. 223, n. 488.

527. Virgil, *Aeneid*, VII.116 from memory ('mensas consumpsimus' for 'etiam mensas consumimus').

528. Gerald has 'qui et vulgari vocabulo brachan dicitur'.

Chapter 11
How the Welsh cut their hair, take care of their teeth and shave off their beards.

Both the men and the women cut their hair short and shape it round their ears and eyes. Like the Parthians the women cover their heads with a flowing white veil, which sticks up in folds like a crown. Both sexes take great care of their teeth, more than I have seen in any country. They are constantly cleaning them with green hazel-shoots and then rubbing them with woollen cloths until they shine like ivory. To protect their teeth they never eat hot food, but only what is cold, tepid or slightly warm. The men shave their beards, leaving only their moustaches. This is not a new habit, but one which goes back to time immemorial. You can find it in the book which Julius Caesar wrote about his exploits, for there we read: the Britons 'shave their whole body except their upper lip'.[529] Sometimes they shave their heads, too, so that they can move more freely, for, when they run through the forest groves, they want to avoid the fate of Absalom.[530] Of all the people I have seen the Welsh are the most particular in shaving the lower parts of the body.

It is Julius Caesar, too, who tells us that, when they were about to fight a battle, the Britons used to daub their faces with shiny warpaint. They made themselves so bright and ghastly that the enemy could hardly bear to look at them, especially if the sun was shining.[531]

Chapter 12
Their natural acumen and shrewdness.

The Welsh are very sharp and intelligent. When they apply their minds to anything, they are quick to make progress, for they

529. Caesar, *De bello Gallico*, V.14, from memory ('abrasa' for 'rasa', 'praeter superius labrum' for 'praeter caput et labrum superius').
530. II Samuel 18.9.
531. Caesar, *De bello Gallico*, V.14, reference only.

have great natural ability. They are quicker-witted and more shrewd than any other Western people.

When they play their instruments they charm and delight the ear with the sweetness of their music. They play quickly and in subtle harmony. Their fingering is so rapid that they produce this harmony out of discord. To save time I repeat what I have written about the three peoples under the heading of 'Musical Instruments' in my *Topography of Ireland*:

It is remarkable[532] how [the Irish] maintain a musical balance while moving their fingers so rapidly. They play their various instruments with consummate artistry, keeping them in close harmony. The resulting melody is complete and satisfying, played softly but at great speed, with what one can only call a smooth unevenness or a discordant concord. Whether they are playing in fourths or fifths, they always begin with B-flat and then come back to it at the end, so that the whole melody is rounded off sweetly and merrily. They begin a movement with much subtlety and end it in the same way. They play the grace notes with great abandon, above the heavier bourdon of the bass strings, and so produce a gay and lilting melody. The essence of all art is to conceal art:

> When hidden, art delights; when obvious, it offends.[533]

It follows that music which gives profound and indescribable pleasure to those who listen carefully and can enjoy its subtleties, can only offend the ears of the inattentive instead of gratifying them. They see, but they do not perceive; they hear, but they do not understand. To such an unappreciative audience, music is no more than a confused and discordant noise, causing them tedium and boredom.

[The Welsh] play three instruments, the harp, the pipe and the crwth.[534]

In their lawsuits, official speeches and civic addresses they use almost all the devices of public speaking: putting a case,

532. Repeated from *The Topography of Ireland*, III.11.

533. Ovid, *Ars Amatoria*, II.313, from memory ('lateat, prosit' for 'latet ars, prodest', and 'ferat ars' for 'affert').

534. This is the 'crwth', from 'crotta', a stringed instrument, whence 'crowder'.

inventing pretexts, shaping an argument, refuting an opponent, supporting a contention.

In their narrative poems and their declamations they are so inventive and ingenious that, when using their native tongue, they produce works of art which are at once attractive and highly original, both in the choice of words and the sentiments expressed. You will find many poets in Wales, bards, as they call them, who devote their energies to this kind of composition:

> Stern bards who many an austere epic song have sung.[535]

More than any other rhetorical figure they delight in alliteration, and especially that which links together the initial letters or syllables of words. The two peoples, both English and Welsh, make such play with this literary device when they are trying to speak elegantly, that any pronouncement is condemned as rough and uncouth if it is not so polished and adorned. Here are two examples in Welsh:

> Dychaun Dyu da dy unic.[536]
> Erbyn dibuilh puilh paraut.[537]

Here are three in English:

535. Lucan, *Pharsalia*, I.499, from memory ('concreti fuderunt' for 'securi fudistis').

536. 'God can provide for the lonely man.' In MS D the words are glossed: 'i.e. facere potest bene Deus unico; ac si diceret, hominem potest juvare Deus, etsi solus sit'. In Modern Welsh this would be 'Dichon Duw da i unig'. I am grateful to Professor A. O. H. Jarman of the University College of Cardiff for help with this note and the following one.

537. 'Guard thyself against evil desire', or possibly, in a more general sense, 'behave prudently even in the face of a frenzied attack'. In MS D the words are glossed: 'i.e. contra insensatum sensum praepares'. Professor Jarman refers me to three variants in different collections of medieval Welsh proverbs: 'hurth pob amhuyll puyll syd oreu', Black Book of Chirk; 'Reit wrth amwyll pwyll barawt', White Book of Rhydderch; and 'reit wrth amhwyll pwyll parawt', Red Book of Talgarth; cp. *Bulletin of the Board of Celtic Studies*, Vol. III, pp. 11 and 27. Gerald, of course, is not really interested in the content of these lines. He quotes them solely as examples of alliteration's artful aid.

God is togedere gamen and wisdom.[538]
Ne halt nocht al sor isaid, ne al sorghe atwite.[539]
Betere is red thene rap, and liste thene lither streingthe.[540]

It is much the same in Latin literature, where you often find this figure. Virgil wrote:

Of such calamities Cassandra sang.[541]

It was Virgil again who addressed the following lines to Augustus:

A boyish girl? Dame Nature is inscrutable!
You're born, a girlish boy, a boy, but beautiful.[542]

In no other of the languages which I know is this device of alliteration used as much as in English and Welsh. It is remarkable, for instance, that French, which is so richly adorned with other figures, should never make use of this particular one, whereas other languages are full of it.[543] I cannot believe that the Welsh and the English, so different from each other and so antagonistic, could ever consciously agree about the rhetorical

538. 'Merriment and wisdom go well together.' In MS D the line is glossed: 'i.e. bona est una cum jocunditate sapientia'. I am grateful to Mr Thorlac Turville-Petre for help with this note and the two following ones.

539. 'There is nothing to be gained by voicing every complaint, or blaming someone else for every misfortune.' In MS D the line is glossed: 'i.e. non attinet omne malum suum alii revelare, nec omne alterius incommodum ei exprobare'. Cp. O. Arngart, *The Durham Proverbs, from Durham Cathedral MS B. III.32*, Lunds Universitets Årsskrift, Lund, 1956, No. 19.

540. 'Deliberation is better than haste, and cunning than misapplied strength.' In MS D the line is glossed: 'hoc est, plus valet deliberatio quam praepropera festinatio, et plus moderatio quam violentia'. Cp. Layamon's *Brut*, 17210–11, and *Ancrene Riwle*, 268/27. Cp. B. J. and Helen W. Whiting, *Proverbs, Sentences and Proverbial Phrases*, 1968, for other parallels, G12, S485, S500, R65, L38.

541. Virgil, *Aeneid*, III.183.

542. According to the Rev. James F. Dimock, in the notes to his edition, p. 188, n. 6, these two lines appear on p. 177 of Scaliger's *Catalecta Virgilii*, 1617, addressed not to Augustus but 'In puerum formosum' ('dubitet' for 'dubitat'). Cp. p. 215, n. 465.

543. This is not true, although OF certainly did not use alliteration as much as contemporary English.

device. It must be just habit: the facile jump from like to like has appealed to each of them separately. It pleases the ear and so it has been used more and more down the years. In his book *On Elocution* Cicero writes about those who speak naturally with no attempt at polish: 'There are people who, when they read good speeches or poems, admire the speakers or the poets without understanding why they are moved. They are incapable of appreciating what it is that pleases them so much, the link with the context or the artistry which lies behind it.' [544]

Chapter 13
Their choral music and part-singing.

When they come together to make music, the Welsh sing their traditional songs, not in unison, as is done elsewhere, but in parts, in many modes and modulations. When a choir gathers to sing, which happens often in this country, you will hear as many different parts and voices as there are performers, all joining together in the end to produce a single organic harmony and melody in the soft sweetness of B-flat.

In the northern parts of Great Britain, across the Humber and in Yorkshire, the English who live there produce the same symphonic harmony when they sing. They do this in two parts only, with two modulations of the voice, one group humming the bass and the others singing the treble most sweetly. The two peoples must have developed this habit not by any special training but by age-old custom, by long usage which has made it second nature. It is now become so common with them both and so firmly established that you never hear a simple melody sweetly sung, for it is always in many parts, as with the Welsh, or in two, as with the English of the north. What is even more remarkable, small children sing in parts, and tiny babies do so, too, from the moment they stop screaming and first begin to sing.

As the English in general do not adopt this way of singing, but

544. Cicero, *De Elocutione*, 'sicut Tullius, in libro *De elocutione*': but I cannot trace the quotation.

only those who live in the north, I think that these latter must
have taken their part-singing, as they did their speech, from the
Danes and Norwegians, who so often invaded those parts of the
island and held them longer under their dominion.

Chapter 14
Their witticisms and plays on words.

In Wales courtiers and even family-men in their own homes are
often very funny in what they say. This amuses their guests and
gains them the reputation of being great wits. They make the
most droll comments, some of which are very clever. They love
sarcastic remarks and libellous allusions, plays on words, sly
references, ambiguities and equivocal statements. Some of these
are just for fun, but they can be very bitter. I thought you would
like me to give you some examples to show you what I mean.

Tegeingl is the name of a cantref in Gwynedd.[545] Dafydd ab
Owain[546] ruled over it, but it had once belonged to his brother.
It was also the name of a woman who had been the mistress of
each in turn. Someone said: 'I don't think David should have
Tegeingl. His brother had Tegeingl first.'

One day when he was going on a journey, Rhys ap Gruffydd,
Prince of that region, went into St David's cathedral to pray.
Quite a few of his men were with him. Mass was said and they
made their oblations. A young man came up to Rhys in church
and threw himself at his feet. With everyone listening, he
announced that he was Rhys' son. He wept and begged that the
truth of what he had said might be tested by the trial of white hot
iron. When this was reported to Rhys' family, one of his two
sons, who had just left the cathedral, replied: 'Well, I am not
surprised. Some gave gold and some gave silver. This man had
neither, so he gave what he had, which was iron.' He was
referring to the man's poverty.

A group of people were talking about a house, which was so

545. The name Tegeingl is probably derived from the tribal name
Deceangli.
546. Dafydd ab Owain Gwynedd. He had many brothers.

strongly built that it could never be entered by force. 'Yes, the house is well-protected,' said one. 'We shall never be able to get at the larder, always assuming that there has ever been any food in it.' In this play on words he was referring to the meanness of the householder. The house was unassailable, and so was the food kept in it.

Someone made a similar remark about a housewife well known for her parsimony: 'I have only one thing to hold against her,' he said. 'She puts too little butter in her salt.' This was an example of the part for the whole. By such subtle play on words the speaker meant that there was too little butter, but he seemed to imply that there was too much salt.

In the *Saturnalia* of Macrobius you will find recorded the witticisms of certain philosophers and other great men. When Cicero 'saw his son-in-law Lentulus, who was a very short man, wearing a very long sword, he asked: "Who attached my son-in-law to that sword?" ' [547] He, too, was using the part for the whole.

It was Cicero again who, 'when he saw a half-length portrait' of his brother Quintus Cicero, 'drawn with enormous features and holding a shield, remarked: "Half of my brother is bigger than the whole!" ' [548]

When the sister of Faustus had just spent the night with a fuller, her brother said: 'I find it odd that she still has her beauty-spot, seeing that she has slept with a fuller.' [549]

Antiochus was on the parade-ground showing Hannibal all the troops and weapons which he had assembled for the attack which he was about to launch on the Romans. ' "Hannibal," said he, "do you think that these are enough for the Romans?" Hannibal inspected the recruits and found them very raw. "Well," he answered, "the Romans are greedy, but I think they will be well satisfied with these." ' That was a sarcastic and highly critical reply. King Antiochus was asking if Hannibal thought that his men would be equal to the task in hand, but Hannibal was already seeing them as captives. [550]

547. Macrobius, *Saturnalia*, II.3.
549. ibid., II.2.

548. ibid.
550. ibid.

Chapter 15
Their boldness and confidence in speaking up for themselves.

Nature has endowed [the Welsh] with great boldness in speaking and great confidence in answering, no matter what the circumstances may be, and even in the presence of their princes and chieftains. This is true of all of them, from the highest to the lowest. We see that the Romans and the Franks had the same facility. It is not true of the English, nor of the Saxons from whom they have descended, nor, indeed, of the Germans. It is no good saying that the reason for this defect in the English is the state of servitude which they now endure. The Saxons and Germans, who still enjoy their liberty, have the same weakness, so that the argument does not hold. The Saxons and the Germans derive their cold nature from the frozen polar regions which lie adjacent to them. In the same way the English, although they now live elsewhere, still retain their outward fairness of complexion and their inward coldness of disposition from what nature had given them earlier on. The Britons, on the contrary, transplanted from the hot and arid regions of the Trojan plain, keep their dark colouring, which reminds one of the earth itself, their natural warmth of personality and their hot temper, all of which gives them confidence in themselves.

They sail the seas, climes change, but they remain the same.[551]

After the fall of Troy three peoples managed to escape from Asia Minor to different parts of Europe,

Those left by pitiless Achilles and the Greeks:[552]

the Romans under their leader Aeneas, the Franks under Antenor and the Britons under Brutus.[553] From this line of

551. Horace, *Epistolae*, I.9.27.
552. Virgil, *Aeneid*, III.87 ('reliquiae' for 'reliquias' and 'Achillis' for 'Achilli').
553. Cp. Geoffrey of Monmouth, *The History of the Kings of Britain*, I.12.

descent comes the great courage of these three nations, their magnanimity, their ancient blood, their quickwittedness and their ability to speak up for themselves. Of the three peoples left alive after the fall of Troy, the Britons alone kept the vocabulary of their race and the grammatical properties of their original tongue. This is because they were held captive in Greece for many years after the destruction of their country and because they migrated much later to these western parts of Europe. You will still find the following names common among them: Oeneus, Rhesus, Aeneas, Hector, Achilles, Heliodorus, Theodorus, Ajax, Evander, Ulysses, Helena, Elissa, Gwendolena, and many others which make you think of ancient times. You must know, too, that all the words in Welsh are cognate with either Greek or Latin. The Greeks say $ὕδωρ$ for water, the Welsh 'dwfr'; $ἅλς$ for salt, the Welsh 'halen'; $μις$ and $τις$ for I and you, the Welsh 'mi' and 'ti'; $ὄνομα$ for name, the Welsh 'enw'; $πέντε$ for five, the Welsh 'pump'; and $δέκα$ for ten, the Welsh 'deg'. The Romans said 'frenum', 'tripos', 'gladius' and 'lorica', and the Welsh say 'ffrwyn', 'tribedd', 'cleddyf' and 'llurig'. The Romans said 'unicus', 'canis' and 'belua', and the Welsh say 'unig', 'ci', and 'bela'.

Chapter 16
Welsh soothsayers, who behave as if they are possessed.

Among the Welsh there are certain individuals called 'awenyddion' who behave as if they are possessed by devils.[554] You will not find them anywhere else. When you consult them about some problem, they immediately go into a trance and lose control of their senses, as if they are possessed. They do not answer the question put to them in any logical way. Words stream from their mouths, incoherently and apparently meaningless and without any sense at all, but all the same well expressed: and if you listen carefully to what they say you will receive the solution to your problem. When it is all over, they will recover from their trance, as if they were ordinary people waking from a heavy

554. Awenyddion = poets, from 'awen' = originally oracular frenzy.

sleep, but you have to give them a good shake before they regain control of themselves. There are two odd things about all this: when they have given their answer, they do not recover from their paroxysm unless they are shaken violently and forced to come round again; and when they do return to their senses they can remember nothing of what they have said in the interval. If by chance they are questioned a second or a third time on the same matter, they give completely different answers. It is possible that they are speaking through demons which possess them, spirits which are ignorant and yet in some way inspired. They seem to receive this gift of divination through visions which they see in their dreams. Some of them have the impression that honey or sugary milk is being smeared on their mouths; others say that a sheet of paper with words written on it is pressed against their lips. As soon as they are roused from their trance and have come round again after their prophesying, that is what they say has happened. It is rather like what Esdras wrote about himself: 'Behold, a voice called me, saying, Esdras, open thy mouth. Then opened I my mouth, and, behold, he reached me a full cup, which was full as it were with water, but the colour of it was like fire. And when I had drunk of it, my heart uttered understanding, and wisdom grew in my breast.' [555]

When they are going into a trance they invoke the true and living God, and the Holy Trinity, and they pray that they may not be prevented by their sins from revealing the truth.

You will only rarely find soothsayers of this sort among peoples other than the Britons, and, of course, the Trojans, from whom they descend. In Troy, at the time of the siege of that noble city, there were two soothsayers endowed with the spirit of prophecy, Calchas [556] and Cassandra, [557] who openly foretold the destruction to come. The result of this was that Priam's son Helenus, who was their high priest, went over to the Greeks in the first year of the siege, taking Calchas with him, for he possessed certain prophetic books written by Calchas himself

555. 2 Esdras, XIV.38.
556. Calchas, son of Thestor.
557. Cassandra, daughter of Priam and twin sister of Helenus.

and by a number of earlier soothsayers, in which the fall of Troy was predicted. Later on Helenus was lavishly rewarded by the Greeks. Cassandra, King Priam's daughter, foretold the fall of the city every day, but the Trojans were far too stubborn and proud to believe what she said. On the very night when Troy was destroyed she described in full detail the act of treachery and how it was to be effected. That is why Virgil wrote:

Of such calamities Cassandra sang.[558]

In the same way, at a time when the kingdom of Britain still existed, the two Merlins, Celidonius and Ambrosius, each foretold its destruction, and the coming first of the Saxons and then of the Normans.

At this point I want to include a story about this sort of thing by Aulus Gellius. 'On the very day when Julius Caesar and Pompey were fighting a pitched battle in Thessaly during the Civil War, a strange thing happened in Italy north of the Po. A priest called Cornelius, well known in the area, respected for his personal conduct and revered as a man of religion, was suddenly moved to proclaim: "Caesar has won." In his pronouncement this soothsayer gave full details of what was happening, the day of the conflict, how the armies took up their positions, the ebb and flow of the battle, and the attacks launched by the two armies.'[559]

If you should ask, careful reader, by what supernatural agency such prophecies are made possible, I do not necessarily say by sorcery or by the intervention of evil spirits. It is true that knowledge of what is to be is the property of God alone, for only He can foretell the future by His omniscience freely dispensed from on high. As the Apostle says, 'Now there are diversities of gifts, but the same Spirit.'[560] Saint Peter says in his second Epistle: 'For the prophecy came not in old time by the will of man: but holy men of God spake as they were moved by the Holy Ghost.'[561] There is a similar statement in the Book of

558. Virgil, *Aeneid*, III.183.
559. Aulus Gellius, *Noctes Atticae*, XV.18.
560. I Corinthians, XII.4.
561. II Peter, I.21.

Daniel, where the Chaldeans answered King Nebuchadnezzar, when he demanded an interpretation of his dream. They said: 'There is not a man upon the earth that can shew the king's matter: therefore there is no king, lord, nor ruler that asked such things at any magician, or astrologer, or Chaldean. And it is a rare thing that the king requireth, and there is none other that can shew it before the king, except the gods, whose dwelling is not with flesh.'[562] Jerome makes the following comment on this passage: 'Prophets and all learned men admit that knowledge of events to come belongs to God above and not to men. Therefore the prophets who foretold the future spoke by the spirit of God.'[563] You will object that, if they were guided by the spirit of God, they would add 'Thus spake the Lord God', or some such words, when they were making their prophecies; and that no such method of prophesying is found in Merlin, so that what he said is merely sorcery. He may well have been a true believer, but, you will say, there is no mention of his sanctity or devoutness. To this I answer that the spirit of prophecy was given not only to the holy but sometimes to unbelievers and Gentiles, to Baal and the Sibyl, for example, and even to the wicked, such as Caiaphas and Baal again. In his homily on the Book of Numbers Origen says: 'Do not wonder if you see him whom I have said to be one of the scribes and Pharisees and doctors among the Jews making prophecies about Christ. Caiaphas said: "It is expedient for us, that one man should die for the people." Saint John adds: "And thus spake he [not of himself: but] being high priest that year." No one should be exalted just because he prophesies and is granted knowledge of the future. Prophecies shall fail, tongues shall cease, knowledge shall vanish away. There remain faith, hope and charity, and the greatest of these is charity, which never fails.'[564] Not only did evil men prophesy, but they performed signs and miracles, which many good men could not do. John the Baptist, who was so great, performed no

562. Daniel, II.10.
563. Saint Jerome, *In Danielem*, 2.9–10, much rewritten.
564. Origen, *In Numeros Homilia*, XIV, much rewritten. The references are to John, 11.50; I Cor., 13.8; and I Cor., 13.4–5.

miracle, as John the Evangelist testifies, when he says: 'And many resorted unto him, and said, John did no miracle,' [565] etc. We do not read that the Mother of God ever performed a miracle. On the other hand we read in the Acts of the Apostles that the sons of Sceva cast out evil spirits 'in the name of the Lord Jesus, when Paul preacheth'. [566] You will find in Matthew and Luke: 'Many will say to me in that day, Lord, Lord, have we not prophesied in thy name? and in thy name have cast out devils? and in thy name done many wonderful works? And then will I profess unto them, I never knew you.' [567] Elsewhere we read: 'And John answered him, saying, Master, we saw one casting out devils in thy name: and we forbad him, because he followeth not us. But Jesus said, Forbid him not: for there is no man which shall do a miracle in my name, that can lightly speak evil of me. For he that is not against us is on our part.' [568]

Alexander of Macedon, a Gentile, crossed the Caspian mountains and by a miracle shut up the ten tribes within their promontories, where they still remain, and will remain until the coming of Elisha and Enoch. [569] We read of the faith of Merlin, and we read of his prophesying; but we do not read that he was saintly or that he performed miracles.

You will object that the prophets were not possessed when they prophesied, whereas we read that when Merlin Silvester made his prophecies he was in a frenzy, and in the same way the other soothsayers about whom I have written in this chapter seem to be possessed. Some prophesied by dreams, visions and enigmatical sayings, like Ezekiel and Daniel. Others did so by words and deeds, as Noah referred to the Church when he had built the Ark, and Abraham to Christ's Passion when he sacrificed his son. Moses said: 'The Lord thy God will raise up unto thee a prophet of thy brethren; unto him ye shall hearken,' [570] etc., meaning Christ. Others, such as Daniel, have prophesied in an even better way, by the inspiration and revelation of the Holy Ghost within them. To those who object I

565. John, X.41.   566. Acts, XIX.14.
567. Matthew, VII.22.   568. Mark, IX.38, and Luke, IX.49.
569. I cannot trace this anecdote.   570. Deuteronomy, XVIII.15.

reply simply that in the First Book of Kings we read about David being persecuted by Saul. When Saul learned that David had fled to Naioth, which is a hill in Ramah, where there was a group of prophets, 'he sent messengers to take David: and when they saw the company of the prophets prophesying, and Samuel standing as appointed over them, the spirit of God was upon the messengers of Saul, and they also prophesied. And Saul sent other messengers and again the third time, and they prophesied also'. Saul was angry and he pursued them, 'and he went on, and he prophesied, until he came to Naioth', as if he had lost his reason. 'And he stripped off his clothes also, and prophesied all that day and all that night' with the others, while David and Samuel watched him.[571] It is not to be wondered at, then, if those who suddenly receive the spirit of God as a sign of grace come down from above should for a time seem to have lost their reason.

Chapter 17
Their respect for noble birth and ancient genealogy.

The Welsh value distinguished birth and noble descent more than anything else in the world. They would rather marry into a noble family than into a rich one. Even the common people know their family-tree by heart and can readily recite from memory the list of their grandfathers, great-grandfathers, great-great-grandfathers, back to the sixth or seventh generation, as I did earlier on for the Welsh princes: Rhys son of Gruffydd, Gruffydd son of Rhys, Rhys son of Tewdwr, and so on.[572]

As they have this intense interest in their family descent, they avenge with great ferocity any wrong or insult done to their relations. They are vindictive by nature, bloodthirsty and violent. Not only are they ready to avenge new and recent injuries, but old ones, too, as if they had only just received them.

They do not live in towns, villages or castles, but lead a solitary existence, deep in the woods. It is not their habit to

571. I Kings, XIX.18–24.
572. Cp. *The Description of Wales*, I.3.

build great palaces, or vast and towering structures of stone and cement. Instead they content themselves with wattled huts on the edges of the forest, put up with little labour or expense, but strong enough to last a year or so.

They do not have orchards or gardens, but if you give them fruit or garden produce they are only too pleased to eat it. Most of their land is used for pasture. They cultivate very little of it, growing a few flowers and sowing a plot here and there. They use oxen to pull their ploughs and carts, sometimes in pairs but more often four at a time. The ploughman walks in front, but backwards. When the bulls pull out of the yoke, as often happens, he falls on his back and is in grave danger. They do not usually use sickles when they reap, for they prefer a short piece of iron in the shape of a knife, which is loosely joined to a stick at either end. If you saw it you would understand this better than you can hope to do by listening to my description.

> We're more impressed by what our eyes see clear
> Than we can ever be by what we hear [573]

For fishing and crossing rivers they make coracles out of withies. These are not oblong but rounded, and they are pointed in front, rather in the shape of a triangle. They are left bare inside, but are covered outside with untanned animal-skins. When a salmon is landed inside one of these coracles, the fish sometimes strikes the boat so hard with its tail that it is turned over, to the great danger of the man who is fishing. When fishermen are on their way to the river, or going home, they have the primitive habit of carrying their coracles on their backs. Bledri, the well-known story-teller, who lived a little before our time, used to describe this in the most amusing way: 'There are among us men who, when they go a-hunting, carry their horse on their shoulders until they come near to their quarry. Then, to catch their prey, they mount their steeds. When they have finished, they lift their horses back onto their shoulders and carry them home again.'

573. Horace, *Ars Poetica*, 180–81 ('aures' for 'aurem').

Chapter 18
How they received the true religion long ago, their piety and their devotion to the Christian faith.

About two hundred years ago, long before the fall of Britain, the Welsh were instructed and confirmed in the Christian faith by Faganus and Duvianus who, at the request of King Lucius, were sent to the island by Pope Eleutherius.[574] Later on, Germanus of Auxerre and Lupus of Troyes were sent over because of the corruption which had gradually resulted from the invasions of the pagan Saxons, and more especially to put an end to the Pelagian heresy, but they found nothing heretical or contrary to the articles of the true faith.[575] Even today the Welsh still keep up some of the practices which Germanus and Lupus taught them. When a loaf of bread is put before them, they break off a piece and give it to the poor. They sit down three to a meal in memory of the Holy Trinity. When they meet a monk or priest, or any religious in his habit, they stretch out their arms, bow their heads and ask his blessing. More than any other people they long to be confirmed by a bishop and to receive that mark with the chrism which is the sign of the grace of the Holy Ghost. When they marry, or go on a pilgrimage, or, on the advice of the clergy, make a special effort to amend their ways, they give a donation of one tenth of all their worldly goods, cattle, sheep and other livestock. This partition of their property they call the Great Tithe. They give two thirds of it to the church in which they were baptized and the remaining third to the bishop of their diocese. Of all pilgrimages they prefer going to Rome, and when they reach St Peter's they pray there most devoutly. As I can bear witness, they pay greater respect than any other people to their churches, to men in orders, the relics of the saints, bishops' crooks, bells, holy books and the Cross itself, for which they show great reverence. This is the reason why the churches in

574. Cp. Bede, *Historia Ecclesiastica*, I.4, and Geoffrey of Monmouth, *The History of the Kings of Britain*, IV.19.
575. Cp. Bede, op. cit., I.17, and Geoffrey of Monmouth, op. cit., VI.13.

Wales are more quiet and tranquil than those elsewhere. Around them the cattle graze so peacefully, not only in the churchyards, but outside, too, within the fences and ditches marked out and set by bishops to fix the sanctuary limits. The more important churches, hallowed by their greater antiquity, offer sanctuary for as far as the cattle go to feed in the morning and can return at evening. If any man has incurred the hatred of his prince and is in danger of death, he may apply to the church for sanctuary and it will be freely granted to him and his family. Many people abuse this immunity and far exceed the indulgence of the church canons, which in such cases offer only safety of life and limb. From their place of sanctuary they sally forth on foraging expeditions, harass the whole countryside and have even been known to attack the prince in question.

Nowhere can you see hermits and anchorites more abstinent and more spiritually committed than in Wales. The Welsh go to extremes in all matters. You may never find anyone worse than a bad Welshman, but you will certainly never find anyone better than a good one.

A happy and prosperous race indeed, a people blessed and blessed again, if only they had good prelates and pastors, and one single prince and he a just one!

Here ends Book I, which concentrates on the good points.

HERE BEGINS BOOK II: THE LESS GOOD POINTS.

Preface to Book II.

In Book I, I set out clearly the character, way of life and customs of the British people. There I collected together and explained in detail all the good points which redound to their credit and glory. In Book II, I must, as a serious historian, arrange my material in proper order and put before you things which seem less praiseworthy and transgress the path of virtue.

I must ask your indulgence if I state the blunt truth, without which history loses all authority and ceases to be worthy of the name. The painter who professes to imitate nature by his artistry loses his reputation if he concentrates too much on those aspects which please him and through very shame leaves out anything which he finds unseemly.

> No man can be born perfect: he is best
> Who has fewest faults.[576]

The wise man must accept all human attributes as inherent in his own nature.[577] In our earthly existence there is no happy perfection under heaven. Evil is never far removed from good, and vice is only with difficulty distinguished from virtue. Any man whose personality is well balanced, by nature or by training, takes pleasure in hearing good things reported, but he must not be offended when he has to listen to the contrary.[578]

The natural propensities of the Welsh may well have been corrupted and changed for the worse by their long exile and their lack of prosperity. Poverty puts an end to many of our vices, but it has been known to encourage us in our wrongdoing.

576. Horace, *Satires*, I.3.68–9 ('vitiis sine nemo' for 'nam vitiis nemo sine').
577. Terence, *Heautontimorumenos*, 77
578. This passage is repeated from *The Conquest of Ireland*, I.46.

Chapter 1
The inconstancy and instability of the Welsh; and their failure to keep their word or carry out their promises.

The Welsh people rarely keep their promises, for their minds are as fickle as their bodies are agile.[579] It is very easy to persuade them to do something wrong, and just as easy to stop them once they have started. They are always quick to take action, and they are particularly stubborn when what they are doing is reprehensible. The only thing they really persist in is changing their minds.

A formal oath never binds them. They have no respect for their plighted word, and truth means nothing to them. They are so accustomed to breaking a promise, held sacrosanct by other nations, that they will stretch out their hand, as the custom is, and with this well-known gesture swear an oath about nearly everything they say, not only in important and serious matters, but on every trifling occasion. They are always prepared to perjure themselves to their own convenience and for any temporary advantage which they hope to gain by concealing the truth. In any lawsuit, civil or ecclesiastic, they are ready to swear anything which seems expedient at the moment, whether they are the accusers or the accused, each side doing all it can to make its point and prove its case. For all that they have laws which have stood the test of time, in which a man's plighted word is held sacred, truth is revered, honest dealing is highly thought of, the accused is given the benefit of the doubt, the accuser is allowed no advantage, and the onus of proving a case lies with the man who brings it. To a people so cunning and crafty this seems no great burden, for they take it all very lightly.

579. This sentence is repeated from *The Conquest of Ireland*, II.39 ('igitur haec gens' for 'itaque', 'minus animo levis' for 'levis minus animo').

Chapter 2
They live on plunder and have no regard for the ties of peace and friendship.

It is the habit of the Welsh to steal anything they can lay their hands on and to live on plunder, theft and robbery, not only from foreigners and people hostile to them, but also from each other. When they see a chance of doing harm, they immediately forget all treaties of peace and ties of friendship. They think much more of material gain, however shameful, than they do of the need to keep a promise or observe an oath. In his book called *The Downfall of the Britons*, Gildas, who revered the truth, as every historian must, was not prepared to gloss over the weakness of his own people. 'In war they are cowards,' he said, 'and you cannot trust them in times of peace.'[580] What do you think then, about Julius Caesar, who bestrode the world like a colossus, yet who, when he fought against them under their leader Cassivelaunus,

In terror showed his back to the Britons he'd attacked?[581]

Were they not brave on that occasion? What about Belinus and Brennius, who captured Imperial Rome and added it to all their other conquests?[582] What of the Britons in the time of the Emperor Constantine, the son of our own Helen?[583] What of them in the reign of Aurelius Ambrosius, whom even Eutropius praises?[584] Were they not brave in the days of our own famous Arthur, call him fabulous if you will?

On the other hand, when they were on the point of being conquered by the Picts and the Scots, people about whom there

580. Gildas, *De excidio Britanniae*, §.6.
581. Lucan, *Pharsalia*, II.572, quoted by Geoffrey of Monmouth, *The History of the Kings of Britain*, IV.9.
582. Geoffrey of Monmouth, op. cit., III.8–9.
583. Constantine II, later Emperor. Cp. Geoffrey of Monmouth, op. cit., V.6–8.
584. Cp. passim, Geoffrey of Monmouth, op. cit., VI.6–VIII.16. I cannot trace the reference in Eutropius.

is nothing good to say, they sent the following desperate message to the auxiliary Roman legions, as we read in Gildas: 'The barbarians are driving us into the sea and the sea drives us back into the hands of the barbarians. We have to choose between being drowned and having our throats cut.'[585] Were they brave then? Have we any reason to admire them for what they did? They summoned the Saxons to their assistance, and when these mercenaries attacked and overwhelmed them, was it then that they were brave? Of all these arguments the strongest evidence for their lack of spirit is the fact that, in all that he wrote about the Britons and their long story, the historian Gildas, a man of religion and one of their own race, had nothing good to say to posterity about them.

With God as my guide, and if my life is spared, I promise to give you a different answer to this problem in my *Topography of Britain*.[586]

Let me just add one further small item of evidence to the more important arguments adduced above. When Maximus, the British leader mentioned at the beginning of this book, had left the armed forces of this island in a very weak position by taking so many men abroad with him, for a great number of years Britain remained destitute of troops and equipment, and so was exposed to the attacks of pirates and freebooters. Until then the country had been famous for the determined way in which it defended itself. With these troops to support him, the tyrant Maximus conquered almost the whole of Cisalpine Gaul and even dared to make an armed attack upon Imperial Rome. As time passed the population increased again: the young men of Britain learned to bear arms again and regained their former reputation for courage.[587] One has to remember how circumstances change down the years, and history will confirm me in this.

585. This is the famous appeal to Aetius. Cp. Gildas, *De excidio Britanniae*, §.20, repeated by Geoffrey of Monmouth, op. cit., VI.3.

586. Gerald never wrote this book.

587. This is the Maximianus of Geoffrey of Monmouth. Cp. *The History of the Kings of Britain*, V.12–16.

The Britons maintain that, when Gildas criticized his own people so bitterly, he wrote as he did because he was so infuriated by the fact that King Arthur had killed his own brother, who was a Scottish chieftain. When he heard of his brother's death, or so the Britons say, he threw into the sea a number of outstanding books which he had written in their praise and about Arthur's achievements. As a result you will find no book which gives an authentic account of that great prince.[588]

Chapter 3
Their weakness in battle: how shamefully and ignobly they run away.

In war the Welsh are very ferocious when battle is first joined. They shout, glower fiercely at the enemy, and fill the air with fearsome clamour, making a high-pitched screech with their long trumpets. From their first fierce and headlong onslaught, and the shower of javelins which they hurl, they seem most formidable opponents. If the enemy resists manfully and they are repulsed, they are immediately thrown into confusion. With further resistance they turn their backs, making no attempt at a counter-attack, but seeking safety in flight. As the poet knew only too well, this is disastrous on the battlefield.

To run away is a cowardly crime.[589]

Elsewhere we read:

Although he may lack skill, only a coward flees.[590]

What was written about the Germans is just as applicable to the Welsh: 'In the first onslaught they are more than men, in the second they are less than women.'[591] Their courage is best seen when they are in retreat, for they will frequently turn back and,

---

588. Apart from the fact that Gildas was born on the south bank of the Clyde, there is no evidence to support any of this.
589. Lucan, *Pharsalia*, IX.283.
590. Horace, *Ars Poetica*, 31 ('culpae ducit' for 'ducit culpae').
591. This is said by Livy of the Gauls.

like the Parthians, shoot their arrows from behind.[592] Just as, after a famous victory, even cowards boast of how bold they have been, so, after defeat, no man is deemed to have fought bravely.

Their sole idea of tactics is either to pursue their opponents, or else to run away from them. They are lightly armed and they rely more on their agility than on brute strength. It follows that they cannot meet the enemy on equal terms, or fight violently for very long, or strive hand-to-hand for victory,

> As shield clangs hard on shield, sharp spear opposing spear,
> And, fighting foot to foot, dread swordsmen cut and shear.[593]

Although beaten today and shamefully put to flight with much slaughter, tomorrow they march out again, no whit dejected by their defeat or their losses. They may not shine in open combat and in fixed formation, but they harass the enemy by their ambushes and their night-attacks. In a single battle they are easily beaten, but they are difficult to conquer in a long war, for they are not troubled by hunger or cold, fighting does not seem to tire them, they do not lose heart when things go wrong, and after one defeat they are ready to fight again and to face once more the hazards of war. The poet Claudian seems to be talking about a people like the Welsh, or at least not very different from them, when he says:

> When dying, they think of their wrongs; but if their breath
> They once recover, they will stolidly face death.
> To them the shedding of much blood is meaningless.[594]

Chapter 4
Their desire to own land and the quarrels between brothers which ensue.

The Welsh people are more keen to own land and to extend their holdings than any other I know. To achieve this they are prepared to dig up boundary ditches, to move stones showing the

592. This is a Parthian shot.
593. Statius, *Thebaid*, VIII. 398–9 ('clipeo clipeus' for 'clypeus clypeis').
594. Claudian, *In Eutropium*, II. 116–18.

edges of fields and to overrun clearly-marked limits. So prone are they to this lust for possession, from which I may say they all suffer, that they are prepared to swear that the land which they happen to occupy on some temporary or longer-established tenancy agreement of lease, hire, renting or any other similar arrangement is their own freehold and has always belonged to their family, even when they and the rightful owner or proprietor have publicly sworn an affidavit about his security of tenure. Quarrels and lawsuits result, murders and arson, not to mention frequent fratricides. Things are made worse by the ancient Welsh custom of brothers dividing between them the property which they have.

Another serious cause of dissension is the habit of the Welsh princes of entrusting the education of each of their sons to a different nobleman living in their territory. If the prince happens to die, each nobleman plots and plans to enforce the succession of his own foster-child and to make sure that he is preferred to the other brothers. The most frightful disturbances occur in their territories as a result, people being murdered, brothers killing each other and even putting each other's eyes out, for as everyone knows from experience it is very difficult to settle disputes of this sort.

It follows that you will find that friendships are much warmer between foster-brothers than they are between true brothers. It is also remarkable how much more people love their brothers when they are dead than they do while they are still alive. They will persecute their living brothers until they bring about their death; but when their brothers die, especially if someone else happens to have killed them, they will move heaven and earth to avenge them. With a slight modification the words spoken by Micah describe them perfectly: 'The good man is perished out of the earth: and there is none upright among men: they all lie in wait for blood; they hunt every man his brother to the death. The evil they do with both hands they declare to be good.' [595]

595. Micah, VII.2. Gerald says Malachi.

Chapter 5
The greediness of the Welsh and the demands which they make on people.

If they come to a house where there is any sign of affluence and they are in a position to take what they want, there is no limit to their demands. They lose all control of themselves, and insist on being served with vast quantities of food and more especially intoxicating drink. With the Apostle they say: 'I know both how ... to abound and to suffer need,'[596] but they do not add with him that they are 'made all things to all men' so that they 'might by all means save some'[597] for God. In times of scarcity their abstinence and frugality are most remarkable, but, when they have gone without food for a long time, their appetite becomes enormous, especially when they are sitting at someone else's table. In this they resemble wolves and eagles, which live by plunder and are rarely satisfied. In difficult times they have to fast, but in times of plenty they glut themselves. All the same, no one in Wales mortgages his property to satisfy his greed and gluttony, as I have seen the English do.

They want everyone else to share their bad habits and then provide the wherewithal to pay for them,

For crime makes us equal, corrupting us all.[598]

Chapter 6
The crime of incest, and the abuse by which church livings are both shared and handed down from father to son.

Incest is extremely common among the Welsh, both in the lower classes and the better educated people. 'There is no fear of God before their eyes',[599] and they have no hesitation or shame in

596. Philippians, 4.12. 597. I Corinthians, 9.20–22.
598. Lucan, *Pharsalia*, V.290.
599. Psalm XIV.7 in the Prayer Book, Psalm XIII in the Vulgate.

marrying women related to them in the fourth or fifth degree, and sometimes even third cousins.[600] Their usual excuse for abusing the ordinances of the Church in this way is their wish to put an end to some family quarrel or other. These are common among them and they pursue them with tremendous bitterness, for 'their feet are swift to shed blood'.[601] Another reason given for their marrying women of their own family is their great respect for noble descent, which means so much to them. They are most unwilling to marry anyone of another family, who, in their arrogance, they think may be their inferior in descent and blood. In most cases they will only marry a woman after living with her for some time, thus making sure that she will make a suitable wife, in disposition, moral qualities and the ability to bear children. They have long had the custom of buying young girls from their parents, with a penalty-clause in case they run away, not in the first instance with a view to marriage, but just to live with them.

A Welsh church has as many incumbents and sharers in the living as there are important families resident in the parish. When fathers die, the sons succeed, not by election, but as if they held these benefices by hereditary right, which is a pollution of God's sanctuary. If a bishop dared to appoint and induct anyone else, the people would avenge this insult both on him and on the man he chose.

These two abuses, incest and the passing on of church benefices from father to son, were once very common in Brittany and, indeed, they still are. Hildebert, Bishop of Le Mans, writes in one of his letters that he was present with the Breton clergy at a council expressly convened to put an end to such enormities in Brittany.[602] From what he says it is clear that the abuses have been practised from time immemorial in both countries, this side

600. As the Rev. James F. Dimock points out in the preface to his edition, p. xlvii, the Welsh did not accept the degrees prohibited by canon law, any more than we do today.

601. Psalm XIV.6 in the Prayer Book, Psalm XIII in the Vulgate.

602. Hildebert, Bishop of Tours 1125–33, had been Archdeacon of Le Mans. The reference is to the reforms of the Council of Nantes of 1127, over which he presided as Metropolitan.

of the water and across the Channel. The words of the psalmist David seem applicable to the Welsh: 'They are corrupt, and become abominable in their doings; there is none that doeth good, no not one . . . But they are all gone out of the way, they are altogether become abominable: there is none that doeth good, no not one. Their throat is an open sepulchre, with their tongues they have deceived: the poison of asps is under their lips. Their mouth is full of cursing and bitterness: their feet are swift to shed blood. Destruction and unhappiness is in their ways, and the way of peace have they not known: there is no fear of God before their eyes.'[603] Solomon says much the same: 'My son, walk thou not in the way with them; refrain thy foot from their path: For their feet run to evil, and make haste to shed blood.'[604]

Chapter 7
The sins of the Welsh, through which they lost first Troy and then Britain.

It was because of their sins, and more particularly the wicked and detestable vice of homosexuality, that the Welsh were punished by God and so lost first Troy and then Britain. We read that when the Emperor Constantine handed over the Western Empire and the city of Rome to Pope Silvester and his successors, he had in mind to rebuild Troy and to establish there the capital of the Eastern Empire; but he heard a voice which said: 'It is Sodom that you are going to rebuild.' Thereupon he immediately changed his plans, and turned his sails and war-pennants towards Byzantium, making that city the capital of his empire and giving to it his own propitious name.[605]

In the *History of the Kings of Britain* we read of Malgo, King of the Britons, who practised homosexuality, and many others with him.[606]

For a long time now this vice has ceased among the Welsh and

603. Psalm XIV.2–7 in the Prayer Book, Psalm XIII in the Vulgate.
604. Proverbs, I.15–16.
605. I cannot trace this reference.
606. Geoffrey of Monmouth, *The History of the Kings of Britain*, XI.7.

hardly anyone can remember it. They maintain that their time of repentance is nearly over, and that, by their successful wars and their seizure of new territory, they have in our own day greatly increased in population, strength and force of arms. As a result they boast, and most confidently predict, that they will soon reoccupy the whole island of Britain. It is remarkable how everyone in Wales entertains this illusion. According to the prophecies of Merlin, the foreign occupation of the island will come to an end and the foreigners themselves will be destroyed. The Welsh will then be called Britons once more and they will enjoy their ancient privileges.[607]

In my own opinion this is completely wrong. It is a true adage that:

> Resistance weakens when things always go our way:
> And we grow soft if life is one long holiday.[608]

The same poet wrote:

> Where means are lacking libido can never thrive:
> Lust is luxurious and needs wealth to survive.[609]

The fact that the Welsh have now given up homosexuality, which they were unable to resist in their more prosperous days, must be attributed, not to any improvement in their morals, but to their indigence now that they are exiled and expelled from the kingdom of Britain. How can they say that they have done penance and more than paid the penalty, when we see them still sunk in sin and in a deep abyss of every vice – perjury, theft, robbery, rapine, murder, fratricide, adultery, incest, and obstinately ensnared and entangled in wrongdoing, which grows worse as day follows day? The words spoken by Hosea might well have been spoken about the Welsh: 'There is no truth, nor mercy, nor knowledge of God in the land. By swearing, and lying, and

607. Geoffrey of Monmouth, op. cit., VII.3: 'Kambria shall be filled with joy and the Cornish oaks shall flourish. The island shall be called by the name of Brutus and the title given to it by the foreigners shall be done away with' (Penguin Classics, p. 175).

608. Ovid, *Ars Amatoria*, II.437–8.

609. Ovid, *Remedia Amoris*, 749 and 746.

killing, and stealing, and committing adultery, they break out, and blood touches blood. Therefore shall the land mourn, and every one that dwelleth therein shall languish. And the people that doth not understand shall fall.'[610]

The other circumstances about which they boast are to be attributed to the untiring efforts of the Norman Kings, who were strongly supported in their invasion by the proud French, rather than to their own great power and strength. If you want proof of this, just consider the English kings before the Normans came. They gave their whole attention to the island of Britain, and they made such a determined effort to subdue the Welsh that they destroyed them almost to a man. King Offa shut the Welsh off from the English by his long dyke on the frontier.[611] King Ethelfrid destroyed Chester and put to the sword the monks of the famous monastery of Bangor Iscoed, who were busy praying that the Britons might win.[612] Then, last of all, and by far the greatest, came Harold. He advanced into Wales on foot, at the head of his lightly clad infantry,[613] lived on the country, and marched up and down and round and about the whole of Wales with such energy that he 'left not one that pisseth against a wall'.[614] In commemoration of his success, and to his own undying memory, you will find a great number of inscribed stones put up in Wales to mark the many places where he won a victory. This was the old custom. The stones bear the inscription: HIC FUIT VICTOR HAROLDUS.[615] It is to these recent victories of the English over the Welsh, in which so much blood was spilt, that the first three kings of the Normans owe the fact that in their lifetime they have held Wales in peace and subjection. Meanwhile the population of the country has

610. Hosea, 4.1-3 and 14.

611. Offa, King of Mercia 757 to 796. For his dyke, see Asser, *De rebus gestis Ælfredi* ch. 14: 'Rex nomine Offa qui vallum magnum inter Britanniam (= Wales) atque Merciam de mari usque ad mare fieri imperavit.'

612. Ethelfrid, King of Northumbria 593 to 617. See Geoffrey of Monmouth, *The History of the Kings of Britain*, XI.13.

613. This was in 1063.

614. I Samuel 25.22 and I Kings 16.11.

615. No such stones have ever been found.

greatly increased. The Welsh have gradually learnt from the English and the Normans how to manage their weapons and to use horses in battle, for they have frequented the court and been sent to England as hostages. They have taken advantage of the fact that the first three Norman kings have been greatly preoccupied with their possessions across the Channel. These are the reasons why they have been able to raise their heads a little higher, recover their lands and cease to bear the yoke which once weighed so heavily upon them.

Chapter 8
How the Welsh can be conquered.

Any prince who is really determined to conquer the Welsh and to govern them in peace must proceed as follows. He should first of all understand that for a whole year at least he must devote his every effort and give his undivided attention to the task which he has undertaken. He can never hope to conquer in one single battle a people which will never draw up its forces to engage an enemy army in the field, and will never allow itself to be besieged inside fortified strong-points. He can beat them only by patient and unremitting pressure applied over a long period. Knowing the spirit of hatred and jealousy which usually prevails among them, he must sow dissension in their ranks and do all he can by promises and bribes to stir them up against each other. In the autumn not only the marches but certain carefully chosen localities in the interior must be fortified with castles, and these he must supply with ample provisions and garrison with families favourable to his cause. In the meantime he must make every effort to stop the Welsh buying the stocks of cloth, salt and corn which they usually import from England. Ships manned with picked troops must patrol the coast, to make sure that these goods are not brought by water across the Irish Sea or the Severn Sea, to ward off enemy attacks and to secure his own supply-lines. Later on, when wintry conditions have really set in, or perhaps towards the end of winter, in February and March, by which time the trees have lost their leaves, and there is no more pasturage to be had in the mountains, a strong force of infantry must have the courage to invade their secret strongholds, which lie deep in the woods and are buried in the forests. They must be cut off from all opportunity of foraging, and harassed, both individual families and larger assemblies of troops, by frequent attacks from those encamped around. The assault troops must be lightly armed and not weighed down with a lot of equipment. They must be strengthened with frequent reinforcements, who have been following close behind to give them support and to provide a base. Fresh troops must keep on replacing those who are tired out, and maybe those who have been killed in battle. If he constantly moves up new men, there need be no break in the assault. Without them this belligerent people will never be conquered, and even so the danger will be great and many casualties must be expected. What does it matter to an army of English mercenaries if their losses are great today? There is enough money to ensure that the ranks of battle will be filled again and more than filled tomorrow. To the Welsh, on the other hand, who have no mercenaries and no foreign allies, those who fall in battle are irreplaceable, at least for the time being.

In an undertaking such as this,[616] just as the workman is to be trusted in his own trade, so advice should be sought of those who are resident in the country, who by experience have become familiar with local conditions and who know the manners and habits of the local people. It is, moreover, to the great advantage of such men that the power of a hostile people, whose implacable enmity and hatred they have incurred by long and continuous warfare, should now be weakened or destroyed.

In my opinion the Welsh marches would have been better controlled under the English occupation if their kings, in governing these regions and in repelling the attacks of a hostile people, had from the beginning taken the advice of the marcher lords, and used their tactics, instead of those of the Angevins and the Normans. For a military expedition such as I have outlined above, and whether it is against the Irish or the Welsh will make no difference, troops who

616. The long passage 'In an undertaking . . . the same sort of warfare' is repeated, with minor changes, from *The Conquest of Ireland*, II.38.

have lived all their lives in the marches will be by far the most suitable, for they have had long practice in waging war in local conditions. They are bold, speedily deployed and experienced in all that they do. As military circumstances dictate, they ride well and they advance quickly on foot. They are not particular about their food and drink, and when it is really necessary they will do without bread or alcohol. It was by men of this calibre that Ireland and Wales were first invaded: and if they are to be subdued completely, it can only be by such men. In their own countries the Flemings, Normans, French routiers and Brabançon mercenaries are bonny fighters and make well-disciplined soldiers, but the tactics of French troops are no good at all in Ireland or Wales. They are used to fighting on the level, whereas here the terrain is rough; their battles take place in the open fields, but here the country is heavily wooded; with them the army is an honourable profession but with us it is a matter of dire necessity; their victories are won by stubborn resistance, ours by constant movement; they take prisoners, we cut off their heads; they ransom their captives, but we massacre them. When troops fight in flat open country, heavy complicated armour, made partly out of cloth and partly of iron, offers good protection and certainly looks smart; but in a marshy or thickly wooded terrain, where foot-soldiers have the advantage over cavalry, light armour is far better. Against men who wear no armour at all and where the battle is almost always won or lost at the first onslaught, light protection is much more suitable. When the enemy is retreating at full speed through narrow defiles and up mountain-sides, the pursuers must be able to move quickly: they need to be protected, but their armour should be very light. If they have high curved saddles and wear heavy complicated equipment, mounting their horses and dismounting will be a great problem, and they will never be able to advance on foot. Against men who are heavily armed, fighting on the flat where victory is won by main force, and relying upon brute strength and the sheer mass of iron which they wear, I have no doubt at all that you must pit armour against armour and weight against weight,

For circumstances must dictate the proper means.[617]

Against an army so mobile and lightly armed as the Welsh, who always prefer to do battle on rough terrain, you need troops with little equipment and who are used to the same sort of warfare.

617. Horace, *Ars Poetica*, 92.

The towns and castles on the banks of the Severn, all the land held by the English on the western side of the river facing Wales, the whole of Shropshire and Cheshire, all this must be protected by a strong army levied for this purpose. Special local honours and privileges should be granted to the same places, as a mark of favour from their ruler.

Every year there must be an inspection of arms, horses and all warlike stores. This should be carried out by honest, experienced men, carefully chosen for the job, who have the defence and safety of their own country at heart instead of wanting to destroy it, and who are not interested in lining their own pockets. The military leaders in the area should be bound by a strict oath to do all in their power to put down the enemy. All soldiers and all civilians, whatever their function, in short the entire population, should be trained to bear arms. In this way freedom would be a match for freedom, and pride would be checked by pride. It must always be borne in mind that the Welsh are not being enervated by daily toil, they are not crushed and dispirited by slavery, they are not being maltreated by unjust taskmasters. They still carry their heads high and are prompt to avenge injuries. They are ready to take up arms and to rebel, and they will defend their country with the utmost courage. Nothing rejoices the hearts of men so much, nothing inspires them and encourages them to behave so nobly as the sheer joy of being free. On the other hand nothing dejects and dispirits them as much as oppression and slavery.

This part of the kingdom, if it were fully armed and bravely defended, might well in time of need offer strong military support to the throne, not only locally and in the neighbouring regions, but even farther afield. It is possible that the public treasury might as a result receive less in taxes, but this decrease in income would be amply compensated for by the peaceful state of the kingdom and the respect in which the sovereign would be held, especially as the heavy and quite alarming expenses of one single military expedition into Wales usually amounts to as much as is levied in taxes from the Welsh over a whole series of years.

Chapter 9
How Wales should be governed once it has been conquered.

Once the Welsh nation[618] has been conquered systematically by the
methods outlined in the previous chapter, it must be ruled with great
moderation in the following way. The governor appointed must be a
man of firm and uncompromising character. In times of peace he will
observe the laws, and never refuse to obey them; he will respect his
terms of appointment and do all in his power to keep his government
firm and stable. Although they have no conception of honour themselves, the Welsh, like all barbarous peoples, want more than anything
else to be honoured. They respect and revere honest dealing in others,
although they lack it themselves. As a race they are mercurial and
unreliable. The moment they show signs of rebellion, no mercy
should be shown to them and they must be punished immediately.
Once they have paid the penalty for their wrongdoing and are at peace
again, their revolt should be forgotten as long as they behave properly,
and they should be restored to their former position of security and
respect, for

> The quarrel over, it is wrong to bear a grudge.[619]

Such kindly treatment will encourage them to keep the peace and
obey the laws, and the knowledge that punishment will follow immediately may well deter them from such rash enterprises. It is easy
to lose sight of reality in these matters and I have myself seen many
people in authority turn a blind eye to lawlessness, allow themselves
to be influenced by flattery, try to ingratiate themselves with their
enemies in time of war, rob the civilian population in time of peace,
despoil those who can offer no resistance and hold revolutionaries in
high regard. They have been sadly wrong in the way in which they
reacted to circumstances, as I have always realized. By confusing
right and wrong in this way, they have themselves been worse confounded in the end.

If we prepare for contingencies they will not be as bad as they
otherwise might. Happy the state which in times of peace is yet prepared for war. In peace-time a successful and prudent ruler will build

618. Much of the passage 'Once the Welsh nation . . . warning to posterity'
is repeated, with changes, from *The Conquest of Ireland*, II.39.
619. I cannot trace this quotation.

castles, widen the trackways through the woodlands and surround himself with well-disposed supporters, so that he is prepared for the hazards of war and in a sense forearmed. Those who are well treated and properly recompensed in time of peace will respond more promptly, reliably and faithfully to the call of war, or whenever danger threatens.

The prince or governor must never entrust his capital or chief stronghold to the Welsh, for, however friendly it may appear, a people which is held in subjection is always plotting treachery. I have seen many great men cruelly put to death, or at least dishonoured and driven out of their castles, as the result of such carelessness and negligence. Treachery on the part of the Welsh is a much greater source of peril than any open warfare: their perfidy is more to be feared than their armed strength, their apparent goodwill more than their open anger, their ingratiating ways more than their animosity, their treason more than their taking up arms, their feigned friendship more than their enmity, which last can be dealt with easily enough.[620] Any governor who is really prudent and provident must find out what pitfalls are to be avoided by taking note of the disasters which have befallen others in the same position. It costs nothing to learn from other people's experience. As Ennodius says: 'We who come after must learn to avoid the mistakes of those who have lived before us. Any catastrophe is a warning to posterity.'[621]

If the ruler concerned is kind-hearted enough to want to achieve all this without head-on conflict and immense bloodshed, he must do as I have said: fortify the marches on all sides; cut off completely all imports by land and sea; and stir the Welsh up to internecine feuds by bribery and by granting away each man's land to someone else. They will soon be reduced by hunger and famine, and by an increasing shortage of almost all the necessities of life; they will quarrel bitterly with each other, and assassinations will become an everyday occurrence; and in a short time they will be forced to surrender.

620. In Gerald's Latin these contrasts are a series of plays on words: ars/Mars, pax/fax, mel/fel, malitia/militia, proditio/expeditio, amicitia/inimicitia. He had used this sentence in *The Conquest of Ireland*, II.39, and again in *The Topography of Ireland*, III.21.

621. Ennodius, *Vita Epifani*, p. 100, lines 26–7 (ed. F. Vogel, *Monumenta Germaniae Historica, Auctorum Antiquissimorum Tomus VII*. Berlin, 1961 reprint) ('et' added).

There are three things [622] which are causing the ruin of the Welsh people and preventing them, generation after generation, from ever enjoying prosperity. The first is that all their sons, both legitimate and illegitimate, insist upon taking equal shares in their patrimony. One result of this, as I have said already, is that they not infrequently kill each other. The second is that they entrust the upbringing of their sons to important people of good family in the neighbourhood. When the fathers die, each foster-parent does all in his power to ensure the succession of his protégé, which leads to murder, arson and wholesale destruction. Thirdly, through their natural pride and obstinacy, they will not order themselves as other nations do so successfully, but refuse to accept the rule and dominion of one single king.

Chapter 10
How the Welsh can best fight back and keep up their resistance.

I have set out the case for the English with considerable care and in some detail. I myself am descended from both peoples, and it seems only fair that I should now put the opposite point of view. I therefore turn to the Welsh in this final chapter of my book, and I propose to give them some brief, but I hope effective, instruction in the art of resistance.

If the Welsh would only adopt the French way of arming themselves, if they would fight in ordered ranks instead of leaping about all over the place, if their princes could come to an agreement and unite to defend their country – or, better still, if they had only one prince and he a good one – living as they do in a country so inaccessible and so well protected, I cannot see how so powerful a people could ever be completely conquered. If they were united, no one could ever beat them. They have three great advantages: their country is fortified by nature; they are accustomed to live on very little, and this satisfies them; and the

622. In Version I, instead of this last paragraph of II.9, Gerald had suggested either the complete re-colonization of Wales or the conversion of the whole country into an unpopulated game preserve. Cp. pp. 51–2.

entire nation, both leaders and the common people, are trained in the use of arms.

The English are striving for power, the Welsh for freedom; the English are fighting for material gain, the Welsh to avoid a disaster; the English soldiers are hired mercenaries, the Welsh are defending their homeland. The English, I say, want to drive the Welsh out of the island and to capture it all for themselves. The Welsh, who for so long ruled over the whole kingdom, want only to find refuge together in the least attractive corner of it, the woods, the mountains and the marshes, to which they have been banished for their sins, so that there for a given time they may in want and poverty do penance for the excesses which they committed when they were prosperous.

The memory which they will never lose of their former greatness may well kindle a spark of hatred in the Welsh and encourage them to rebel from time to time; for they cannot forget their Trojan blood and the majesty of their kings who once ruled over Britain, a realm which was so great and a dynasty which lasted so long. During the military expedition which Henry II, King of the English, led against them in South Wales in our own lifetime,[623] an old man living in Pencader (which means the Head of the Chair), who had joined the King's forces against his own people, because of their evil way of life, was asked what he thought of the royal army, whether it could withstand the rebel troops and what the outcome of the war would be. 'My Lord King,' he replied, 'this nation may now be harassed, weakened and decimated by your soldiery, as it has so often been by others in former times; but it will never be totally destroyed by the wrath of man, unless at the same time it is punished by the wrath of God. Whatever else may come to pass, I do not think that on the Day of Direst Judgement any race other than the Welsh, or any other language, will give answer to the Supreme Judge of all for this small corner of the earth.'

Here ends [the Description of Wales]

623. This was in 1163. Cp. pp. 121–2.

APPENDIX 1

The additions made in Versions II and III
of The Journey through Wales

There are twenty-two additions in Version II:

i. First Preface, pp. 63–9. With the original dedication to William de Longchamp, these pages of the First Preface are, however, added at the end of the text of Version I.

ii. I.1, pp. 76–7. One §. How the canons of St David's tried to persuade Rhys ap Gruffydd not to allow Baldwin to continue his mission and above all not to visit St David's. ('As soon as . . . the Archbishop's feelings').

iii. I.1, pp. 79–80. Five §§. Various marvels: Saint David's handbell in Glascwm; the burning of Llywel church; the two pools in Elfael; the pool near Séez in Normandy; feuds in Maelienydd, Elfael and Gwrthrynion. ('In the church at Glascwm . . . Gwrthrynion').

iv. I.2, pp. 82–3. Part of one §. How William de Braose larded his letters with pious remarks. ('William de Braose . . . God's assistance').

v. I.2, p. 88. Two §§. More marvels. How Gilbert Hagurnell gave birth to a calf; the horse/deer hybrid. ('In the same region . . . those of a deer').

vi. I.2, pp. 95–6. One §. How Brecknock Mere changes colour and other marvels. ('The local inhabitants . . . imperceptible to the eye').

vii. I.2, p. 96. Concluding sentence. The violent deeds done in the Black Mountains. ('I leave it to others . . . acts of violence').

viii. I.3, p. 97. Three sentences. The salubrious air of Llanthony. ('When, sadly afflicted . . . temperate and healthy').

ix. I.5, pp. 116–21. Six §§. The prophecies of Meilyr. ('It is worth relating . . . by shameful perfidy').

x. I.6, pp. 123–5. One §. The prophecy made to Henry II in Cardiff. ('On his return . . . *How to Bring Up a Prince*').

xi. I.7, p. 130. One §. Gerald's own observation of dogs. ('To all that has gone before . . . heals itself').

xii. I.8, p. 133. One §. The monks' little joke about Welsh quicksands. ('That same night . . . the quicksands').

xiii. I.11, pp. 146–7. Four §§. More prophecies from rams' shoulderblades. ('On another occasion . . . to the ears').

xiv. I.12, pp. 154–5. One §. Elidyr of Stackpole and the son of the incubus. ('At about the same time . . . it was all true').

xv. II.2, pp. 170–71. One §. Rhys ap Gruffydd and events which happened in Llanhyver Castle in 1191–4. ('I must tell you . . . shameful crime').

xvi. II.2, p. 171. One §. Saint Cynog's torque. ('At the time . . . judgement of God').

xvii. II.3, p. 175. Half of each of two §§. Additional material on the habits of beavers. ('When they are building . . . an adze').

xviii. II.8, pp. 193–4. One §. The sons of Owain ap Gruffydd and events which happened in 1194. ('I shall pass over . . . eyes of God').

xix. II.9, p. 195. Two sentences. The one-eyed mullets in Scotland. ('It is worth noticing . . . right one').

xx. II.9, p. 195. One §. The eagle of Snowdon. ('There is a remarkable eagle . . . but not the place').

xxi. II.11, p. 200. Four sentences. The handless sempstress of Chester. ('Still in our own lifetime . . . all who saw her').

xxii. II.12, p. 202. Half of one §. The wisdom of Owain Gwynedd. ('The previous day . . . could bring').

In Version III there are nineteen more additions:

i. I.1, p. 74. Two sentences. The list of monarchs who were reigning in 1188. ('At that time . . . in Palestine').

ii. I.1, p. 75. One sentence and a few words. Additional details of how Gerald took the Cross in Radnor. ('. . . was the first to stand up . . . I acted . . . Cross of Christ').

iii. I.2, pp. 80–81. Two sentences. How Baldwin read *The Topography of Ireland*. ('The Archbishop . . . of his retainers').

iv. I.2, p. 82. Three sentences. Quotations from the Acts of the Apostles and the Epistle of Saint James. ('We learn from Saint Paul . . . will and ordinance').

v. I.2, pp. 84–6. Three §§. Miracles which occurred in Bury St Edmunds, Howden and Winchcombe. ('In our own lifetime . . . to this day').

APPENDIX I

vi. I.2, pp. 86–7. Most of one §. The long quotation from *The Topography of Ireland* about Saint Patrick's horn. ('In Wales . . . recovered fully').

vii. I.3, pp. 104–5. One §. King Richard's *bon mot* about the Templars, the Benedictines and the Cistercians. ('I have thought it . . . the White Monks" ').

viii. I.11, p. 141. One sentence. How Gerald preached in Latin and French at Haverfordwest. ('Many found it odd . . . the sign of the Cross').

ix. I.12, pp. 153–4. One §. The French knight and the Cistercian abbot. ('In our own times . . . towards the monks').

x. I.12, pp. 155–6. One §. How a Danish bishop was served by a demon. ('A somewhat similar case . . . in human guise').

xi. II.1, pp. 163–4. Two sentences. How Geoffrey of Llanthony became Bishop of St David's in 1203. ('So also . . . consecrated him').

xii. II.1, pp. 167–8. Three §§. The long quotation from *The Conquest of Ireland* concerning Henry II's visit to St David's in 1172. ('The King had left . . . twelve miles away').

xiii. II.3, p. 176. Three sentences. The three quotations about beavers from Cicero, Juvenal and Saint Bernard. ('In his oration . . . hunters need').

xiv. II.6, p. 183. One sentence. The faulty statement about the Rivers Dysynni and Artro. ('Before this . . . Traeth Bychan').

xv. II.10, p. 196. One sentence. The reference by Trogus Pompeius to the spring which runs hot and cold. ('Trogus Pompeius . . . and the day').

xvi. II.12, p. 201. Half a sentence. Robert de Belesme. ('. . . tracing its descent . . . long ago').

xvii. II.12, p. 203. One §. The list of Welsh princes. ('At this point . . . the Welsh and the English').

xviii. II.14, p. 206. One sentence. Pope Urban III's rebuke to Archbishop Baldwin. ('When Pope Urban . . . Archbishop, etc." ').

xix. II.14, pp. 207–8. Half of one §. The deathbed vision of Archbishop Richard, and how he and Archbishop Baldwin failed to follow the lead of Thomas Becket. ('When the martyr's first successor . . . the winnowing-fans').

APPENDIX 2

The additions made in Versions II and III of The Description of Wales

There are thirteen additions in Version II:

i. Second Preface, p. 217. The quotation from Horace. ('To this the poet . . . should revere').

ii. I.4, pp. 223–4. The explanatory words: 'from "cant" meaning a hundred and "tref" meaning a vill'.

iii. I.5, p. 229. The three quotations about beavers from Cicero, Juvenal and Saint Bernard. ('In his oration . . . hunters need').

iv. I.5, p. 230. The words: 'In the same way the Dysynni and the Artro . . .'

v. I.8, p. 233. The sentence, with the quotation: 'They agree with . . . perishes with peace.'

vi. I.17, p. 253. The long passage on coracles. ('For fishing . . . home again" ').

vii. II.2, p. 258. The § about Maximus. ('Let me just add . . . confirm me in this').

viii. II.2, p. 259. The § about Gildas and Arthur. ('The Britons maintain . . . great prince').

ix. II.4, p. 261. The quotation from Micah. ('With a slight modification . . . to be good" ').

x. II.6, p. 264. The quotations from Proverbs. ('Solomon says . . . blood" ').

xi. II.7, pp. 265–6. The quotation from Hosea. ('The words . . . shall fall" ').

xii. II.9, p. 271. Two sentences on the short-sightedness of the policy of the Welsh marcher-lords. ('They have . . . in the end').

xiii. II.9, p. 273. The three things which are causing the ruin of the Welsh people. ('There are three things . . . one single king'). This is the repetitive passage which replaces the one struck out from Version I.

APPENDIX 2

There are four new changes in MS Rd, which I count as Version III.

    i. Second Preface, p. 217. The words 'says Seneca again' are replaced by 'as a certain moral philosopher remarks'. The quotation is really from Cicero.

    ii. I.2, p. 222. The words 'who is the present prince' are replaced by 'who was the prince during our own lifetime'. Prince Rhys ap Gruffydd died in 1197.

    iii. I.3, p. 222. The words 'Dafydd ab Owain' are replaced by 'Lywelyn ab Iorwerth, Iorwerth ab Owain'. Lywelyn expelled Dafydd in 1194.

    iv. II.2, p. 258. The words 'Maximus, the British leader' are replaced by 'Maximus, great in name and great in deed'.

APPENDIX 3

Gerald of Wales and King Arthur

Gerald makes a number of references to the historical Arthur, real or alleged, and to the fictional King Arthur, in the two books translated in this volume. Naturally enough, he does not distinguish between them. Whenever he has occasion to mention Geoffrey of Monmouth, he is uncomplimentary, but, as my notes show, his debt to the *Historia Regum Britanniae* is considerable. All this can be followed from the index.

Two of Gerald's statements merit a word or two of discussion. He seems to have been one of the first, if not the first, [624] to imagine that there were two Merlins: the magician and soothsayer who plays so big a part in Geoffrey's *Historia* and whom Gerald calls 'iste qui et Ambrosius dictus est';[625] and a second and older Merlin 'qui et Celidonius dictus est . . . et Silvester',[626] whose prophecies – one assumes that he means the prophecies – he himself discovered when he was in Nefyn with Archbishop Baldwin.[627] Again this can be followed from the index.

The second interesting statement for Arthurian scholars is Gerald's attempt to explain why Gildas never mentioned Arthur in the *De excidio Britanniae* (*Desc.*, II.2) [628]

More important are the two long passages in the *De principis instructione* and the *Speculum Ecclesiae* in which Gerald twice gives

624. See E. K. Chambers, *Arthur of Britain*, 1927, p. 99.

625. *Itin.*, II.8. This is a memory of the *Historia Regum Britanniae*, VI.19, where Geoffrey wrote 'qui et Ambrosius dicebatur'. As I have suggested in my Penguin Classics translation, p. 169, n. 1, Geoffrey's words have all the air of being a gloss.

626. *Itin.*, II.8.

627. The sentence is odd: 'Ubi Merlinum Silvestrem, diu quaesitum desideratumque, archidiaconus Menevensis dicitur invenisse' (*Itin.*, II.6). This is Version III. Why 'dicitur invenisse'? In Versions I and II he had written 'invenit'.

628. This passage is added in Version II.

what seems to be an authoritative account of the discovery of the tomb of the fictional King Arthur and his wife Guinevere in the grounds of Glastonbury Abbey, and of his own visit there to inspect the remains. These descriptions are so graphic and they are of such interest that I print a translation:

1. *De principis instructione*, I.20:
The memory of Arthur, that most renowned King of the Britons, will endure for ever. In his own day he was a munificent patron of the famous Abbey at Glastonbury, giving many donations to the monks and always supporting them strongly, and he is highly praised in their records. More than any other place of worship in his kingdom he loved the Church of the Blessed Mary, Mother of God, in Glastonbury, and he fostered its interests with much greater loving care than that of any of the others. When he went out to fight, he had a full-length portrait of the Blessed Virgin painted on the front of his shield,[629] so that in the heat of battle he could always gaze upon Her; and whenever he was about to make contact with the enemy he would kiss Her feet with great devoutness.

In our own lifetime[630] Arthur's body was discovered at Glastonbury, although the legends had always encouraged us to believe that there was something otherworldly about his ending, that he had resisted[631] death and had been spirited away to some far-distant spot. The body was hidden deep in the earth in a hollowed-out oak-bole and between two stone pyramids which had been set up long ago in the churchyard there. They carried it into the church with every mark of honour and buried it decently there in a marble tomb. It had been

629. Cp. *The History of the Kings of Britain*, IX.4, where the shield is called Pridwen.
630. What does Gerald mean by his tantalizing 'his nostris diebus'? He seems to have written the first book of *De principis instructione* between 1193 and 1199. Henry II died on 6 July 1189, but there is nothing in this passage to imply that he was still alive. Henry de Soilli became Abbot of Glastonbury on 15 September 1189, but, of course, he is not named in this passage. In the *Chronicon Anglicanum* (ed. J. Stevenson, 1875, p. 36), Ralph of Coggeshall records the discovery of Arthur's tomb *sub anno* 1191. In the *Historia de rebus gestis Glastoniensibus* (ed. T. Hearne, 1727, p. 341), Adam of Domerham says that Arthur's body had lain in the tomb for 648 years. Starting from Geoffrey of Monmouth's date of 542 for the Battle of Camlann, this gives 1190.
631. The text says 'its ending' and 'it had resisted', referring back to 'body'.

provided with most unusual indications which were, indeed, little short of miraculous, for beneath it – and not on top, as would be the custom nowadays – there was a stone slab, with a leaden cross attached to its under side. I have seen this cross myself and I have traced the lettering which was cut into it on the side turned towards the stone, instead of being on the outer side and immediately visible. The inscription read as follows: HERE IN THE ISLE OF AVALON LIES BURIED THE RENOWNED KING ARTHUR, WITH GUINEVERE, HIS SECOND WIFE.

There are many remarkable deductions to be made from this discovery. Arthur obviously had two wives, and the second one was buried with him. Her bones were found with those of her husband, but they were separate from his. Two thirds of the coffin, the part towards the top end, held the husband's bones, and the other section, at his feet, contained those of his wife. A tress of woman's hair, blond, and still fresh and bright in colour, was found in the coffin. One of the monks snatched it up and it immediately disintegrated into dust. There had been some indications in the Abbey records that the body would be discovered on this spot, and another clue was provided by lettering carved on the pyramids, but this had been almost completely erased by the passage of the years. The holy monks and other religious had seen visions and revelations. However, it was Henry II, King of England, who had told the monks that, according to a story which he had heard from some old British soothsayer,[632] they would find

632. Gerald's words are: '. . . sicut ab historico cantore Britone audierat antiquo . . .' Henry II's motives for persuading the Glastonbury monks to dig up what could plausibly be taken for the bodies of King Arthur and Queen Guinevere would be obvious enough: the discovery would, he might have hoped, put an effective end to Welsh dreams that their hero would come back one day to help them in their resistance to the Norman kings. How could he possibly know that these bones lay there sixteen feet in the ground, and all the attendant circumstances? The monks may have known that some very distinguished man and woman had been buried centuries before in their grounds, as, indeed, were Edmund I, d. 946, Edgar, d. 975, and Edmund Ironside, d. 1016. They may have been clever enough to plant the remains there. They could have had ready suitable bones, a stone slab, a leaden cross with an inscription, and all the other paraphernalia, and introduced them at dead of night when the hole was down to sixteen feet. Adam of Domerham says significantly that Abbot Henry de Soilli kept curtains round the hole, 'locum cortinis circumdans'. The lock of blond hair, and the monk who so conveniently destroyed it, were masterly touches. It would have been a modest elaboration to let it be known that Henry II, so recently dead and

Arthur's body buried at least sixteen feet in the ground, not in a stone coffin but in a hollowed-out oak-bole. It had been sunk as deep as that, and carefully concealed, so that it could never be discovered by the Saxons, whom Arthur had attacked relentlessly as long as he lived and whom, indeed, he had almost wiped out, but who occupied the island [of Britain] after his death. That was why the inscription, which was eventually to reveal the truth, had been cut into the inside of the cross and turned inwards towards the stone. For many a long year this inscription was to keep the secret of what the coffin contained, but eventually, when time and circumstance were both opportune the lettering revealed what it had so long concealed.

What is now known as Glastonbury used in ancient times to be called the Isle of Avalon. It is virtually an island, for it is completely surrounded by marshlands. In Welsh it is called 'Ynys Avallon', which means the Island of Apples.[633] 'Aval' is the Welsh word for apple,[634] and this fruit used to grow there in great abundance. After the Battle of Camlann, a noblewoman called Morgan, who was the ruler and patroness of these parts as well as being a close blood-relation of King Arthur, carried him off to the island now known as Glastonbury, so that his wounds could be cared for. Years ago the district had also been called 'Ynys Gutrin'[635] in Welsh, that is the Island of Glass, and from these words the invading Saxons later coined the place-name 'Glastingebury'.[636] The word 'glass' in their language means 'vitrum' in Latin, and 'bury' means 'castrum' or 'civitas'.

You must know that the bones of Arthur's body which were discovered there were so big that in them the poet's words seem to be fulfilled:

All men will exclaim at the size of the bones they've exhumed. [637]

The Abbot showed me one of the shin-bones. He held it upright on the ground against the foot of the tallest man he could find, and it

now beyond questioning, had told them where to dig. The credulous reader is advised to read *The Piltdown Forgery*, J. S. Weiner, 1955.

633. There is much debate about the origin of the place-name Avalon.
634. In Modern Welsh this is 'afal'.
635. In Modern Welsh this is 'gwydr'; 'gwydryn' is a drinking glass.
636. Glastonbury < 'Glastingebury' < 'Glaestingas' (OE), the people of 'Glastonia' = the place where woad grows + 'bury' < 'glasto' (O Celt), 'glastum' (Gall) = woad. As E. Ekwall points out, *English Place-names*, p. 199, the Latin word 'vitrum' is used for woad as well as glass.
637. Virgil, *Georgics*, I.497.

stretched a good three inches above the man's knee. The skull was so large and capacious that it seemed a veritable prodigy of nature, for the space between the eyebrows and the eye-sockets was as broad as the palm of a man's hand. Ten or more wounds could clearly be seen, but they had all mended except one. This was larger than the others and it had made an immense gash. Apparently it was this wound which had caused Arthur's death.

2. *Speculum Ecclesiae*, II.8–10:

In our own lifetime,[638] when Henry II was reigning in England, strenuous efforts were made in Glastonbury Abbey to locate what must have once been the splendid tomb of Arthur.[639] It was the King himself who put them on to this,[640] and Abbot Henry, who was later elected Bishop of Worcester, gave them every encouragement.[641] With immense difficulty Arthur's body was eventually dug up in the churchyard dedicated by Saint Dunstan.[642] It lay between two tall pyramids with inscriptions on them, which pyramids had been erected many years before in memory of Arthur. The body was reduced to dust, but it was lifted up into the fresh air from the depths of the grave and carried with the bones to a more seemly place of burial. In the same grave there was found a tress of woman's hair, blond and lovely to look at, plaited and coiled with consummate skill,[643] and belonging no doubt to Arthur's wife, who was buried there with her husband. The moment that [he saw][644] this lock of hair, [one of the monks], who was standing there in the crowd, jumped down into the deep grave[645] in an

638. The *Speculum Ecclesiae* is dated c. 1216, so that Gerald wrote this second account a quarter of a century after the discovery.

639. Henry II died on 6 July 1189. Maybe the 'strenuous efforts' were begun while he was still alive.

640. Cp. n. 632.

641. In the *De principis instructione* Gerald did not name the Abbot. Henry de Soilli became Abbot of Glastonbury on 15 September 1189. He was elected Bishop of Worcester on 4 December 1193 and consecrated on 12 December.

642. According to William of Malmesbury there was a church in Glastonbury as early as AD 166. There was certainly a Celtic monastery there before the Saxon conquest. Saint Dunstan became Abbot c. 943.

643. This is a new elaboration.

644. The *Speculum Ecclesiae* exists in one manuscript only, British Library, Cotton, Tiberius B.XIII, and this is badly damaged. There will be many gaps in my translation.

645. Again, in his earlier account in the *De principis instructione*, Gerald

attempt to snatch hold of it before any of the others. It was a pretty shameless thing to do and it showed little reverence for the dead. This monk, then, of whom I have told you, a silly, rash and impudent fellow, who had come to gawp at what was going on, dropped down into the hole, which was a sort of symbol of the Abyss from which none of us can escape. He was determined to seize hold of this tress of woman's hair before anyone else could do so and to touch it with his hand. This was a fair indication of his wanton thoughts, for female hair is a snare for the feeble-minded, although those with any strength of purpose can resist it.[646] Hair is considered to be imperishable, in that it has no fleshy content and no humidity of its own, but as he held it in his hand after picking it up and stood gazing at it in rapture, it immediately disintegrated into fine powder. All those who were watching were astounded by what had happened. By some sort of miracle, not to say ..., it just disappeared, as if suddenly changed back into atoms, for it could never have been uncoiled and examined closely ...: this showed that it was even more perishable than most things, proving that all physical beauty is a transitory thing for us to stare at with our vacant eyes or to grope for in our lustful moments, empty and availing nothing. As the philosopher says: 'Physical beauty is short-lived, it disappears so soon, it fades more quickly than the flowers in springtime.'[647]

Many tales are told and many legends have been invented about King Arthur and his mysterious ending. In their stupidity the British people maintain that he is still alive. Now that the truth is known, I have taken the trouble to add a few more details in this present chapter. The fairy-tales have been snuffed out, and the true and indubitable facts are made known, so that what really happened must be made crystal clear to all and separated from the myths which have accumulated on the subject.

---

does not say that the monk snatched up the tress of blond hair after he had jumped down sixteen feet into the hole in the ground. Nothing would have been easier than for him to have replaced the hair by a handful of human dust. Indeed, the hair may never have existed, for only the monk need have seen it, and he could have lied.

646. This is an interesting example of hair fetish: there were not many things which Gerald did not know.

647. I cannot trace this quotation.

After the Battle of Camlann ... killed his uncle ... Arthur: the sequel was that the body of Arthur, who had been mortally wounded, was carried off by a certain noble matron, called Morgan, who was his cousin, to the Isle of Avalon, which is now known as Glastonbury. Under Morgan's supervision the corpse was buried in the churchyard there. As a result the credulous Britons and their bards invented the legend that a fantastic sorceress called Morgan had removed Arthur's body to the Isle of Avalon so that she might cure his wounds there. According to them, once he has recovered from his wounds this strong and all-powerful King will return to rule over the Britons in the normal way. The result of all this is that they really expect him to come back, just as the Jews, led astray by even greater stupidity, misfortune and misplaced faith, really expect their Messiah to return.

It is worth noting ... just as, indeed ... placed by all, as ... are called islands and are known to be situated in salt water, that is to say in the sea. It is called Avalon, either from the Welsh word 'aval', which means apple, because apple-trees and apples are very common there,[648] or from the name of a certain Vallo who used to rule over the area long ago.[649] In remote times the place used to be called 'Ynys Gutrin' in the Welsh language, that is the Island of Glass, no doubt from the glassy colour of the river which flows round it in the marshland. As a result the Saxons who occupied the area later on called it 'Glastonia' in their language, for in Saxon or English 'glass' corresponds to the Latin word 'vitrum'. From what I have said you can see why it was called first 'the Isle of Avalon' and then 'Glastonia'.[650] It is also clear how this fantastic sorceress came to be adopted by the story-tellers.

It is worthy of note that the Abbot called[651] ... also from the letters inscribed on it, although they had been almost obliterated long ago by the passing of the years, and he had the aforesaid King Henry to provide the main evidence.

The King had told the Abbot on a number of occasions[652] that he had learnt from the historical accounts of the Britons and from their bards that Arthur had been buried in the churchyard there between

648. Cp. n. 633.

649. Nothing is known of this Vallo, although folklorists have taken him up.

650. Cp. n. 636.

651. Henry de Soilli.

652. Cp. n. 630. Henry de Soilli became Abbot two months after the death of Henry II.

two pyramids which had been erected subsequently, very deep in the ground for fear lest the Saxons, who had striven to occupy the whole island after his death, might ravage the dead body in their evil lust for vengeance. Arthur had attacked them on a great number of occasions and had expelled them from the Island of Britain, but his dastardly nephew Mordred had called them back again to fight against him.[653] To avoid such a frightful contingency, to a large stone slab, found in the tomb by those who were digging it up, some seven feet[654] . . . a leaden cross had been fixed, not on top of the stone, but underneath it, bearing this inscription: HERE IN THE ISLE OF AVALON LIES BURIED THE RENOWNED KING ARTHUR, WITH GUINEVERE, HIS SECOND WIFE. They prised this cross away from the stone, and Abbot Henry, about whom I have told you, showed it to me. I examined it closely and I read the inscription. The cross had been attached to the under side of the stone and, to make it even less easy to find, the surface with the lettering had been turned towards the stone. One can only wonder at the industry and the extraordinary prudence of the men of that period, who were determined to protect at all costs and for all time the body of this great man, their leader and the ruler of this area, from the possibility of sudden desecration. At the same time they ensured that at some moment in the future, when the troubles were over, the evidence of the lettering cut into the cross might be discovered as an indication of what they had done.

. . . it had indicated, so Arthur's body was discovered, not in a stone sarcophagus, carved out of rock or of Parian marble, as would have been seemly for so famous a King, but in wood, in an oak-bole hollowed out for this purpose and buried deep in the earth, sixteen feet or more down, for the burial of so great a Prince, hurried no doubt rather than performed with due pomp and ceremony, as this period of pressing disturbance made only too necessary.

When the body was discovered from the indications provided by King Henry, the Abbot whom I have named had a splendid marble tomb built for it, as was only proper for so distinguished a ruler of the area, who, moreover, had shown more favour to this church than to any other in his kingdom, and had endowed it with wide and extensive lands. By the judgement of God, which is always just and which in this case was certainly not unjustified, who rewards all good deeds not

653. Cp. *The History of the Kings of Britain*, XI.1.
654. The figure VII comes just where the manuscript is damaged and it may have been misread by the editor.

APPENDIX 3

only in Heaven above but on this earth and in our terrestrial life . . .,
church . . . others of his kingdom . . . the genuine [remains] and the
body . . . of Arthur to be buried in a seemly fashion . . . and gloriously
. . . and . . . inhumed.

INDEX

What follows is at once an index and an *index raisonné* of my translation of *The Journey through Wales* and *The Description of Wales*. Every proper name and place-name mentioned in the text is listed in this index; and all the major events and most of the minor ones which occur are given in succinct form under the names of the persons concerned in them.

INDEX

Aaron, Saint, martyred at
Caerleon, 115

Abbots, abuses committed by,
180–81

Abelard, Peter, 43, 153 and
n. 247

'Aber', meaning of word, 80, 226

Aberconwy, Battle of, 186 n. 358

Aberffraw, ancient royal
stronghold, 139, 223

Abergavenny
journey to, 25–6, 32, 33,
108–13, 131
Massacre of, AD 1175, 109–11
and n. 145

Abergavenny Castle
course of River Usk past, 226
origins of name, location of, 108

Abergavenny, Lord of, see
William de Braose

Aberhonddu, Welsh for Brecon, 80;
see also Brecon

Aberhonddu Castle, location of,
226 and n. 502

Aberhotheni (Hotheni), 226,
n. 502

Abertawe see Swansea

Abertawe Castle, site of, 226

Aberteivi see Cardigan

Abraham, dreams, visions, 250

Abraham, Bishop of St David's,
163 and nn. 269, 271–2

Absalom, 238 and n. 530

Acre
death of Baldwin at, 16, 38
n. 116, 208 and n. 445

death of Ranulf de Glanville at,
75 n. 39
siege of, 208

Acts of the Apostles, quoted from,
referred to, 82 and n. 57, 190
and n. 371, 250 and n. 566

Adam of Domerham, evidence on
Arthur's tomb, 281 n. 630,
282 n. 632

Adwenhelye see Eluned

Aeneas, accounts of links with
early history of Wales, 223 and
n. 488, 231–2 and
nn. 513–14, 245–6

Aeneid see Virgil

Aetius, appeal of Britons to, 258
and n. 585

Afandreg (Anaudreg, Anaudrech)
ap Mertyn, 222 and n. 485

Agnes see Nest

Agriculture, patterns of, 47, 57,
233, 252

Aidan, son of Rhodri Mawr, 221
n. 479

Alan of Britanny, 108 n. 143

Alba Domus (Alba Landa) see
Whitland

Albanactus, son of mythical Brutus,
232

Albania (North Britain), origins of
name, 232

Albanus (Saint Alban), 115

Aled see Eluned

Alexander, Abbot of Ford,
candidate for See of St
David's, 18, 19

evidence as to cause of death, 284
family relationships, 159 n. 255,
160
Gerald's references to, 96 and
n. 101, 280–88
killer of own brother, 259
link with Merlin Silvester, 193
miraculous conception, 193
n. 379
reference to 'three principal
courts', 139 n. 215
references to, omitted from
Version II of *Description*, 51
shield, 281 and n. 629
supposed court at Caerleon, 115
Arthur's Chair (Cadair Arthur), 96
and n. 100
Artro, River, confusion over course
of, 37 n. 113, 39, 42, 51 n. 155,
183 n. 344, 230
Arts, liberal, Gerald's admiration
for practice of, 64–9, 213, 214,
215–17
Arwistel (Augustus), Bishop of
St David's, 163 and n. 269
Asaph, Saint, 224
Ascanius, accounts of links with
early history of Wales, 223
and n. 488, 231–2 and
nn. 513–14, 237 and n. 526
Aser (Asser), Bishop of St David's,
161–2 and nn. 263, 266,
266 n. 611
Athens, reference to, 212 and
n. 454
Augustine, Saint, of Canterbury,
meeting with Welsh bishops,
164 and n. 280
Augustine, Saint, of Hippo,
references to, quotations from,
81–2, 136 and n. 205, 152–3
and n. 245
Augustine's Oak, 164 n. 280
Augustinian Rule, recognition of,
101 and n. 113

Augustus, Emperor, 241 and n. 542
Aulus Gellius, quoted, 64 n. 7,
248 and n. 559
Aurelius Ambrosius, 257
Aust (Gloucestershire), site of
Augustine's Oak, 164 n. 280
*Autobiography of Giraldus
Cambrensis*, H. E. Butler, 9 n. 2
Avalon, Isle of
Arthur's body removed to, 283,
286
origins of name, 283 and n. 633,
286
see also Glastonbury
Avon, River
crossing of, 33, 71, 130
quicksands in vicinity of, 42, 226
source, course, 226
'Awenyddion', meaning of word,
246 and n. 554

Baal, 249 and n. 564
Bala, Lake, source of Dee in, 198
and n. 405, 230
Baldwin, Archbishop of
Canterbury
attitude of canons of St David's
to mission, 38, 76–7
crusading zeal, 16, 24, 28, 208
death, 16, 38 n. 116, 208 and
n. 445
ecclesiastical appointments, 24
enthronement at Canterbury,
206 and n. 438
Gerald's assessment of, comments
on, 42, 54–5, n. 162, 55–6, 58,
68, 74, 164, 184
meeting with Arthenus, 109
origins, purpose, impact of
journey, 12, 16, 24, 25–6 and
n. 93, 27
physical, mental attributes, 24–5,
27
quarrel with Convent of Christ
Church, Canterbury, 30 n. 110

Britons (*contd*)
  origins of language, 246
  origins of name, 231–2 and
    nn. 513–14
  resistance to Saxons, Normans, 220
  retreat to Wales, Cornwall,
    Brittany, 220–21 and
    nn. 476–7
Britanny
  incidence of incest, abuse of
    benefices in, 263–4 and n. 602
  language akin to Welsh, 231
  retreat of Britons to, 220–21 and
    nn. 476–7
Bromfield
  journey to, 32, 36, 72, 204
  Welsh name for, 203 n. 421ˉ
Bromfield Priory, journey to, 32, 36
Bromwich, Rachel, 91–2 n. 90,
  139 n. 215, 182 n. 339, 186
  n. 359, 220 n. 473, 223 n. 489
Bronllys Castle, death of Mahel de
  Neufmarché at, 89 n. 78, 91
  n. 89
Brutus (mythical)
  alleged distribution of Britain to
    sons, 232 and n. 514
  escape from Troy, link with early
    history of Welsh princes,
    231–2 and nn. 513–14, 245–6
Brychan, ruler of Brecknock, 86 n.
  68, 91–2 and nn. 90–91
'Brychan', Welsh sheet, 237 and
  n. 528
Brycheiniog *see* Brecknockshire
Builth, conquest of, 77
Bury St Edmunds, story of miracle
  in, 43, 84
Butler, H. E., 9 n. 2, 23 n. 73, 60

Cadell ab Einon, 222 and n. 484
Cadell ap Gruffydd, 144 n. 227
Cadel ap Rhodri Mawr
  family relationships, 221 and
    n. 479, 222 and n. 484

  lands given to, 221 and n. 481
Cador (old man at Swansea), gift
  for crusade, 34, 132–3
Cadwaladr ap Gruffyd ap Cynan
  burial in Bangor Cathedral,
    192
  death, 192 n. 376, 203 n. 420
  wise rule praised, 203
Cadwaladr ap Seisyll ap Dyfuwal,
  killed, 109–10 n. 145
Cadwallon ap Caradog ap Iestin,
  quarrels with brothers, 128
    and n. 188
Cadwallon ab Owain Cyfeiliog,
  201 n. 415
Cadwallon ab Owain Gwynedd
  blinded by order of Henry II,
    201–2 n. 417
  family relationships, 193
    n. 382
Caeo, commote of
  defeat of Gwenllian in, 139; *see
    also* Gwenllian
  Gruffydd ap Rhys's lands in, 94
    and n. 96
'Caer', meaning of word, 114
Caerleon
  capture by Hywell and Iorwerth,
    119 and n. 116
  course of River Usk past, 226
  Gerald's knowledge of, 115
    n. 155
  journey through, 32, 33, 114–21
  reference to court of Arthur at,
    139 n. 215
  Roman remains, 114–15 and
    n. 155
  rulers of, 108 n. 144
  site of royal palace, 223 and
    n. 489
Caerleon, see of
  concepts of metropolitan status,
    115. 159–60 nn. 255–6, 179
  removal of metropolitan status to
    St David's, 159 n. 255, 160

Caernarfon, journey to, 32, 35, 72,
183, 184–5
Caiaphas, 249 and n. 564
Caius Marius, 64–5 and n. 11
Calchas (Trojan soothsayer),
247–8 and n. 556
Caldy Island (Ynys Byr), 150
Cambrenses, origin of name, 232
Camber (son of mythical Brutus),
232
Cambria
boundary between southern
England and, 225
origins of name, 47, 220, 231–2
and n. 513
see also Wales
Camden, William, editions of
Gerald's works, 44, 45, 52, 53
Camlann, Battle of, 281 n. 630,
283, 286
Camrose, journey through, 32, 34,
156–7
Canterbury, Canterbury Cathedral
consecration of Bishops of St
David's at, 163
Gerald's visit to, 12
monks of Christ Church, 14–15,
30 n. 110
Canterbury, Archbishops of
conflict with Crown, 206–8
Gerald's resistance to
subservient role of St David's,
14, 18 and n. 41, 19, 22, 41,
159–60 and n. 255, 162–3, 164
relation to Church in Wales, 26
see also Baldwin, Becket,
Langton, Ralph Richard,
Theobald, Walter
Cantref
administrative unit, 47, 94 and
n. 95, 186, 223
etymology of term, 51, 223–4
Cantref Bychan
boundary between Cantref
Mawr and, 226

Gruffydd ap Rhys's lands in, 94
n. 96
mountains of, 96
rivers of, 121, 226
tidal spring, 139
Cantref Einon, origins of name,
88 n. 73
Cantref Mawr
boundary between Cantref
Bychan and, 226
Gruffydd ap Rhys's lands in, 94
and n. 96
proximity of Carmarthen to, 139
rivers of, 227
Cantref Selyf, origins of name,
88 n. 73
Cantref Tewdos, origins of name,
88 n. 73
Caracute, unit of land, 165
n. 282
Caradog, Saint (Fynach), 144–5
and nn. 228–9
Caradog ap Iestin
death, 130 n. 193
family relationships, 81 and n. 51
quarrelsome sons, 128 and n. 188
Cardiff, journey to, 33
Cardiff Castle
assault on, by Ifor Bach, 122–3
and nn. 174–5, 142 n. 224
course of River Taff past, 226
journey to, 121
Cardigan
journey to, 25–6, 171–2
response to mission, 171–2
Cardiganshire
boundary between Dyved and,
227
fertility, 230
journey through, 25–6, 27–8, 31
n. 111, 32, 34–5, 71, 173,
177
rivers of, 227, 230
ruled by Richard FitzGilbert,
108 and n. 142

Carmarthen
  besieged by Rhys ap Gruffydd,
    138 and n. 212
  discovery of Merlin in, 192, 226
    and n. 503
  journey to, 32, 34, 138–9
  location, description of, 138–9
  origins, meaning of name, 138,
    192, 226 and n. 503
  Roman remains, 138 and n. 214
Carmarthen Castle, course of River
  Tywi past, 226
'Carn', meaning of word, 121
Carn Madryn Castle, 183 and n. 343
Carreg Iago (Carreg yr Archjagon),
  site of sermon in Anglesey,
    185 n. 353
Carquit, William, excommunication
  of, 12
Cassandra, 247–8 and n. 557
Cassivelaunus, 257 and n. 581
'Castor', origin of term, 176 and
  n. 312
Catalus (Catulus), Bishop of St
  David's, 161–2 and n. 263
Celliwig, Cornwall
  reference to court of Arthur at,
    139 n. 215
  site of royal palace, 223 n. 489
Cemais
  journey through, 34, 71,
    169–72
  Norman rulers of, 170 n. 299
Cenarth Mawr, salmon fishing at,
  173
Cenwulf, King of Mercia, 85
  nn. 66–7
Cerrig y Borth, site of meeting
  with Rhodri in Anglesey,
    185 n. 353
Chaldeans, answer to
  Nebuchadnezzar, 248–9
Chambers, E. K., 280 n. 624
Chapter-headings
  of Description, 218–19 and n. 220

of Journey, 40 and nn. 122–3,
    71–2 and n. 28, 74 n. 29
Châteauroux (Castellum Radulphi)
  conflict between Henry II and
    Louis VII, 142 n. 225
  scene of sorrows, 143
  story of blind prisoner of, 43,
    142–3
Châtillon-sur-Seine, Gerald's
  imprisonment at, 20–21
Chester
  course of River Dee past, 230
  journey to, 26, 30, 31, 32, 36, 72,
    198–9
Chester, Countess of, cheese from
  deer's milk, 199 and n. 408
Chester, Earls of, see Hugh,
  Ranulf (bis)
Chesterton, Oxon, living of, held
  by Gerald, 12 n. 11, 23 n. 78
Childebert, King of the Franks,
  162 n. 268
Children, Gerald's loving
  attitude to, 59
China, folklore associated with
  bones, 145 n. 231
Chinon, Touraine
  Gerald's visit to, 16
  Henry II's death at, 79 n. 49
Choral music see Music-making,
  Part-singing
Christ Church see Canterbury
Christianity, conversion of Welsh
  to, 47, 253–4
Churches, Welsh respect for, 253–4
Cicero, quotations from, references
  to, 51 n. 154, 52, 56, 90 and
    n. 83, 176 and n. 313, 206
    and n. 439, 212 n. 450, 217
    n. 470, 229, 242 and n. 544, 244
Cilgerran, 173 and n. 305
Cistercian abbot (nameless),
  anecdotes about, 41
Cistercian Order
  attitude to almsgiving, charity, 126

Baldwin a member of, 206 and
n. 437
comments of attitude to wealth,
property, 103–4, 105–7 and
n. 138
origins, aims, 101 and n. 115
Richard I's reference to, 105 and
n. 135
spread in Wales, 118 n. 162,
119 n. 165, 178 nn. 323–4,
195 and n. 389, 196 n. 394
Cîteaux, foundation of Cistercian
Order in, 101 n. 115
City of the Legions see Caerleon
Clamosus, Lake (Brecknock Mere,
Llangors Lake, 93–5 and
n. 93, 95–6
Clare, Suffolk, 108 n. 142
Clare, Earl of, 142; see also
FitzGilbert, Gilbert
Claudian, quotation from, 260 and
n. 594
Cledauc, Bishop of St David's,
161–2 and n. 263
'Cleddau', meaning of word, 141
Cleddau streams, river
crossing of, 34, 140
source, course, 227
Clement III, Pope, tenure of Holy
See, 74 n. 30
Clement of Gloucester, Prior of
Llanthony Prima, 98 and
n. 105
Clent, Worcestershire, murder of
St Kenelm at, 85 n. 66
Clifford, course of River Wye past,
225–6 and n. 501
Clothes, Welsh, described, 47, 57,
237
Clovis, King of the Franks, 162
n. 268
Cluniac Order
comments on attitude to wealth,
property, 105–7 and n. 138
origins, 105 n. 136

Cluny Abbey, foundation of, 105
n. 136
Clwyd, River, source, course, 196,
230
Coed Eulo, Battle of, 189 and
n. 364, 196
Goed Grwyne, journey through, 33,
71, 108–13
'Coelibes' monks, 183–4 and
n. 347
Coleshill
course of River Dee past, 230
defeat of Henry II at, 189 and
n. 364, 196
'Colidei' monks, 183–4 and n. 347
'Combroges', origins of name,
220 n. 472
Commote, administrative unit, 94
and n. 95
Conquest of Ireland (Expugnatio
Hibernica)
aims in writing of, 15, 67–8
n. 22, 211–13 and n. 460
editions, 18 n. 41, 44
Gerald's name for, 149 and
n. 240
material from repeated in
Journey, 41, 56, 156 n. 250,
157 n. 253, 166 and n. 287,
167 n. 288, 189 and n. 368,
206 n. 435, 215 n. 466, 255
and n. 578, 256 and n. 579,
268–9 and n. 616, 271–2 and
nn. 618, 620
reference to Lech Lafar Stone,
166 and n. 286
revisions of, 37
translations of, 45
written for Richard I, 67–8
Constance of Brittany, 199 n. 408
Constantine, Emperor, 264
Constantine II, Emperor, 257 and
n. 583
Conway, Cistercian monastery at,
195

Conway, River
crossing of, 36, 72, 192, 195
source, course, 230
Coracles, fishing from, 51, 252
Corineus, British leader in
Cornwall, 220 and n. 475
Corinthians, I, quotations from,
references to, 82 and n. 55,
248 n. 560, 249 n. 564, 262
and n. 597
Cornwall
language akin to Welsh, 231
retreat of Britons to, 220–21 and
nn. 476–7
Court, life at, comments on, 66–7
Cristin, wife of Owain Gwynedd,
192 and n. 376, 193 and
n. 382, 196
Croesus, King of Lydia, references
to, 65 and n. 14, 107 and
n. 141, 217
Crooked Greek, 232 and n. 514
Crooks, bishops', Welsh respect
for, 253–4
Cross, taking of see Crusade, Third
Cross of Christ, Welsh reverence
for, 253
Crug Mawr, journey past, 177 and
n. 319
Crug Mawr, Battle of, 177 and
n.320
Cruker Castle, journey to, 25, 32–3,
77
Crusade, Third
Gerald's part in, 16, 24, 37, 41,
75
numbers, character of recruits,
26, 204
reasons for difficulties, 204–5
and nn. 430–2
siege of Acre, 16, 208 and n. 445
story of castellan of Radnor
Castle, 77–8
taking of the Cross, response to
journey, 32–3, 34, 75–6, 80,

109, 114, 121, 126, 132, 140,
141, 178–9 and n. 327, 182–3,
184, 185, 186, 196, 200, 201,
202
Crwth (stringed instrument),
Welsh love of, 239 and n. 534
Cuhelyn see Alexander, Archdeacon
'Culdei' monks, 183–4 and n. 347
Cunedda, Brythonic chieftain,
182 n. 339
Curig, Saint, miraculous staff of,
78–9
Cwenthryth (Quendrada), sister of
Saint Kenelm, 85–6 and n. 66
Cydweli Castle, held by Maurice
of London, 126 n. 185, 137
n. 209
Cydweli, commote of, held by
Roger, Bishop of Salisbury,
99 n. 108
Cyfeiliog, commote in Powys, 202
n. 418
'Cymri', origin of name, 220 and
n. 471, 232
Cymric language, 232; see also
Welsh language
'Cymwd' see Commote
Cynan, Abbot of Margam, 126 and
n. 186
Cynan, Abbot of Whitland, 119
and n. 165, 126 n. 186
Cynan ab Iago family
relationships, 222 and n. 485
Cynan ab Owain 193 n. 382
Cynan, land of
journey through, 72, 181 and
n. 336, 182
rivers of, 230
rugged character. 230
spearmen of, 230–31
see also Merionethshire
Cynfyn ap Gwerstan, family
relationships, 223 n. 486
Cynog, Saint, miraculous torque,
86 and n. 68, 171

Cynwrig ab Owain
  blinded by order of Henry II,
    201–2 n. 417
  family relationships, 193 n. 382
Cywwrig ap Rhys ap Gruffydd,
  meeting with Baldwin and
  Gerald, 25, 35, 178–9 and
  nn. 326–7

Dafydd ab Owain Gwynedd
  defeat at Battle of Aberconwy,
    186 n. 358
  exile, death in England, 50, 52,
    193–4, 203 n. 423, 203 n. 423
  family relationships, 193 and
    nn. 382, 384, 222 and n. 485,
    243 and n. 546
  Gerald's description of, 50
  host to Baldwin and Gerald at
    Rhuddlan, 36, 196
  observation of neutrality between
    English, Welsh, 203
  territories in Gwynedd, 243
Daiville (De Eyville), Dean of
  Shrewsbury, 204 and n. 427
Danes
  effect of invasions on English
    language, 231
  musical traditions derived from,
    243
Daniel, dreams, visions, 250
Daniel, Saint see Deiniol
Daniel, Book of, quotations from,
  references to, 120–21 and
  n. 170, 248–9 and n. 562
David and Saul, references to, 251
David, Bishop of St David's see
  FitzGerald
David, Saint
  dates, 161 n. 262
  election as Archbishop, 179
  miracles associated with, 79, 161
    and n. 261, 168 n. 294, 179
  patron saint of St David's
    Cathedral, 224

reception of metropolitan
  responsibilities, 115
removal of archbishopric to St
  David's, 159 n. 255, 160
saintliness, 161
tenure of see, 159 n. 255, 160,
  161
Davies, Elwyn, 46, 61, 62
Davies, J. C., 61
Davies, W. S., 60
Deceangli see Tegeingl
Decretals, Gratian, Gerald's
  lectures on, 14 and n. 17
Dee, River
  boundary between England and
    Wales, 198, 230
  crossing of, 30, 36, 72, 198 and
    n. 403
  source, course, 230
Deer, cheese from milk of, 199
Deer-cow, story of, 199 and n. 409
De excidio Britanniae see Gildas
Degannwy, journey through, 72,
  195
Degannwy Castle, course of River
  Conway past, 230
Deheubarth
  divisions of Wales into Gwynedd,
    Powys and, 47
  extent of, 221
  meaning of name, 94 and n. 97,
    221
  princes, rulers of 47, 221
  see also Wales, South
Deiniol, Saint, Bishop of Bangor,
  184 and n. 348, 224
De iure et statu Menevensis
  ecclesiae, autobiographical
  content, 9 n. 3
Demetia see Dyved
Denmark, story of unnatural
  priest in, 155–6
De principis instructione
  date of, 281 n. 630
  Gerald's account of visit to

Fish
fighting, story of, 79–80
one-eyed, 195
plentiful in Brecknock, 93
Fishing, in Welsh way of life, 51,
57, 252
FitzAlan, William, of Oswestry
and Clun, 36, 200–201 and
n. 414
FitzAldelm, William, 167
FitzBernard, Robert, 167
FitzCount, Brian, 108 and n. 143
FitzGerald, David, Bishop of St
David's
appointment of Gerald to
archdeaconry, 12
death, 9–10 n. 5, 13, 163
n. 275
elevation to see, consecration, 10,
163 and nn. 275, 277
encouragement of Gerald, 10
family relationships, 11, 135
n. 203
persecution by Mahel FitzWalter,
91 and n. 88
relations with canons, 84 n. 63,
91 n. 88
stories about, 84, 131–2, 135,
167–8 and n. 293
value of Gerald's estimate of,
55–6
FitzGerald, Maurice
defeated at Battle of Crug Mawr,
177 n. 320
family relationships, 11, 167
n. 290
with Henry II in Ireland, 167
FitzGerald, William
defeated at Battle of Crug Mawr,
177 n. 320
family relationships, 11
FitzGilbert, Richard (Richard de
Clare)
ambush, murder of 108–9 and
n. 142, 177 n. 320

capture of Usk Castle, 116
n. 159, 120 and n. 169
FitzGilbert, Robert (Robert de
Clare), 123 n. 175, 142 n. 224
FitzHenry, Henry
family relationships, 189 and
n. 367
killed in Anglesey, 189–90 and
n. 36
FitzJohn, Payn, story of Gruffydd
ap Rhys, Milo FitzWalter
and, 94–5
FitzMartin, William
capture of Llanhyvor Castle
from, 170–71
family relationships, 170–71
and n. 299
FitzPeter, Geoffrey, Justiciar, 19,
22
FitzPons, Richard, 91 n. 89
FitzRichard, Osbern, 89 n. 75
FitzStephen, Robert
family relationships, 167
nn. 189–90
with Henry II in Ireland, 167
wounded at Battle of Coed Eulo,
189, 190
FitzTancard, Richard, I, castellan
of Haverfordwest, 143–4 and
n. 226, 144–5
FitzTancard, Richard, II, castellan
of Haverfordwest, 143 n. 226
FitzWalter, Bertha, 81 n. 53
FitzWalter, Milo, Earl of Hereford
death, 89 n. 77, 94 n. 98
family relationships, 81 n. 53,
89–90 and n. 76, 90–91, 94
n. 99
foundation of Llanthony
Secunda, 100 and n. 112
story of Gruffydd ap Rhys, Payn
FitzJohn and, 94–5
Flanders see Flemings
Flemings
exemption from tithes in Rhos, 13

Merfyn ap Rhodri Mawr
family relationships, 221 n. 479,
222
lands given to, 221
Merfyn Frych, family relationships,
221 n. 479, 222 and n. 485,
223 n. 486
Merioneth
description of, 182, 230
origins of name, 182 n. 339
rivers of, 230
rulers, 24, 181 n. 336
spearmen of, 230–31
Merlin, Merlins
concept of two, 280 and
nn. 625–7
Gerald's intention to write on,
67–8 n. 22
origins of name, 226 and n. 503
prophecy on death of English
King at Talking Stone, 167,
168
prophecy on resurgence of
Britons, 265 and n. 607
see also Merlin Ambrosius,
Merlin Silvester
Merlin Ambrosius
contemporary of Vortigern, 192
origins in Carmarthen, 138 and
n. 213, 192, 226 and n. 503
prophecy on destruction of
Britain, 248
prophecy on Menevia dressed in
pall of City of the Legions,
115 and n. 156, 159 n. 255
sources for tales of, 192
nn. 377–8, 193 n. 379
Merlin Silvester (Celidonius)
origins, 192
prophecies in time of Arthur,
192–3
prophecies uttered while in
frenzy, 250
prophecy on destruction of
Britain, 248

prophecy on Rhyd Pencarn, 121
works found by Gerald, 183 and
n. 346, 280 and n. 627
Merthyr Cynog, burial place of
Saint Cynog, 86 n. 68
Meurig ab Anaudreg (Afandreg),
222 and n. 485
Meurig ab Idwal Foel, 222 n. 485
Meuruc, son of Rhodri Mawr, 221
n. 479
Micah, quotation from, 261 and
n. 595
Milford Haven, 144 n. 228
Military science, Gerald's
comments on, 57, 267–70
Miracles, local, Gerald's interest in,
42–3, 78–9, 83–4, 94–6, 127–8,
136, 141, 145, 172
Molesme, Benedictine Order in,
Cistercians' breakaway from,
101 n. 115
Molossi, hounds of, 88 and n. 71
'Môn mam Cymru', 230; see also
Anglesey
Monmouth Castle, journey past,
114
Montgomery, Arnulf de, builder of
Pembroke Castle, 148 and
n. 234, 149
Montgomery, Hugh de, Earl of
Shrewsbury, ravager of
Anglesey, 187 and n. 360, 188
n. 361
Montgomery, Roger de, Earl of
Shrewsbury, 148 n. 234
Morbiu, Bishop of St David's, 163
n. 269
Mordred, nephew of Arthur, 287
Morgan, removal of body of
Arthur, 283, 286
Morgan ap Caradog ap Iestin
family relationships, 128 and
n. 188
with Baldwin on part of journey,
25, 130 and n. 193, 131

Talgarth, Black Mountains of, 96

Talking Stone, 166 and n. 285, 167–8

Tawe, River, source, course, 132, 226

Tayled *see* Eluned

Teeth, Welsh habits in care of, 47, 57, 238

Tegeingl
tidal spring at, 196 and n. 391
tribal name, 243 and n. 545

Teifi, River
crossing of, 35
described, 173–4
journey to bridgehead, 35, 171–2
site of Abbey of Strata Florida on, 178 n. 324
source, course, 171, 227

Teilo, Saint
origins, 126 n. 184
patron saint of Llandaff, 126 and n. 184, 224
see of St David's, 161–2 and n. 264

Templars, Saladin's defeat of, 74–5 n. 37, 208 and n. 444

Tenby, living of, held by Gerald, 12 n. 11

Tench, abundance in Brecknock, 93 and n. 93

Terence, quotations from, references to, 63 n. 4, 255 and n. 577

Tewdwr, father of Rhys, 221–2 and n. 482

Tewdwr ap Cadell, 222 and n. 484

Thebes, reference to, 212 and n. 453

Theliau *see* Teilo

Theobald, Archbishop of Canterbury
consecration of David as Bishop of St David's, 163 n. 277
resistance to metropolitan status for St David's, 165 n. 281

Thestor, father of Calchas, 247 n. 556

Thomas, W. J., 133 n. 200

Tiberias, Saladin's victory at, 74–5 n. 37

Tithes
Gerald's concern for proper payment of, 12, 13, 81–2
Great, Welsh custom, 253

Toads, plague of, 169–70

Topography of Ireland (Topographia Hibernica)
account of Saint Patrick's horn, 86–7 and nn. 69, 70
dating of, 67–8 n. 22
editions, translations, 44, 45
material from, repeated in other works, 41, 56, 97, 173 and n. 307, 174 and n. 309, 177 and n. 316, 199 and n. 409, 239 and n. 532, 268–9 and n. 616, 271–2 and nn. 618, 620
origins, 15
presentation to Baldwin at Brecon, 41, 67–8 n. 22, 80–81, 205–8
revisions of, 37
written for Henry II, 67–8 and n. 22

Topography of Britain, projected work, 258 and n. 586

Torque of Saint Cynog, miraculous power of, 86 and n. 68, 171

Tostig, Welsh campaign, 89 n. 75

Towyn, journey to, 25, 32, 35, 182

'Traeth', meaning of word, 183

Traeth Bychan
course of River Mawddach through, 230
crossing of, 35, 37 n. 113, 72, 183 and n. 344

Traeth Mawr
course of River Mawddach through, 230
crossing of, 35, 37 n. 113, 72, 183 and n. 344

Trajan, reference to, 215
Tramerin, Bishop of St David's,
163 and n. 269
Triads, Gerald's frequent memories
of, 55
Trogus Pompeius, quotation from,
196
Trout, abundance in Brecknock, 93
Troy
fall of, 212 and n. 452
link with early history of Wales,
231-2 and nn. 513-14, 247-8
and nn. 556-8, 264, 274
Troyes, Gerald's visit to, 21
'Tud', early judicial unit in Wales,
94 n. 95
Turf, miraculous, in
Haverfordwest, 141
Turville-Petre, Thorlac, 62, 241
n. 538
Tydeus, reference to, 197 and
n. 401
Tyfrydog, Saint, 188
Ty Gwyn see Whitland
Tywi, River
crossing of, 34, 71, 138
source, course, 226

'Uchelwr', meaning of word, 221
and n. 480
Uchtryd ab Edwin, leader of revolt
of 1096, 148 n. 236
Unclean spirits, accounts of, 43,
151-3
Urban III, Pope, 42, 74 and n. 30,
206 and n. 440
Usk Castle
captured by Richard de Clare,
116 n. 159, 120 and n. 169
course of River Usk past, 226
journey to, 25-6, 29 n. 104, 32,
33, 114
Usk, River
abundance of fish, 93
crossing of, 33, 114

source, course, 80, 108, 121, 226
Utrecht, death of Henry V, Holy
Roman Emperor at, 198 n. 406

Valley of Roses, 166 and n. 284
*Vatinical History see Conquest of
Ireland*
Vere, Alberic de, III, Earl of
Oxford, 191 and n. 373
Vere, Alberic de, IV, Second Earl
of Oxford, 43, 191 and n. 373
Vice, unnatural, Welsh habits,
47-8, 264-5
Virgil, quotations from, references
to, 64-5 and nn. 8, 12, 67 and
n. 19, 111 and n. 151, 116 and
n. 158, 125 and n. 182, 131
and n. 194, 139 and n. 217,
194 and n. 387, 212 and
nn. 452, 455, 215, 216 and
n. 467, 233 and nn. 517, 519,
235 nn. 522-3, 237 and n. 527,
241 and n. 541, 245 n. 551,
248 and n. 558, 283 n. 637
Vortigern, association with Merlin
Ambrosius, 192

Wales
borders between England and,
198, 225, 226, 230
campaign of Harold and Tostig,
89 n. 75
cantrefs, 223
cathedral sees, 224
church in, *see under* St David's,
see of
dating of Baldwin's journey,
30-36
description of extent, 220
division into three, 221-2
early administrative units, 94
n. 95
fertility, attractiveness, 47, 230-31
Gerald's role in journey, 27-9
Gerald's solution to problems of

Welsh language (*contd*)
Gerald's knowledge of, 29 and
nn. 104, 106
origins, distribution, 231
translator into, on journey *see*
Alexander, Archdeacon
Welsh people
acumen, shrewdness, 238–9
attitude to canonically prohibited
degrees, 263 n. 60
comments on how to conquer,
and rule, 48, 51–2, 57, 267–70,
271–3
conduct in battle, 234, 259–60,
267, 270
conversion to Christianity, 47,
253–4
family relationships, 261, 263,
273
frugality, parsimony, 235
Gerald's advice to, on art of
resistance, 273–4
greed, 262
Henry II's comments on, 234–5
and n. 522
hospitable character, 236–7
incidence of incest,
homosexuality, 262–3, 264–5
inconstancy and instability, 256,
271
musical traditions, 47, 57, 236,
239 and nn. 533–4, 242–3
nature of comments on
characteristics, way of life,
47–8, 51, 56–7
physical attributes, 230, 233, 234
plundering habits, 47, 257–9, 262
punishment for sins, 264–7
quarrelsomeness, 96, 103, 189,
251, 260–61, 263, 273
respect for noble birth, 47, 223,
251
reverence for holy things, places,
87, 253–4
self-confidence, 245–6

treatment by local rulers, 142
warlike attitudes, 233–4, 235
wit, 47, 243–4
Wenlock Edge, journey to, 36, 72,
204
Wentloog (Gwynllwg)
in Newport area, 121 and n. 171
rulers of, 108 n. 144
Westminster Abbey
consecration of Bishops of St
David's at, 163 n. 277, 164
n. 278
Gerald's manuscripts destroyed
by fire in, 49, 53
Wexford, English garrison in, 167
Wexford, see of, offered to Gerald,
15
Wharton, Henry, 44, 52–3
Whitchurch Abbey, journey to, 32,
36, 72, 200
Whitchurch, Abbot of, Baldwin's
desire to meet, 24
White monks *see* Cistercian Order
Whiting, B. J. and H. W., 241
n. 540
Whitland, Abbey of (Alba Domus,
Alba Landa, Blanchland)
Abbot of, Baldwin's desire to
meet, 24
foundation, refoundation, 119
n. 165, 178 n. 323
journey to, 32, 34, 140 and
n. 221
Wight, Isle of, 186–7
Wilfred (Wilfre, Wilfridus), Bishop
of St David's, 163 and
nn. 269, 273
William I, King of England
alleged orders for burial of
Harold, 198–9 n. 407
charter to Battle Abbey, 88 n. 74
references to reign of, 54
William II, King of England
gift of Ewias to Hugh de Laci,
100 and n. 111

READ MORE IN PENGUIN

In every corner of the world, on every subject under the sun, Penguin represents quality and variety – the very best in publishing today.

For complete information about books available from Penguin – including Puffins, Penguin Classics and Arkana – and how to order them, write to us at the appropriate address below. Please note that for copyright reasons the selection of books varies from country to country.

In the United Kingdom: Please write to *Dept. EP, Penguin Books Ltd, Bath Road, Harmondsworth, West Drayton, Middlesex UB7 0DA*

In the United States: Please write to *Consumer Sales, Penguin Putnam Inc., P.O. Box 12289 Dept. B, Newark, New Jersey 07101-5289.* VISA and MasterCard holders call 1-800-788-6262 to order Penguin titles

In Canada: Please write to *Penguin Books Canada Ltd, 10 Alcorn Avenue, Suite 300, Toronto, Ontario M4V 3B2*

In Australia: Please write to *Penguin Books Australia Ltd, P.O. Box 257, Ringwood, Victoria 3134*

In New Zealand: Please write to *Penguin Books (NZ) Ltd, Private Bag 102902, North Shore Mail Centre, Auckland 10*

In India: Please write to *Penguin Books India Pvt Ltd, 11 Community Centre, Panchsheel Park, New Delhi 110017*

In the Netherlands: Please write to *Penguin Books Netherlands bv, Postbus 3507, NL-1001 AH Amsterdam*

In Germany: Please write to *Penguin Books Deutschland GmbH, Metzlerstrasse 26, 60594 Frankfurt am Main*

In Spain: Please write to *Penguin Books S. A., Bravo Murillo 19, 1° B, 28015 Madrid*

In Italy: Please write to *Penguin Italia s.r.l., Via Benedetto Croce 2, 20094 Corsico, Milano*

In France: Please write to *Penguin France, Le Carré Wilson, 62 rue Benjamin Baillaud, 31500 Toulouse*

In Japan: Please write to *Penguin Books Japan Ltd, Kaneko Building, 2-3-25 Koraku, Bunkyo-Ku, Tokyo 112*

In South Africa: Please write to *Penguin Books South Africa (Pty) Ltd, Private Bag X14, Parkview, 2122 Johannesburg*